T0244561

THE BRITISH POETS,

PUBLISHED BY

LITTLE, BROWN & COMPANY.

A COMPLETE COLLECTION,

FROM CHAUCER TO WORDSWORTH,

Handsomely Printed in Neat 16mo. Volumes.

Price 75 Cents Per Volume.

Each Work Sold Separately.

THIS Collection, of which more than one hundred volumes are already issued, is intended to embrace the whole works of the most distinguished authors, from Chaucer to Wordsworth, with selections from the minor poets; accompanied with biographical, historical, and critical notices and portraits, — the whole forming a far more complete, elegant, and cheap edition of the British Poets than has ever appeared before.

The numerous testimonials to the excellence of this series, which the publishers have received, both from the press and the public, in all parts of the country, would seem to indicate that a popular want has been met by this edition, which is universally acknowledged to be the best ever issued, both in point of editorship and mechanical execution.

Notices of the Press.

" We cannot speak too highly in praise of this edition — the only one that deserves the name of ' complete ' — of the British Poets." — *Boston Daily Advertiser.*

" We really know nothing more worthy of the cordial support of the American public than the Boston edition of the English poets." — *New York Times.*

" A fairer printed, a more tasteful or more valuable set of books, cannot be placed in any library." — *New York Courier and Inquirer.*

"The best, the most permanently valuable, the most convenient, and the cheapest edition of the standard poetical literature of Great Britain ever published." — *Home Journal.*

"We regard it as the most beautiful and convenient library edition of the British Poets yet published." — *Philadelphia Evening Bulletin.*

"We do not know any other edition of the English Poets which combines so much excellence." — *Bibliotheca Sacra.*

The following volumes are already issued: —

AKENSIDE	1 vol.	MILTON	3 vols.
BALLADS	8 vols.	MONTGOMERY	5 "
BEATTIE	1 vol.	MOORE	6 "
BUTLER	2 vols.	PARNELL & TICKELL	1 vol.
CAMPBELL	1 vol.	POPE	3 vols.
CHATTERTON	2 vols.	PRIOR	2 "
CHURCHILL	3 "	SCOTT	9 "
COLERIDGE	3 "	SHAKSPEARE	1 vol.
COLLINS	1 vol.	SHELLEY	3 vols.
COWPER	3 vols.	SKELTON	3 "
DONNE	1 vol.	SOUTHEY	10 "
DRYDEN	5 vols.	SPENSER	5 "
FALCONER	1 vol.	SURREY	1 vol.
GAY	2 vols.	SWIFT	3 vols.
GOLDSMITH	1 vol.	THOMSON	2 "
GRAY	1 "	VAUGHAN	1 vol.
HERBERT	1 "	WATTS	1 "
HERRICK	2 vols.	WHITE	1 "
HOOD	4 "	WORDSWORTH	7 vols.
KEATS	1 vol.	WYATT	1 vol.
MARVELL	1 "	YOUNG	2 vols.

*** We have in Press, and shall issue soon, the Works of

BYRON,   BURNS,   CHAUCER.

The remainder of the series will be published as fast as the volumes can be prepared.

THE BRITISH ESSAYISTS,

PUBLISHED BY

LITTLE, BROWN & COMPANY,

110 WASHINGTON STREET, BOSTON.

THE

BRITISH ESSAYISTS;

WITH PREFACES, HISTORICAL AND BIOGRAPHICAL,

BY A. CHALMERS, F.S.A.

In 38 vols. 16mo.

TATLER,	ADVENTURER,	MIRROR,
SPECTATOR,	WORLD,	LOUNGER,
GUARDIAN,	CONNOISSEUR,	OBSERVER,
RAMBLER,	IDLER,	LOOKER-ON.

THE volumes are of the exact size and style of LITTLE, BROWN & Co.'s edition of the " British Poets," and sold at the same price, — seventy-five cents per volume.

The want of a neat and uniform edition of these Essays, the productions of the best writers of the English tongue, has long been felt, and the present issue is intended to supply the deficiency.

The volumes are of convenient size, handsomely printed from the last English edition, and the price is such as to recommend them to the favor of the public, and especially of those who are engaged in making selections for school and college libraries.

(3)

Notices of the Press.

"These works, the flower of the best English literature for a century, merit a place in every library. They have borne a large office in the culture of mind and style for past generations, and for our elders now upon the stage; and we can wish for those entering active or literary life, access to no purer, or more copious, or more stimulating fountains of thought, sentiment, and motive, than are here." — *N. A. Review.*

"The judgment of the most competent and respected authority has been passed upon these works, and has decided that they are eminently worthy of being kept in constant use." — *Christian Examiner.*

"The value and popularity of the works included in this series will increase as those who read the English language become cultivated, and wish for compositions of the highest rank. For school and family libraries, these books are just what is needed; they are of convenient size, and attractive outward appearance, — their contents are models of composition, their spirit is liberal and manly, — their tone and influence moral and religious, without cant, or a weakness of any kind." — *Boston Transcript.*

"It is superfluous to praise the essays, — they are by general consent esteemed models of pure English style, and are full of entertainment, knowledge of the world, and moral instruction, — they will be read with pleasure as long as the English language lives." — *N. Y. Commercial Advertiser.*

"No greater service can be done in the cause of good letters than the extensive dissemination of these standard compositions. They embrace the best models of style in the English Language." — *Boston Daily Advertiser.*

"As models of English prose they stand unrivalled, and deserve a place in every library, public or private, but especially in every school and town library in the country." — *Boston Atlas.*

"A series of standard works, the value and popularity of which have only increased with time." — *N. Y. Times.*

"No more desirable edition has ever been published." — *N. Y. Evening Post.*

H.W. Smith Sc.

Even in our ashes live &c

Gray

THE

POETICAL WORKS

OF

THOMAS GRAY.

EDITED,

WITH A LIFE,

BY REV. JOHN MITFORD.

———

BOSTON:
LITTLE, BROWN AND COMPANY.
NEW YORK: BLAKEMAN AND MASON.
CINCINNATI: RICKEY AND CARROLL.
M.DCCC.LXII.

TO

SAMUEL ROGERS, ESQ.

THIS EDITION OF

GRAY

IS INSCRIBED

WITH FEELINGS OF RESPECT AND ESTEEM

BY THE EDITOR.

SONNET.

A LONELY Man he was, from whom these lays
Flow'd in his cloister'd musings: He in scorn
Held them, the unfeeling multitude, who born
For deeds of nobler purpose, their ripe days
Waste amidst fraudful industry, to raise
Inglorious wealth. — But He, life's studious morn
Gave to the Muse, so best might he adorn
His thoughtful brow with never-dying bays.
And well the Muse repaid him.   She hath given
An unsubstantial world of richer fee ;
High thoughts, unchanging visions, that the leaven
Of earth partake not ; — Rich then must he be,
Who of this cloudless world, this mortal heaven,
Possesseth in his right the Sovereignty.

CONTENTS.

	Page.
MEMOIR OF GRAY, by the Rev. J. Mitford	i
Appendix to the Memoir	xciii

POEMS.

Ode. On the Spring	1
Ode. On the Death of a favourite Cat, drowned in a Tub of Gold Fishes	6
Ode. On a Distant Prospect of Eton College	10
Hymn to Adversity	17
The Progress of Poesy	22
The Bard	38
Ode for Music	61
The Fatal Sisters	70
The Vegtam's Kivitha; or, the Descent of Odin . . .	75
The Triumphs of Owen	84
The Death of Hoel	87
Sonnet on the Death of Mr. Richard West	90
Epitaph on Mrs. Jane Clerke	91
Epitaph on Sir William Williams	93
Elegy written in a Country Churchyard	94
A Long Story	111

POSTHUMOUS POEMS AND FRAGMENTS.

Ode on the Pleasure arising from Vicissitude	120
Translation of a Passage from Statius	126
The Fragment of a Tragedy, on the Subject of the Death of Agrippina	128
Hymn to Ignorance	140
The Alliance of Education and Government	143
Stanzas to Mr. Bentley	153
Sketch of his own Character	155
Amatory Lines	156
Song	157
Tophet. An Epigram	159
Impromptu, on the Seat of a deceased Nobleman . .	161
The Candidate	163

EXTRACTS.

Page.

Propertius, Lib. iii. Eleg. v. 165
Propertius, Lib. ii. Eleg. i. 167
Tasso Gerus. Lib. cant. xiv. 170

POEMATA.

Hymeneal on the Marriage of His Royal Highness the
    Prince of Wales 173
Luna Habitabilis 177
Sapphic Ode: To Mr. West 183
Alcaic Fragment 187
Latin Lines, addressed to Mr. West, from Genoa . . . 188
Elegiac Verses, occasioned by the sight of the Plains
    where the Battle of Trebia was fought 188
Carmen ad C. Favonium Zephyrinum 189
Fragment of a Latin Poem on the Gaurus 192
A Farewell to Florence 196
Imitation of an Italian Sonnet of Signior Abbate Buon-
    delmonte 197
Alcaic Ode 198
Part of an Heroic Epistle from Sophonisba to Masinissa 200
De Principiis Cogitandi, Liber Primus 204
                        Liber Quartus 216
Greek Epigram 218

EXTRACTS.

Petrarca, Part I. Sonetto 170 219
From the Anthologia Græca :
    In Bacchæ Furentis Statuam 220
    In Alexandrum, ære effictum 220
    In Medeæ Imaginem, Nobile Timomachi Opus . . 220
    In Niobes Statuam 221
    A Nymph offering a Statue of herself to Venus . . 221
    In Amorem Dormientem 221
    From a Fragment of Plato 222
    In Fontem Aquæ Calidæ 222
    " Irrepsisse suas murem," &c. 222
    " Hanc tibi Rufinus mittit," &c. 223
    Ad Amorem. 223

THE LIFE OF THOMAS GRAY.

BY JOHN MITFORD.

THOMAS GRAY, the subject of the present narrative, was the fifth child of Mr. Philip Gray, a respectable citizen and money-scrivener in London. His grandfather was also a considerable merchant in that place. The maiden name of his mother was Dorothy Antrobus. Thomas was born in Cornhill, the 26th of December, 1716; and was the only one of twelve children who survived. The rest died in their infancy, from suffocation, produced by a fullness of blood; and he owed his life to a memorable instance of the love and courage of his mother, who removed the paroxysm, which attacked him, by opening a vein with her own hand: an instance of affection that seems to have been most tenderly preserved by him through his after life, repaid with care and attention, and remembered when the object of his filial solicitudes could no longer claim them. Mason informs us, " that Gray seldom mentioned his mother without a sigh."

He was educated at Eton, under the protection of Mr. Antrobus, his maternal uncle, who was at

b

that time assistant to Dr. George, and also a fellow of Pembroke College, at Cambridge, where Gray was admitted as a pensioner in 1734, in his nineteenth year.   I should be unwilling to pass over this period of his life, without mentioning that while at Eton, as well as at Cambridge, he depended for his entire support on the affection and firmness of his mother; who, when his father had refused all assistance, cheerfully maintained him on the scanty produce of her separate industry. At Eton his friendship with Horace Walpole, and more particularly with Richard West,* commenced.   In him he met with one, who, from the goodness of his heart, the sincerity of his friendship, and the excellent cultivation of his mind, was worthy of his warmest attachment.   The purity of taste, indeed, as well as the proficiency in literature which the letters of West display, were re-

* Richard West was the son of the right honourable Richard West, lord chancellor of Ireland; who died in 1727 or 1728, aged 36; and his grandfather, by the mother's side, was Bishop Burnet. His father was the maternal uncle of Glover the poet, and is supposed to be the author of a tragedy called 'Hecuba,' published in 1726. Mason says that, when at school, West's genius was thought to be more brilliant than his friend's. A portrait of the father is in the hall of the Inner Temple, given by Richard Glover. He was appointed Lord Chancellor in the reign of George the First, in 1725. He wrote on Treasons and Bills of Attainder, also on the Manner of Creating Peers. See this last tract highly praised in Quarterly Review, No. lxxxiv. p. 303. See King's poem, The Toast, p. 117.

markable at his age; and his studious and pensive habits of mind, his uncertain health, and his early and untimely death, have all contributed to throw " a melancholy grace" over the short and interesting narrative of his life. With him, for the period of eight years, Gray enjoyed what the moralist calls " the most virtuous as well as the happiest of all attachments — the wise security of friendship: ' Par studiis, ævique modis.' " Latterly, when West's health was declining, and his prospects in life seemed clouded and uncertain, Gray's friendship was affectionate and anxious, and only terminated by the early death of his friend in his twenty-sixth year.

When Gray removed to Peter House, Horace Walpole* went to King's College in the same university, and West to Christ Church at Oxford. From this period the life of Gray is conducted by his friend and biographer Mr. Mason, through the

---

* In H. Walpole's Works are some letters between West and Walpole at College (vol. iv. p. 411). The intimacy between Gray, Walpole, West, and Asheton, was called the quadruple alliance; and they passed by the names of Tydeus, Orosmades, Almanzor, and Plato. Thomas Asheton was afterwards fellow of Eton College, rector of St. Botolph, Bishopsgate Street, and preacher to the Society of Lincoln's Inn. He wrote an answer to a work of Dr. Conyers Middleton. Walpole addressed a poetical epistle from Florence to him. See Gray's Letters; and Walpole's Works, vol. v. p. 386. Asheton died in 1775. His niece of the same name married Dr. William Cleaver, Bishop of St. Asaph. See an account of him in Sir Egerton Brydges's Restituta, vol. iv. p. 249.

medium of his Letters;* concerning which it may be said, that from the humour, the elegance, and the classical taste displayed in them; from the alternate mixture of serious argument, animated description, just criticism, and playful expression; notwithstanding the incidents of his life were peculiarly few in number, nor any of them remarkable,. yet a more interesting publication of the kind never appeared in English literature.

Gray's Letters commence, as I have said, from the time when he left Eton for Cambridge; but from them it is difficult to trace the line of study which he pursued at College. His letters treat chiefly of his poetry, and other private pursuits; and he seems to have withdrawn himself entirely from the severity of mathematical studies, and to have confined his inquiries to classical literature, to the acquisition of modern languages, to history, and other branches of what is called polite learning. West describes himself and his friend as walking hand in hand,

> " Through many a flow'ry path and shelly grot,
> Where Learning lull'd us in her *private* maze."

During Gray's residence at College, from 1734 to September, 1738, his poetical productions were —'A Copy of Latin verses,' inserted in the '*Musæ*

* Mason followed the plan of C. Middleton in his Life of Cicero, and of Quirini in his Life of Cardinal Pole. See Pye's Life of Pole, p. 177.

Etonenses;' another 'On the Marriage of the Prince of Wales;' and 'A Sapphic Ode to West.' A small part of his 'Translation from Statius,' Mr. Mason has given; but has withheld a Latin Version of the *'Care Selve beate'* of the Pastor Fido, and an English translation of part of the fourteenth canto of Tasso's *'Gerusalemme Liberata,'* which is inserted in the present edition. From September till the following March, Gray resided at his father's house; but his correspondence with West, who was then with his mother at Epsom, his biographer has thought it unnecessary to insert.

At the request of Horace Walpole, Gray accompanied him in his travels through France and Italy, and deferred his intended study of the law. From letters to his friend West, and to his own family, we have an account of his pursuits while abroad. He seems to have been, as we might have expected, a very studious and diligent traveller. His attention was directed to all the works of art that were curious and instructive. Architecture both of Gothic and Grecian origin, painting, and music, were all studied by him. He appears to have applied diligently to the language; nor did the manners and customs of the inhabitants escape his attention. Like Addison, he compared with the descriptions of ancient authors the modern appearance of the countries through which he passed. There are, indeed, few gratifications more exquisite than those which we experience in being able **to** identify the scenes, and realize the descriptions, which have been long consecrated in the mind by genius and by virtue; which have supplied the fancy with its earliest images, and are connected in the memory with its most lasting associations. In such moments as these, we appear to be able suddenly to arrest the progress and lessen the devastations of time. We hardly contemplate with regret the ages that have passed in silence and oblivion; and we behold, for the first time, the fading and faint descriptions of language, stamped with the fresh impressions of reality and truth. The letters which Gray wrote from Italy were not intended for publication, and do not contain a regular account of the observations which he made: but are rather detached and entertaining descriptions, intended for the amusement of his friends at home. Every thing which he thought of importance was committed to his journal. "He catalogued," says Mr. Mason, "and made occasional short remarks on the pictures which he saw. He wrote a minute description of every thing which he saw in his tour from Rome to Naples; as also of the environs of Rome, Florence, &c. They abound with many uncommon remarks, and pertinent classical quotations.'

The route chosen by the travellers was one usually taken: — from Paris, through Rheims (where they stayed three months, principally to accustom themselves to the French language) to Lyons, whence they took a short excursion to Geneva, over the mountains of Savoy; and by Turin, Genoa, and Bologna to Florence. There they passed the winter in the company of Mr. Horace Mann, the envoy at that court.* In March, 1740, Clement the Twelfth, then Pope, died; and they hastened their journey to Rome, in the hope of seeing the installation of his successor.† That Gray would have wished to have extended his travels, and enlarged his prospect beyond these narrow limits, if he had possessed the power, we know from his subsequent advice to a friend who was commencing his travels: "Tritum viatorum compitum calca, et, cum poteris, desere." And the following passage sketches the outline of an Italian tour, which, I believe, few of our travellers have ever completed: "I conclude, when the winter is over, and you have seen Rome and Naples, you will strike out of the beaten path of English travellers, and see a little of the country. Throw yourselves into the bosom of the Apennine; survey the horrid lake of Amsanctus; catch the breezes on the coast of Taranto and Salerno; expatiate to the very toe of the continent; perhaps strike over the faro of Messina; and having measured the gigantic co-

* See Walpole's Works, vol. iv. p. 423. Sir Horace Mann died in 1786 at Florence, where he had resided forty-six years as his Britannic Majesty's minister, at the Court of the Grand Duke.
† Ibid. p. 440.

lumns of Girgenti and the tremendous cavern of Syracusa, refresh yourselves amidst the fragrant vale of Enna. — *Oh! che bel riposo!*"

In May, after a visit to the Frascati and the Cascades of Tivoli, Gray sent his beautiful 'Alcaic Ode' to West. In June he made a short excursion to Naples; and was charmed with the scenery that presented itself in that most delightful climate. He describes the large old fig-trees, the oranges in bloom, the myrtles in every hedge, and the vines hanging in festoons from tree to tree. He must have been among the first English travellers who visited the remains of Herculaneum,* as it was discovered only the preceding year; and he pointed out to his companion, the description in Statius that pictured the latent city :

> "Hæc ego Chalcidicis ad te, Marcelle, sonabam
> Litoribus, fractas ubi Vesbius egerit iras,

---

* Some excavations were made in Herculaneum in 1709 by the Prince D'Elbeuf : but thirty years elapsed after the orders given to the Prince to dig no farther, before any more notice was taken of them. In December, 1738, the King of the two Sicilies was at Portici, and gave orders for a prosecution of the subterraneous labours. There was an excavation in the time of the Romans; and another in 1689. In a letter from H. Walpole to West on this subject (see Walpole's Works, vol. iv. p. 448), dated Naples, June 14, 1740, is a passage which shows Mr. Mason's conjecture, that the travellers did not recognise the ancient town of Herculaneum by name, to be unfounded. H. Walpole calls it by that name in his letter.

Æmula Trinacriis volvens incendia flammis.
Mira fides ! credetne virum ventura propago,
Cum segetes iterum, cum jam hæc deserta virebunt,
Infra urbes, populosque premi ? "

Statii Sylv. IV. iv. 78.*

At Naples the travellers stayed ten days; and
Gray's next letter to his father, in which he talks
of his return to England, is dated again from Florence; and whence he sent, soon after, his Poem
on the 'Gaurus' to West. He remained, however,
at that place about eleven months; and during this
time commenced his Latin poem '*De Principiis
Cogitandi.*' He then set off with Walpole, on the
24th of April, for Bologna and Reggio,† at the latter of which towns an unfortunate difference took
place between them, and they parted. The exact
cause of this quarrel has been passed over by the
delicacy of his biographer, because H. Walpole was
alive when the Memoirs of Gray were written. The
former, however, charged himself with the chief
blame; and lamented that he had not paid more
attention and deference to Gray's superior judg-

* See also Martial. Epig. Lib. iv. Ep. 43, ed. Delph. and
the note by Stephens on Statii Sylv. v. 3. 205, p. 155.

Jamque et flere pio Vesuvina incendia cantu
Mens erat, &c.

† Dr. Johnson has two slight mistakes in his 'Life of Gray.'
He says that they quarrelled at *Florence* and parted, instead of
Reggio. He says also, that Gray began his poem '*De Principiis Cogitandi*' after his return: but it was commenced in the
winter of 1740, at Florence

ment and prudence. In the '*Walpoliana*' (vol. i.
p. 95, art. cx.) is the following passage: "The
quarrel between Gray and me arose from his being
too serious a companion. I had just broke loose
from the restraint of the University, with as much
money as I could spend; and I was willing to in-
dulge myself. Gray was for antiquities, &c.;
whilst I was for perpetual balls and plays;—the
fault was mine." Perhaps the freedom of friendship spoke too openly to please: for in a letter from
Walpole to Mr. Bentley, some years afterwards, he
says: "I was accustomed to flattery enough when
my father was minister: at his fall I lost it all at
once: and since that I have lived with Mr. Chute,
who is all vehemence; with Mr. Fox, who is all
disputation; with Sir C. Williams, who has no time
from flattery, himself; *and with Gray, who does
not hate to find fault with me.*" * Whatever was
the cause of this quarrel, it must have been very
serious, if the information is correct which is given
in the manuscript of the Rev. W. Cole, a person
who appears to have lived in terms of intimacy with

---

* See Walpole's Works, vol. v. p. 334. In a letter from
Gray to Walpole in 1751, is a sentence which seems to point
towards this quarrel: "It is a tenet with me, (he says) — a
simple one, you will perhaps say, — that if ever two people
who love one another come to breaking, it is for want of a
timely *eclaircissement*, a full and precise one, without witnesses
or mediators, and without reserving one disagreeable circumstance for the mind to brood upon in silence." See Walpole's
Works, vol. v. p. 389.

Gray during the latter part of his life. "When matters (he says) were made up between Gray and Walpole, and the latter asked Gray to Strawberry Hill, when he came, he without any ceremony told Walpole, that he came to wait on him as civility required, but by no means would he ever be there on the terms of his former friendship, which he had totally cancelled." Such is the account given by Mr. Cole, and which I suppose is worthy of credit: at any rate, it does not seem at all inconsistent with the independence and manly freedom which always accompanied the actions and opinions of Gray.*

Having thus lost his companion, and, with the separation of friendship, all inducement to remain abroad, Gray went immediately to Venice, and returned through Padua and Milan, following almost the same road through France, which he had travelled before. If he sent any letters to West on his return,† it was not thought requisite to publish them: those to his father were only accounts of his health and safety. Though he returned to England

* For a further elucidation of this subject, the reader is referred to the second volume of *the Aldine edition of Gray's Works*, p. 174–5, where I have stated what are the *supposed* causes of the quarrel; and the terms of the reconciliation will be best learned, from the expressions which Gray uses in his letter to Mr. Wharton on this subject.

† Some letters from Walpole to West, while the former was on his travels with Gray, are in Walpole's Works, vol. iv. p. 419—463. There is one letter from Reggio, May 10th, but not mentioning any quarrel, nor even Gray by name.

as speedily and directly as he could, yet he once diverged from his way, between Turin and Lyons, again to contemplate the wild and magnificent scenery that surrounded the Grande Chartreuse; and in the Album of the Fathers he wrote his beautiful 'Alcaic Ode,' which bears strong marks of proceeding from a mind deeply impressed with the solemnity of the situation; where "every pre-cipice and cliff was pregnant with religion and poetry." *

In two months after the return of Gray in 1741, his father died,† his constitution being worn out by repeated attacks of the gout; and Gray's filial duty was now solely directed to his mother. To the friend who condoled with Pope on his father's death, he answered in the pious language of Euryalus, — " Genitrix est mihi," — and Gray, in the like cir-cumstances, assuredly felt no less the pleasure that arose from contributing to preserve the life and hap-piness of a parent. With a small fortune, which her husband's imprudence had materially impaired,‡ Mrs. Gray and a maiden sister retired to the house

* See Letter XI. dated Turin, November 16, 1739.

† Gray came to town about the 1st of September, 1741. His father died on the 6th of November following, at the age of 65. *Mason.*

Mr. Philip Gray built a country house at Wanstead, at a very considerable expense, which was sold after his death at £2000 less than its original cost. It was purchased by Alder-man Ball, who was still resident in it in 1776. *Isaac Reed*

of Mrs. Rogers,* another sister, at Stoke, near Windsor: and Gray, thinking his fortune not sufficient to enable him to prosecute the study of the law, and yet unwilling to hurt the feelings of his mother, by appearing entirely to forsake his profession, changed or pretended to change the line of study, and went to Cambridge to take his degree in civil law. That in his own mind, however, he had entirely given up all thoughts of his profession, seems to appear from a letter to West: "Alas for one (he says) who has nothing to do but to amuse himself! I believe my amusements are as little amusing as most folks'; but no matter, it makes the hours pass, and is better than ἐν ἀμάθια καὶ ἀμούσια καταβιῶναι."

"But the narrowness of his circumstances," says Mr. Mason, "was not the only thing that distressed him at this period. He had, as we have seen, lost the friendship of Mr. Walpole abroad. He had also lost much time in his travels; a loss which application could not easily retrieve, when so severe and laborious a study as that of the Common Law was to be the object of it; and he well knew that whatever improvement he might have made in this interval, either in taste or science, such improvement would stand him in little stead with regard to his present situation and exigencies.

* Mason describes Mrs. Rogers as the widow of a clergyman, but Isaac Reed, in a MS. note, has said that he was a gentleman of the law.

This was not all: his other friend, Mr. West, he
found on his return oppressed by sickness and a
load of family misfortunes. These the sympathiz-
ing heart of Mr. Gray made his own. He did all
in his power (for he was now with him in London)
to soothe the sorrows of his friend, and try to alle-
viate them by every office of the purest and most
perfect affection: but his cares were vain. The
distresses of Mr. West's mind had already too
far affected a body from the first weak and delicate."

West was indeed at this time rapidly declining
in health, and had gone into Hertfordshire for the
benefit of the air. To him Gray sent part of his
Tragedy of 'Agrippina,' then commenced; and
which, Mr. Mason thinks, was suggested by a favourable impression left on his mind from a representation of the *Britannicus* of Racine. His friend
objected to the length of Agrippina's speech; and
the Fragment is now published, not exactly as
Gray left it, but altered by Mr. Mason from the
suggestions of West. The plan of this play seems
to have been drawn after the model of the plays of
Racine; though it displays perhaps more spirit and
genius than ever informed the works of that elegant and correct tragedian. Mr. Mason, in a letter to Dr. Beattie, mentions among the Poetry left
by Gray, "the opening scene of a tragedy called
Agrippina, with the first speech of the second,
written much in Racine's manner, and with many

masterly strokes."* The language resembles
rather that of Rowe or Addison, than of Shakespeare; though it is more highly wrought, and
more closely compacted. If finished, it would, I
think, have delighted the scholar in the closet;
but it is too descriptive to have pleased upon the
stage. Βαστάζονται δὲ οἱ ἀναγνωστικοί . . . . . . Καὶ παρα-
βαλλόμενοι, οἱ μὲν τῶν γραφικῶν, ἐν τοῖς ἀγῶσι στενοὶ φαίνον-
ται.†

Gray now employed himself in the perusal of the
ancient authors. He mentions that he was reading
Thucydides, Theocritus, and Anacreon. He translated some parts of Propertius with great elegance
of language and versification, and selected for his
Italian studies the poetry of Petrarch. He wrote
an Heroic Epistle in Latin, in imitation of the manner of Ovid; and a Greek Epigram, which he
communicated to West: to whom also in the summer, when he retired to his family at Stoke, he sent

* I have said that Gray kept an attentive eye upon Racine
during the composition of his tragedy; an assertion, I think,
that the notes will serve to prove: but the learned Mr. Twining, in his notes on Aristotle's Poetics, (p. 385, 4to.) says:
"I have often wondered what it was that could attach Mr.
Gray so strongly to a poet whose genius was so little analo-
gous to his own. I must confess I cannot, even in the Dramatic
Fragment given us by Mr. Mason, discover any other resemblance to Racine, than in the length of the speeches. The
fault, indeed, is Racine's; its beauties are surely of a higher
order," &c.

† Aristotelis Rhetorica, lib. γ. cap xii.

his ' Ode to Spring,' which was written there, but which did not arrive in Hertfordshire till after the death of his beloved friend.* West died only twenty days after he had written the Letter to Gray, which concludes with " *Vale, et vive paulis-per cum vivis.*" So little (says Mr. Mason) was the amiable youth then aware of the short time that he himself would be numbered amongst the living.

I shall here insert a very correct and judicious criticism, on a censure made by Johnson of an expression in Gray's Ode to Spring, by the late

* West was buried in the chancel of Hatfield church, beneath a stone, with the following epitaph: "Here lieth the body of Richard West, esq. only son of the right honourable Richard West, esq. lórd chancellor of Ireland, who died the 1st of June, 1742, in the 26th year of his age." West's poems have never been fully collected. There is one, ' An Ode to Mary Magdalene,' in Walpole's Works, vol. iv. p. 419: another in Dalrymple's Songs, p. 142. In the European Magazine for January, 1798, p. 45, is a poem said to be written by him, called 'Damon to Philomel; ' and a Copy of Verses on his Death, supposed to be written by his uncle, Judge Burnet. In Walpole's Works, vol. i. p. 204, is a well known Epigram which was written by West, ' Time and Thomas Hearne,' which was printed by Mr. Walpole in a paper intended for the ' World,' but not sent, and which is commonly attributed to Swift. It appears also, that part of the tragedy of Pausanias is extant in MS. See the editor's note in Walpole's Works, vol. iv. p. 458; also his translation of Tibullus. See Mason's Gray, vol. i. p 22. The collection of his poems by Dr. Anderson, in the edition of the British Poets, is very incomplete: and Mr. Alexander Chalmers, in his subsequent edition, has omitted them entirely.

Lord Grenville, a criticism which does credit to his Lordship's learning and taste *

"'There has of late arisen,' says Johnson, in his Life of Gray, 'a practice of giving to adjectives derived from substantives, the termination of participles: such as the *cultured* plain, the *daisied* bank; but I was sorry to see in the lines of a scholar like Gray, the *honied* spring.'

"A scholar, like Johnson, might have remembered that *mellitus* is used by Catullus, Cicero, and Horace, and that *honied* itself is found both in Shakspeare and in Milton. But to say nothing of the general principles of all language, how could the writer of an English Dictionary be ignorant that the ready conversion of our substantives into verbs, participles, and participial adjectives, is of the very essence of our own tongue, derived to it from its Saxon origin, and a main source of its energy and richness?

"1st. In the instances of verbs and participles, this is too obvious to be dwelt upon for a moment. Such verbs as to *plough*, to *witness*, to *pity*, to *ornament*, together with the participles regularly formed from them are among the commonest words in our language. Shakspeare, in a ludicrous but expressive phrase, has converted even a proper name into a participle of this description: 'Petruchio,' he says, 'is kated.' — The epithet of a *hectoring* fellow is a more familiar instance of a

* See Nugæ Metricæ, by Lord Grenville, privately printed

c

participle similarly formed, though strangely distorted in its use to express a meaning almost the opposite of its original.

" 2ndly. These participles of verbs thus derived, like all other participles, when used to denote *habitual* attributes, pass into adjectives. Winged, feathered, thatched, painted, and innumerable others are indiscriminately used in both these forms, according to the construction of the sentence, and its context. And the transition is so easy, that in many passages it may be doubted to which of these two parts of speech such words should properly be referred.

" 3rdly. Between these participial adjectives, and those which Johnson condemns, there is the closest analogy. Both are derived from substantives; and both have the termination of participles. The latter, such words for instance, as *honied, daisied, tapestried, slippered,* and the like, differ from the others only in not being referable to any yet established verb; but so little material is the difference, that there is hardly one of these cases, in which the corresponding verb might not, if it were wanted, be formed and used, in strict conformity with the genius of our language. *Sugared* is an epithet frequent in our ancient poetry, and its use was properly long anterior to that of the verb, of which it now appears to be a participle. But that verb has since been fully adopted into our language. We now *sugar* our cups, as freely as our ancestors *spiced* and *drugged* them, and no reason can be assigned, why, if such were our practice, we might not also *honey* them, with equal propriety of speech.

"4thly. On the same analogy we form another very numerous and very valuable class of adjectives, compound epithets, derived like the others, from substantives, and like them terminating as participles, but having prefixed to them the signification of some additional attribute. Such are in common speech, four-footed, open-hearted, short-sighted, good-natured, and the like. In poetry we trace them from the *well-envyned* franklin of Chaucer, through the most brilliant pages of all his successors to the present hour. What reader of Shakspeare or Milton needs to be reminded of even-handed, high-flighted, and trumpet-tongued, or of full-voiced, flowery-kirtled, and fiery-wheeled? All these expressive and beautiful combinations, Johnson's canon would banish from our language.

" His criticism therefore recoils on himself. The poet has followed the usage of his native tongue, and the example of its best masters. The grammarian appears unacquainted both with its practice and its principles. The censure serves only to betray the evil passions, which in a very powerful and well-intentioned, but very ill-regulated mind, the success of a contemporary had been permitted to excite.

" The true spirit indeed of this criticism appears

with no less force in what almost immediately follows, where Johnson attempts to ridicule a passage
which few other men have read without delight,
Gray's beautiful invocation of the Thames, in the
Ode on Eton College — ' Say, Father Thames,'
&c. ' This is useless,' he says, ' and puerile.' Father
Thames had no better means of ' knowing than
himself.' He forgets his own address to the Nile
in Rasselas, for a purpose so very similar; and he
expects his readers to forget one of the most affecting passages in Virgil. Father Thames might well
know as much of the sports of boys as the ' great
Father of Waters' knew of the discontents of men,
or the Tiber himself of the obsequies of Marcellus."

In the autumn of 1742, Gray composed the ode
on ' A distant Prospect of Eton College,' and the
' Hymn to Adversity.' The ' Elegy in a Country
Church-yard' was commenced. An affectionate
Sonnet in English, and an Apostrophe which opens
the fourth book of his poem ' *De Principiis Cogitandi*,' (his last composition in Latin verse,) bear
strong marks of the sorrow left on his mind from
the death of West; and of the real affection with
which he honoured the memory of his worth, and
of his talents.

Mr. Mason thinks that Gray did not finish this
poem, on account of the unfavourable reception, or
rather neglect, of the Anti-Lucretius * of the Car-

* This poem had the honour of being corrected by Boileau,
and altered by Louis the XIVth. The author was so long

dinal Melchior de Polignac; a poem which had
been long expected, and appeared about that time.
The failure, however, of M. de Polignac's poem
may be attributed partly to its length, (for it contains above thirteen thousand verses,) and to a
want of sufficient variety and digression in the
composition. The versification is not always finished and compact, and the language has lost
much of its elegance in the endeavour to accom-
modate it with precision to the subject.

Gray's residence at Cambridge was now continued, not from any partiality to the place where he
received his education, but partly from the scantiness of his income, and in a great measure, no
doubt, for the convenience which its libraries afforded.* Original composition he almost entirely

employed on it, and recited it so often, that many parts were
stolen, and inserted in the works of other authors. Le Clerc
got a fragment by heart, and published it in one of his literary
journals. The cardinal died while his work was unfinished,
and before he could add two more books to it against the Deists.
See Anecdotes par Grimm, vol. i. p. 455. The line written
under Franklin's picture, "Eripuit cœlo fulmen, sceptrumque
tyrannis"—is an imitation of one in the Anti-Lucretius, "Eri-
puitque Jovi fulmen, Phœboque sagittas."

* In a note to the Spital Sermon, p. 117, Dr. Parr says:
"After the opportunities which Mr. Gray enjoyed, and of which
he doubtless had availed himself, for observing the state of
literature and the characters of literary men upon the Conti
nent, he did not merely visit the University, but fixed his
chief residence there. And of a choice to which he adhered
so steadily and so long, the scantiness of his fortune, the love
of books, and the easy access he had to them in many libraries,

neglected; but his time was so assiduously occupied in a regular and studious perusal of the best Greek authors, that in six years he had read all the writers of eminence in that language, digesting and arranging their contents, remarking their peculiarities, and noting their corrupt and difficult passages with great accuracy and diligence. In the winter of 1742, he was admitted a bachelor of civil law; and a short recreation of his studies appears in a 'Fragment of an Address to Ignorance,' which contains a satire on the University where he resided,* whose system of education he always disliked and ridiculed, and against which he used to speak so openly, as to create many enemies. It is plain, from his Letters, that he

will hardly be considered as the *sole motives*." Dr. Parr, however, does not assign any other motives that influenced Gray, in his choice of the University for a residence.

Nec tu credideris urbanæ commoda vitæ
Quærere Nasonem, quærit et illa tamen.
Ov. Ep. ex Pont. 1. 8. 29.

* In p. 117 of the Spital Sermon, Dr. Parr says: " At that very time in which Mr. Gray spoke so contemptuously of Cambridge, that very University abounded in men of erudition and science, with whom the first scholars would not have disdained to converse: and who shall convict me of exaggeration, when I bring forward the names of Bentley, Davies, Asheton — of Jesus: Provost Snape, Middleton, Tunstall the public orator, Baker — of St. John's: Edmund Law, John Taylor, Thomas Johnson, Waterland, Whaley (afterwards regius professor of divinity), Smith (the nephew of Cotes), afterwards master of Trinity, Roger Long, Colson, the correspondent of Sir Isaac Newton, and Professor Saunderson ? "

thought the attention and time bestowed there on mathematical and metaphysical pursuits, would have been more profitably spent in classical studies. There is some resemblance in the style of this Fragment to part of Pope's Dunciad; the fourth book of which had appeared but a year or two before: and Gray, I should think, had that poem in his mind when he wrote these lines, to ridicule what he calls "that ineffable Octogrammaton, the power of laziness."

In 1744 the difference between Walpole and Gray was adjusted by the interference of a lady who wished well to both parties. The lapse of three years had probably been sufficient, in some degree, to soften down, though not entirely obliterate, the remembrance of supposed injuries on either side; natural kindness of temper had reassumed its place, and we find their correspondence again proceeding on friendly and familiar terms. About this time Gray became acquainted with Mr. Mason, then a scholar of St. John's College, whose poetical talents he had noticed; and some of whose poems he revised at the request of a friend. He maintained a correspondence with his intimate and respectable friend, Dr. Wharton, of Durham; and he seems to have lived on terms of familiarity with the celebrated Dr. Middleton,* whose loss

* Dr. Middleton died the 28th of July, 1750, in the sixty-seventh year of his age, at Hildersham, in Cambridgeshire.

he afterwards laments. " I find a friend (he says) so uncommon a thing, that I cannot help regretting even an old acquaintance, which is an indifferent likeness of it.

In the year 1747, the 'Ode to Eton College,' the first production of Gray that appeared in print, was published in folio, by Dodsley. Dr. Warton, in his Essay on Pope, informs us, that "little notice was taken of it, on its first publication."

Walpole wished him to print his own poems with those of his deceased friend West. This, however, he declined, thinking the materials not sufficient: but he complied with another wish of Walpole, in commemorating in an Ode the death of his favourite cat. To this little poem I may be permitted to apply the words of Cicero, when speaking of a work of his own : " Non est enim tale, ut in arte poni possit, quasi illa Minerva Phidiæ ; sed tamen, ut ex eâdem officinâ, exisse appareat."* Soon after this, he sent to Dr. Wharton a part of his poem 'On the Alliance of Education and Government.' He never pursued this subject much further. About a hundred lines remain ; and the commentary proceeds a little beyond the poem. Mr. Mason thinks that he dropped it from finding some of his best thoughts forestalled by M. de Montesquieu's L'Esprit des Loix,† which ap-

* *Vide* Ciceronis Præf. Paradoxa. ed. Olivet, vol. iii. p. 356. Paris.

† Compare Montesquieu, L'Esprit des Loix, liv. xiv. chap ii

peared at that time : and other reasons, which I have elsewhere stated, probably concurred in inducing him to leave unfinished, a very fine specimen of a philosophical poem. Some time after, says Mr. Mason, he had thoughts of resuming his plan, and of dedicating his poem by an introductory Ode to M. de Montesquieu ; but that great man's death, which happened in 1755, made him drop his design finally.

Gray was now forming for his own instruction a Table of Greek Chronology, which extended from the 30th to the 113th Olympiad, a period of 332 years ; and which, while it did not exclude public events, was chiefly designed to compare the time of all great men, their writings and transactions. Mr. Mason, who saw this work, says, "that every page was in nine columns : one for the Olympiad, the next for the Archons, the third for the Public Affairs of Greece, the three next for the Philosophers, and the three last for Poets, Historians, and Orators." *

Greek literature about this time seems to have been his constant study. He says in a letter : "I have read Pausanias and Athenæus all through ; and Æschylus again. I am now in Pindar, and Lysias ; for I take verse and prose together like bread and cheese."

* See Gibbon's Rome, vol. iii. p. 248. A plan similar to this has been executed by Edv. Corsinus, in his ' Fasti Attici,' four volumes 4to. Florence, 1764.

In the year 1749, on the death of Mrs. Antrobus, his mother was deprived of a sister and affectionate companion; which loss, if we may judge by
a letter of Gray, was a most severe affliction. It is
not improbable that this circumstance may have
turned his thoughts towards finishing his ' Elegy,'*
which was commenced some time before. Whether
that were the case or not, it now however received
his last corrections, was communicated to Walpole,
and handed about in manuscript with great applause, among the higher circles of society. It was
so popular, that when it was printed, Gray expressed his surprise at the rapidity of the sale;
which Mr. Mason attributed, and, I think, justly,
to the affecting and pensive cast of the subject.
" It spread," he said, " at first, on account of the
affecting and pensive cast of the subject, just like
Hervey's Meditations on the Tombs. Soon after
its publication, I remember sitting with Mr. Gray
in his College apartment, he expressed to me his

---

* The thought of that fine stanza in the Elegy, especially of
the latter lines —

"Some village-Hampden, that with dauntless breast
    The little tyrant of his fields withstood;
Some mute inglorious Milton here may rest,
    Some Cromwell guiltless of his country's blood " —

is expressed more briefly in the following passage of Plautus:

" Ut sæpe summa ingenia in occulto latent.
Hic qualis imperator, nunc privatus est."

                                Captiv. act. iv. sc. 2.

surprise at the rapidity of its sale.　I replied:

Sunt lacrymæ rerum, et mentem mortalia tangunt.'

He paused awhile, and taking his pen, wrote the line on a printed copy of it lying on his table. 'This,' said he, 'shall be its future motto.'　'Pity,' cried I, 'that Dr. Young's Night Thoughts have preoccupied it.'　'So,' replied he, 'indeed it is.'　He had more reason to think I had hinted at the true cause of its popularity, when he found how different a reception his two odes at first met with."*

Pathetic composition, which is employed in describing to us our own griefs, or the sufferings of others, makes its way to the heart at once; it always finds some disposition of the mind favourable to receive it, some passion which cannot resist its power, some feelings which participate in its sorrows.　Much time elapses, before works of elaborate structure, of lofty flight, and of learned allusion, gain possession of the public mind, and are placed in their proper rank in literature. While the 'Bard' and the 'Progress of Poetry' were but little read on their first appearance, Gray received at once the full measure of praise from the 'Elegy:' and perhaps even at this time, the Elegy † is the most popular of all his poems.　Dr.

* Mason's Life of Whitehead, p. 84.

† This Elegy was translated into Latin verse by Messrs. Anstey and Roberts, and not so successfully by Mr. Lloyd.　It has been translated also into Greek by Dr. Cooke, of King's College,

Gregory, in a letter to Beattie, says: "It is a sentiment that very universally prevails, that Poetry
is a light kind of reading, which one takes up
only for a little amusement; and that therefore it
should be so perspicuous as not to require a second reading. This sentiment would bear hard on
some of your best things, and on all Gray's except
his ' Church-yard Elegy,' which, he told me, with
a good deal of acrimony, owed its popularity entirely to the subject, and that the public would
have received it as well if it had been written in
prose." And Dr. Beattie, writing to Sir William
Forbes, says: "Of all the English poets of this
age, Mr. Gray is most admired, and I think with
justice; yet there are comparatively speaking, but
a few who know any thing of his, but his ' Church-
yard Elegy,' which is by no means the best of his
works." This production was the occasion of the
author's acquaintance with Lady Cobham, who
lived in the manor-house at Stoke; and the way
in which it commenced, was described by him in
a poem called the 'Long Story.' The Elegy hav-

and published at the end of his edition of Aristotle's Poetics.
Since that time, it has been translated into the same language
by Dr. Norbury, and Mr. Tew of Eton, Mr. Stephen Weston,
and Dr. Coote. Its imitators also have been very numerous.
The Bard was translated into Latin verse, in 1775. It is said
that within the precincts of the church of Granchester, about
two miles from Cambridge, Gray wrote his Elegy. The curfew
mentioned by the poet was of course the great bell of St.
Mary's. V. Gent. Mag. May, 1814, p. 453.

ing now appeared in some of the periodical publications and magazines, and having been published
with great inaccuracies, Gray requested Walpole
to have it printed in a more respectable and accurate manner, by Dodsley, but without the apparent
knowledge or approbation of the author. It is to
be observed, that in the early editions, the Elegy
is not printed in stanzas of four lines, but con-
tinuously. It is also written in the same manner
by Gray in the Pembroke and Wharton manuscripts. By this connected system of metre, the
harmony of the poem acquires a fuller compass.
Mason adopted it in his four Elegies; and it has
been lately used by Mr. Roscoe in his translation
of the Greek poem of Musurus, which Aldus prefixed to his edition of Plato.*

His thoughts, however, were for a short time
called off from poetry, by the illness of his mother;
and he hastened from Cambridge to attend upon
her. Finding her better than he expected, he
employed himself, during his stay, in superintend-
ing an edition of his poems, which was soon after
published, with designs by Mr. Bentley,† the

---

* Some remarks on this Elegy, which were originally printed
by me in the Gent. Mag. for April, 1836, will be found in the
Appendix to this Life. — Ed.

† Bentley's original drawings are in the library of Strawberry-Hill. See Walpole's Works, vol. ii. p. 447; and Lett.
to G. Montagu, p. 97. Mr. Cumberland, in the Memoirs of
his Life, vol. i. p. 33, thinks that he sees "a satire in copper-

only son of the learned Dr. Bentley, and the
friend of Walpole; a person of various and elegant acquirements, as well as of very considerable talents. To him Gray addressed a Copy of
Verses, highly extolling his powers as a painter.
The original drawings in Walpole's possession,
Mr. Mason says, are infinitely superior to the
prints; but even with this allowance, the praise
must be considered rather friendly than just;
since their merit consists in the grotesque and
quaint fancy which marks the designs; in the
whimsical manner in which the painter has embellished the images of the poet; and which, if it
were intended to correspond to the style of the
'Long Story,' would not be an unsuccessful effort
of the sister-art. The tributes, however, which
are paid by Friendship to Genius, ought not to
be sparing or scanty: and Gray might remember
the example of Dryden and of Pope, in their
complimentary eulogies on Kneller.

In March 1753, he lost the mother, whom he
had so long and so affectionately loved; and he

plate in the etchings of Bentley; and that his uncle has completely libelled both his poet and his patron without intending
to do so." Mr. Cumberland says, at p. 216 of the same volume, that Gray wrote an elaborate critique on a play of Bentley's writing called 'Philodamus,' which was acted at Covent
Garden. For an account of R. Bentley see Brydges' Restituta, vol. iv. p. 364. Scott's Lives of the Novelists, vol. ii.
p. 235. Boaden's Life of Mrs. Siddons, i. p. 360. R. Bentley
died Oct. 1782.

placed over her remains an inscription which strongly marks his piety and sorrow:

> Beside her Friend and Sister,
> Here sleep the Remains of
> DOROTHY GRAY,
> Widow; the careful tender Mother
> Of many Children; one of whom alone
> Had the Misfortune to survive her.
> She died March xi. MDCCLIII.
> Aged LXXII.*

It is usually supposed that Gray's ' Ode on the Progress of Poetry' was written in 1755. From a letter to Walpole it appears that it was then finished, excepting a few lines at the end. He mentions his being so unfortunate as to come too late for Mr. Bentley's edition, and talks of inserting it in Dodsley's Collection. In 1754, it is supposed that he wrote the Fragment of 'An Ode to Vicissitude,' as it is now called. The idea and some of the lines are taken from Gresset's '*Epitre sur ma Convalescence.*' Another Ode was also sketched, which might be called 'The Liberty of Genius,' though some of Gray's biographers, for what reasons I am ignorant, have called it 'The Connection between Genius and

---

* The latter part of Gray's epitaph has a strong resemblance to an inscription on a sepulchral cippus found near the Villa Pelluchi, at Rome, now (I believe) in the British Museum. ——D. M. Dasumiæ. Soteridi. Libertæ. Optimæ. et. Conjugi. Sanctissimæ. bene. mer. fec. L. Dasumius. Callistus. cum. qua. vixit. An xxxv. sine. ulla. querella. optans. ut. ipsa. sibi. potius. superstes. fuisset. quam. se. sibi. superstitem. reliquisset

Grandeur.' The argument of it, the only part which was ever written, is as follows: "All that men of power can do for men of genius is to leave them at their liberty; compared to birds that, when confined to a cage, do but regret the loss of their freedom in melancholy strains, and lose the luscious wildness and happy luxuriance of their notes, which used to make the woods resound." The supplement to this Poem is very inferior to the original, so that we may unite in opinion with an eminent critic, that it is better to leave the unfinished creations of genius in their imperfect form. 'Nobis placet exemplum Priscorum, qui Apelleam Venerem imperfectam maluerunt, quam integram manu extraneâ.' * Gray, as Walpole remarked, was indeed "*in flower*" these last three years. The 'Bard' was commenced, and part of it communicated to Mr. Stonehewer and Dr. Wharton, 1755. In these letters he for the first time complains of listlessness and depression of spirits, which prevented his application to poetry: and from this period we may trace the course of that hereditary disease in his constitution, which embittered in a considerable degree the remainder of his days; and the fatal strength of which, not even the temperance and regularity of a whole life could subdue. In his pocket journal for this year, besides a diary of the weather, and a very accurate calendar of observations on

* Vide Gruteri not; ad Plautum, vol. i. p. 295, 4to.

natural history, he kept a regular account of his health in Latin. By this it appears that his constitution was much enfeebled and impaired, that alarming attacks of the gout were perpetually recurring and disordering his frame. He speaks constantly of the sleepless night, and the feverish morning; and seems seldom to have been free from pain, debility, and disease. Expressions similar to the following, are in almost every page: 'Insomnia crebra, atque expergiscenti surdus quidam doloris sensus; frequens etiam in regione sterni oppressio, et cardialgia gravis, fere sempiterna."

"The Bard" was for some time left unfinished; but "the accident of seeing a blind harper (Mr. Parry) perform on a Welsh harp,* again (he says) put his Ode in motion, and brought it at last to a conclusion."† This poem appears to have been submitted to the critical opinion of his friends. He mentions a remark upon it by Dr. Hurd; and he had recourse to the judgment of Mr. Mason, "whose cavils (Walpole says) almost induced him to destroy his two beautiful and sublime Odes."

Some time previous to this, Dodsley had published his Collection of Poems, in three volumes,‡

* For an Account of Parry, see Smith's Life of Nollekens, vol. ii. p. 213.

† See *Walpoliana*, vol. i. p. 46.

‡ Dodsley published *three* volumes of this Collection, in 1752:

which Walpole sent to Gray. The observations made by the latter, as they were not published in Mr. Mason's Life, and as it is interesting to read the opinions which he entertained of his poetical contemporaries, I shall extract from the letter to his friend, in as short a compass as I can.

"To begin, (he says,) with Mr. Tickell:—This is not only a state poem (my ancient aversion), but a state poem on the Peace of Utrecht. If Mr. Pope had wrote a panegyric on it, one could hardly have read him with patience. But this is only a poor short-winded imitator of Addison, who had himself not above three or four notes in poetry; sweet enough indeed, like those of a German flute, but such as soon tire and satiate the ear with their frequent return. Tickell has added to this a great poverty of sense, and a string of transitions that hardly become a school-boy. However, I forgive him for the sake of his Ballad, which I always thought the prettiest in the world. All there is of Mr. Green here, has been printed before; there is a profusion of wit every where. Reading would have formed his judgment, and harmonized his verse; for even his wood-notes often break out into strains of real poetry and music. The 'School-Mistress'* is excellent in its kind

the fourth volume was published in 1755; and the fifth and sixth volumes, which completed the Collection, in 1758.

* The School-Mistress is by far the best of Shenstone's poems. The variations from the first edition are very curious.

and masterly: and 'London' is one of those few imitations that have all the ease and all the spirit of the original. The same man's * Verses at the Opening of Garrick's Theatre are far from bad. Mr. Dyer has more of poetry in his imagination, than almost any of our number; but rough and injudicious. I should range Mr. Bramston only a step or two above Dr. King, who is as low in my estimation as in yours. Dr. Evans is a furious madman; and 'Pre-existence' is nonsense in all her altitudes. Mr. Lyttleton is a gentle elegiac person.† Mr. Nugent sure did not write his own Ode. I like Mr. Whitehead's little poems, (I mean The Ode on a Tent, The Verses to Garrick, and particularly those to Charles Townshend,) better than any thing I had ever seen before of him. I gladly pass over H. Brown and the rest, to come at you. You know I was of the publishing side, and thought your reasons against it — none: for though, as Mr. Chute said extremely well, 'the still small voice' of Poetry was not made to be heard in a

His writings in prose abound with sound reflection, and knowledge of human nature; and are written in a neat and unaffected manner, displaying great benevolence of mind and gentleness of disposition. Mr. Graves (the author of the Spiritual Quixote) wrote a pamphlet, called ' Recollections of some Particulars in the Life of William Shenstone, Esq. &c.' to vindicate his friend from the censure of Dr. Johnson, *Gray*, and Mason.

* Dr. Samuel Johnson. See W. S. Landor's Satire on Satirists, p. 14.

† See Walpole's Noble Authors, vol. i. p. 549, and Warton's Pope, vol. iv. 309

crowd, yet Satire will be heard, for all the audience are by nature her friends. . . . . . What shall
I say to Mr. Lowth, Mr. Ridley, Mr. Rolle, the
Rev. Mr. Brown, Seward, &c. . . . If I say, 'Mes-
sieurs! this is not the thing: write prose, write
sermons, write nothing at all,' they will disdain
me and my advice. Mr. S. Jenyns now and then
can write a good line or two, such as these:

> 'Snatch us from all our little sorrows here,
> Calm every grief, and dry each childish tear.'

I like Mr. Aston Hervey's Fable; and an Ode the
last of all, by Mr. Mason; a new acquaintance of
mine, whose *Musæus* too seems to carry with it the
promise at least of something good to come. I was
glad to see you distinguished who poor West was
before his charming Ode, and called it any thing
rather than a Pindaric. The Town is an owl, if it
don't like Lady Mary; and I am surprised at it. We
here are owls enough to think her Eclogues very
bad: but that, I did not wonder at. Our present
taste is Sir Thomas Fitzosborne's Letters," &c. *

In 1756 Gray left Peter-house, where he had
resided above twenty years, on account of some
incivilities he met with, which are slightly mentioned in his correspondence. He removed to
Pembroke-hall, where his most intimate friends
resided; and this he describes, " as an æra in a
life so barren of events as his."

---

* See Walpole's Works, vol. v. p. 393.

In July 1757, he took his Odes to London, to be published. "I found Gray (says H. Walpole) in Town, last week. He brought his two Odes* to be printed. I snatched them out of Dodsley's hands, and they are to be the first-fruits of my press." Although the genius of Gray was now "in its firm and mature age," and though his poetical reputation was deservedly celebrated; it is plain that these Odes were not favourably received. "His friends (he says) write to him, that they do not succeed," and several amusing criticisms on them are mentioned in the Letters. Yet there were not wanting some better judges who admired them. They had received the judicious and valuable approbation of Mason and of Hurd;† and if Gray felt any pleasure in the poem which Garrick wrote in their praise, he must have been yet more gratified, when Warburton, while he bestowed on them his honest applause, shewed his indignation at those who condemned, without being able to understand them.‡

* Of these Odes, a thousand copies were printed at Strawberry-Hill.

† It is, I believe, to *Gray* that Hurd alludes in the Essay on the Marks of Imitation, as to the " common friend of Mason and himself," who had suggested an imitation of Spenser, by Milton: see vol. iii. p. 48.

‡ Gray's Odes were reviewed in the Monthly Review for 1757, p. 239. They were also reviewed in the Critical Review, vol. iv. p. 167; in which the critic mistook the Αἰολήια μολπὴ (the Æolian lyre), for the Æolian harp, the instru-

About ten years before this time, the Odes of Collins * were published, and received with the most unmerited neglect. The public had been so long delighted with the wit and satire of Pope, had formed their taste so much on his manner of versification, and had been so accustomed to dwell upon the neat and pointed style of that finished writer; that they were but ill prepared to admire the beauties of the lofty and magnificent language, in which Collins arrayed his sublime conceptions; and which was tasteless to those, who, but a few years before, had received the last book of the Dunciad, from the dying hands of their favourite poet; and who could not pass from wit, and epigram, and satire, to the bold conceptions, the animated descriptions, and the wild grandeur of lyric poetry. † The very works which have now raised

ment invented by Kircher about 1649; and, after being forgotten for a century, discovered by Mr. Oswald. A passage in this Review, suggested to Dr. Johnson an objection of which he made use, in his criticism on Gray; viz. "Is there not, (says the Critical Review) a trifling impropriety in this line, 'Weave the warp, and weave the woof;' — Is not the warp laid, and the woof afterwards woven? Suppose he had written 'Stretch the warp, and weave the woof.'" Compare Johnson's Life of Gray, vol. xi. p. 377, ed. Murphy.

* The Odes of Collins were published in 1746. The open manner in which Goldsmith in his Threnod. Aug. borrowed whole lines and stanzas from Collins, is a strong proof how little Collins' Poems were then known.

† See T. Warton's Preface to Milton's Minor Poems, p. 1. 10, for a support of this opinion, and Mason's Life of Whitehead, p 12.

Gray and Collins to the rank of our two greatest lyric poets, were either neglected, or ridiculed by their contemporaries; while to appreciate the justness of their thoughts, the harmony of their numbers, and the splendid creations of their genius, was left for the more correct decisions of time.

Those who are really competent judges of the merit of poetry, in any age, are necessarily but few; the great and general mass of poetical readers are constantly varying among the favourites of the time; raising with their breath the bubble of that reputation to-day, which they take the same pains to destroy to-morrow.

> Quod dedisti
> *Viventi* decus, atque sentienti
> Rari post cineres habent Poetæ.*

But a poet who receives the praise of an enlightened age, may with confidence expect its continuance; if he write, not for the fluctuation of taste, nor the caprice of fashion; but on his own extended views of nature, on his own confirmed knowledge and experience, and on the solid principles of the art. He who acquires the admiration of the present time, by addressing himself to their taste, by following their judgment, and by soliciting their applause, may be sure that his productions will be superseded by the favourite rivals of the age to come. Πῶς ἂν ὁ μέτ᾽ ἐμὲ πᾶς ἀκούσειεν αἰών,

---

* See Martial. Eleg. Lib. i. 2, 4, and Bentivoglio's Letters, p. 144, and Johnson's Life of Cowley, p. 62.

was the sensible advice of Longinus,* to those, who "with a noble ambition aim at immortality."

There is a passage in the Life of Thomson written by his friend, in which he mentions the reason of the discouragement shewn, by some critics of that day, to the poetry of that interesting writer; and which applies equally in the case of Collins and of Gray; as the same cause that impeded the favourable reception of the Seasons, still continued to exert its powerful influence. "The Poem of Winter, (says Mr. Murdoch, who speaks from his own observation,) was no sooner read, than universally admired; those only excepted, who had not been used to feel, or to look for any thing in poetry beyond a point of satirical or epigrammatic wit; a smart antithesis richly trimmed with rhyme; or the softness of an elegiac complaint. To such his manly classical spirit could not readily recommend itself; till after a more attentive perusal, they had got the better of their prejudices, and either acquired, or affected a truer taste. A few others stood aloof, merely because they had long before fixed the articles of their poetical creed, and resigned themselves to an absolute despair of ever seeing any thing new and original." From that time, till after the death of Gray, the strong and almost exclusive influence of Pope's versification was felt on English poetry. Mason, speaking of

* Vide Longinum περὶ 'Υψοῦς. Sect. XIV. iii. p. 57.

Gray's Hymn or Address to Ignorance, says, —
" Many of the lines are so strong, and the general
cast of the versification so musical, that I believe
it will give the generality of readers a higher
opinion of his poetical talents, than many of his
lyrical productions would have done. I speak of
the generality; for it is a certain fact, that their
taste is founded upon the ten syllable couplet of
Dryden and Pope, and of these only."

In this year Cibber died at an advanced age,
and the Laureatship was offered by the Duke of
Devonshire, then Lord Chamberlain, to Gray;
with a remarkable and honourable privilege, to
hold it as a mere sinecure. This he respectfully
declined; and some of his reasons for refusing it,
he gives in a letter to Mr. Mason: " The office
itself (he says) has always humbled the possessor
hitherto : — if he were a poor writer, by making
him more conspicuous; and if he were a good one,
by setting him at war with the little fry of his own
profession; for there are poets little enough, even
to envy a poet-laureat." *

Upon Gray's refusal, the laurel was accepted
by Mr. Whitehead, who joined to very competent
talents, what made those talents respectable — modesty and worth. Mr. Mason had by him letters
of Gray, in which he gave Whitehead's first and
second odes great encomiums. To Cibber indeed,

* See Mason's Life of Whitehead, vol. i. p. 92, and G.
Colman's Works, vol. iii. p. 161.

he was in every respect infinitely superior: but it
is no disgrace to Mr. Whitehead to affirm, that
to the genius of that poet who succeeded him, we
are indebted for the finest productions that have
ever ennobled an office, in itself not most friendly
to the Muses. Mr. Mason was not quite overlooked on this occasion. "Lord John Cavendish
(he says) made an apology to him, 'that being in
orders, he was thought less eligible than a lay
man.'" A little tinge of that satire which occa-
sionally darted its shafts into the world from the
retirement of Aston, is now visible in Mr. Mason's
narrative,* when he adds, "that he wonders the
same privilege, of holding the office as a sinecure, was not offered to Mr. Whitehead; as the
king would readily have dispensed with hearing
poetry, for which he had no taste, and music, for
which he had no ear." †

In 1758, Gray describes himself as composing,
for his own amusement, the little book which he
calls 'A Catalogue of the Antiquities, Houses,
&c., in England and Wales;' and which he drew
up on the blank pages of Kitchen's English Atlas. After his death it was printed and distri-
buted by Mr. Mason to his friends. ‡

* See Mason's Life of Whitehead, p. 87, and on T. Warton's Lyrical merits, p. 93.
† See Johnson's Epigram, in his Poems by Park, p. 72.
‡ A new edition was printed in 1787 for sale. Mr. Mason's
was only intended for presents.

About this period, much of his time seems to
have been employed in the study of architecture;
in which his proficiency, as indeed in all other
branches of learning which he pursued, was accurate and deep. Some of his observations on this
subject afterwards appeared in Mr. Bentham's
History of Ely. In the Gentleman's Magazine
for April 1784, a letter from Gray to Mr. Bentham is published, which contains all the information afforded to the latter. It was printed in
consequence of the circulation of a report, that
the whole of the Treatise on Saxon, Norman, and
Gothic Architecture, published in the History of
Ely, was written by Gray.* On the 15th of January 1759, the British Museum was opened to the
public; and Gray went to London to read and
transcribe the manuscripts which were collected
there from the Harleian and Cottonian libraries.
A folio volume of his transcripts was in Mr. Mason's hands; out of which, one paper alone — The
speech of Sir Thomas Wyatt † before the Privy
Council — was published in the second number
of Lord Orford's Miscellaneous Antiquities; but,

* See Bentham's preface to the History of Ely, (new
edit.) p. 13; Selections from the Gentleman's Magazine, vol.
ii. p. 249; and Nichols's Literary Anecdotes, vol. iii. p. 489;
and Gentleman's Magazine, vol. liii. p. 37, 138, 301, 375:
vol. liv. p. 243.

† See Chalmers's Life of Sir Thomas Wyatt in the British
Poets, vol. ii. p. 363.

as I understand from a note in Dr. Nott's Edition of Lord Surrey, very imperfectly. *

He was, as Dr. Johnson observed, but little affected by two Odes of Obscurity and Oblivion † written by Messrs. Colman and Lloyd, which then appeared in ridicule of him, and Mr. Mason. The humour of these poems, in my opinion, has been much over-praised. Warburton calls them " two miserable buffoon Odes." ‡ Like all other productions of a personal and satirical nature, their subject ensured to them a short period of popularity. We know with what avidity those works are perused, which hold up to the derision of the public the peculiarities of genius and learning. Almost every author of talent, at some time or other, becomes the mark at which ridicule is aimed. In this particular case, the most modest and retired habits, as well as the most exalted talents, were dragged out with circumstances of laughter and contempt, by men very inferior to Gray, either in the strictness of their moral character, or in the depth and extent of their literary attainments. Yet, while I think their ridicule was not happy or successful, I do not see those marks of rancour and malevolence in their design, which

* See Nott's Surrey, vol. ii. p. lxiv.

† The Ode to *Obscurity* was directed chiefly against Gray; that to *Oblivion* against Mason. See Lloyd's Poems, vol. i. p. 120.

‡ See Warburton's Letters, by Hurd, Lett. cxli

so often imbitter and disgrace the Satires of Churchill;* which the intemperance of youth, I am afraid, can hardly excuse; and which must raise constant disgust in those, who read the works of that powerful, though unfinished writer. Dr. Warton, in his notes on Pope,† says, "The Odes of Gray were burlesqued by two men of wit and genius; *who, however, once owned to me, that they repented of the attempt.*"

During Gray's residence in London, he became slightly acquainted with the amiable naturalist Mr. Stillingfleet, whose death took place a few months after his own.‡ At the request of Mr. Montagu, he wrote an 'Epitaph on Sir William Williams,' who was killed at the siege of Belleisle. In 1762 the professorship of modern history became vacant by the death of Mr. Turner. By the

* Churchill mentions Gray in the Ghost — "And plaintive fops debauched by Gray;" — also in the Journey, in which poem Armstrong is satirized, in language of unbecoming and inexcusable asperity. Mrs. Chapone, in a Letter dated 1764, says, — "You keep my genius down continually by throwing cold water on its dying embers; and terrifying my poor muse, as much as Churchill does that of Gray." Chapone's Letters, vol. ii. p. 164, date 1764.

† See Warton's Pope, vol. i. p. 236. See also G. Colman's Works, vol. i. p. xi.

‡ Mr. Benjamin Stillingfleet died December 15, 1771, aged 69. A very pleasing tribute to his memory has lately been paid by the Rev. Mr. Coxe; by a careful selection from his unpublished Works, and a Life of him, and his literary friends, in three volumes 8vo. 1811.

advice of his friends, he applied to Lord Bute for
the place, through the medium of Sir Henry
Erskine. He was refused; and the professorship was given to Mr. Brocket, the tutor of Sir
James Lowther. "And so (says Gray, humour-
ously passing over his disappointment) I have
made my fortune like Sir Francis Wronghead."

In the summer of 1765, he took a journey
into Scotland, to improve his health, which was
becoming more weak and uncertain, as well as to
gratify his curiosity with the natural beauties and
antiquities of that wild and romantic country. He
went through Edinburgh and Perth to Glamis-
Castle, the residence of Lord Strathmore, where
he stayed some time. Thence he took a short
excursion into the Highlands, crossing Perthshire
by Loch-Tay, and pursuing the road from Dunkeld to Inverness, as far as the pass of Gillikran-
kie. Then returning to Dunkeld, he travelled on
the Stirling road to Edinburgh. "His account of
his journey, (says Dr. Johnson,) so far as it extends, is curious and elegant: for as his compre-
hension was ample, his curiosity extended to all
the works of art, all the appearances of nature, and
all the monuments of past events." In Scotland he
formed an acquaintance with Dr. Beattie; who
had been the first to welcome him on his arrival
in the North, with a testimony of the high admiration in which he held his genius and his character; and which was truly valuable, because it

was the voluntary praise of one, who himself possessed the feeling and power of a poet. I transcribe Dr. Beattie's Letter, from his Life, published by Sir William Forbes:—

"Marischal College of Aberdeen,
30th of August, 1765.

"If I thought it necessary to offer an apology for venturing to address you in this abrupt manner, I should be very much at a loss how to begin. I might plead my admiration of your genius, and my attachment to your character; but who is he that could not with truth urge the same excuse for intruding upon your retirement? I might plead my earnest desire to be personally acquainted with a man, whom I have so long and so passionately admired in his writings; but thousands, of greater consequence than I, are ambitious of the same honour. I, indeed, must either flatter myself that no apology is necessary, or otherwise, I must despair of obtaining what has long been the object of my most ardent wishes. I must for ever forfeit all hopes of seeing you, and conversing with you.

"It was yesterday I received the agreeable news of your being in Scotland, and of your intending to visit some parts of it. Will you permit us to hope, that we shall have an opportunity at Aberdeen, of thanking you in person, for the honour you have done to Britain, and to the poetic art, by your inestimable compositions, and of offering you all that we have that deserves your acceptance; namely, hearts full of esteem, respect and affection? If you cannot come so far northward, let me at least be acquainted with the place of your residence, and permitted to wait on you. Forgive, sir, this request: forgive me, if I urge it with earnestness, for indeed it concerns me nearly: and do me the justice to believe, that I am with the most sincere attachment, and most respectful esteem," &c.

Gray declined the honour which the University of Aberdeen was disposed to confer on him, (of the degree of doctor of laws,) lest it might appear a slight and contempt of his own University, "where (he says) he passed so many easy and happy hours of his life, where he had once lived from choice, and continued to do so from obligation." In one of his conversations with Dr. Beattie,* who expressed himself with less admiration of Dryden than Gray thought his due; he told him, "that if there was any excellence in his own numbers, he had learned it wholly from that great poet; and pressed him with great earnestness to study him, as his choice of words and versification was singularly happy and harmonious." — "Remember Dryden, (he also wrote,) and be blind to all his faults." †

* See Beattie's Essay on Poetry and Music, 4to. p. 360 (note).

† Mr. Mason, in his Life of Whitehead, p. 17, says "that

Part of the summer of 1766 Gray passed in a
tour in Kent, and at the house of his friend Mr.
Robinson, on the skirts of Barham Down.   In a
letter in my possession, from Mrs. Robinson to a
friend, dated June 2, 1766, she says: " I have
met with several interruptions, partly owing to
our having had for almost a fortnight a very
agreeable gentleman in the house, whose conversation is both instructive and entertaining; after
what I have said, you will wish to know his
name — 'tis Mr. Gray — who is well known for
having wrote several pretty elegies; he is also an
acquaintance of your friend Mr. Rycroft," &c. *
In 1767 he again left Cambridge, and went to
the North of England, on a visit to Dr. Whar-

Gray, who admired Dryden almost beyond bounds, used to say
of a very juvenile poem of his, in Tonson's Miscellany, written
on the Death of Lord Halifax, that it gave not so much as the
slightest promise of his future excellency, and seemed to indicate a bad natural ear for versification.   I believe Derrick
reprinted this poem in his edition of Dryden."   There is no
poem that I can discover by Dryden on the Death of Lord
Halifax; but I suppose Mr. Mason meant a Poem on the Death
of Lord Hastings, (See Scott's Life of Dryden, p. 28.) written
when Dryden was only eighteen, and at Westminster School,
and which is the first poem in Derrick's Collection; and is also
in p. 116 of the first volume of Tonson's Miscellany.   These
lines are certainly most singularly inharmonious, with much of
the strained allusion and rough style of Donne.   At the end
of 'Halifax's Miscellanies,' there is an anonymous poem to his
memory, of considerable merit; but I am not able to say by
whom it was written.   See also Mason's Works, vol. i. p. 451.
    * See Miss Carter's Letters to Mrs. Montagu, vol. i p. 364.

ton. He had intended a second tour to Scotland, but returned to London without accomplishing his design. At Dr. Beattie's desire, a new edition of his Poems was published by Foulis at Glasgow; and at the same time Dodsley was also printing them in London. In both these editions, the 'Long Story' was omitted, as the plates from Bentley's designs were worn out: and Gray said, "that its only use, which was to explain the prints, was gone." Some pieces of Welch and Norwegian Poetry, written in a bold and original manner,* were inserted in its place: of which the 'Descent of Odin' is undoubtedly the most valuable, though in many places it is exceedingly obscure. I have mentioned, in the notes to this poem, that Gray translated only that part of it which he found in the Latin version of Bartholinus; and to this cause much of the obscurity is owing. In a letter to Walpole † he says, "As to what you say to me civilly, — that I ought to write more, — I reply in our own words, like the pamphleteer who is going to confute you out of your own mouth; 'What has one to do, when turned of fifty, but really to think of finishing?' However, I will be candid, for you seem to be so with me, and avow to you, that

* See Mason's Life of Whitehead, p. 84. See also Dryden's Miscell. v. vi. p. 387, for a translation that may have turned Gray's thoughts to the Northern Poetry.

† See Walpole's Works, vol. v. p. 374, Letter viii

till fourscore and upward, whenever the humour takes me, I will write; because I like it, and because I like myself better when I do so. If I do not write much, it is because I cannot."—"Gray," says Walpole, "has added to his Poems three ancient odes from Norway and Wales. The subjects of the two first are grand and picturesque, and there is *his* genuine vein in them; but they are not interesting, and do not, like his other poems, touch any passion: our human feelings, which he masters at will in his finer pieces, are not here affected. Who can care through what horrors a Runic savage arrived at all the joys and glories they could conceive, — the supreme felicity of boozing ale out of the skull of an enemy in Odin's Hall?" * To his Odes, Gray now found it necessary to add some notes, "Partly (he says) from justice, to acknowledge a debt when I had borrowed anything: partly from ill-temper, just to tell the gentle reader, that Edward the First was not Oliver Cromwell nor Queen Elizabeth the Witch of Endor." † Walpole, in a letter to G. Montagu, says: "You are very particular, I can tell you, in liking Gray's Odes; but you must remember the age likes Akenside, and did like Thomson. Can the same people like both? Milton was forced to wait till the world had done admiring Quarles. Cam-

* See Letter to G. Montagu, p. 405.
† See Southey's Life of Cowper, vol. i. p. 325.

bridge told me t'other night, that my Lord Ches-
terfield had heard Stanly read them as his own,
but that must have been a mistake of my Lord's
deafness.   Cambridge said—' Perhaps they are
Stanly's, and not caring to own them, he gave
them to Gray.'   I think this would hurt Gray's
dignity ten times more than his Poetry not suc-
ceeding."

In 1768 the professorship of modern history
again became vacant by the accidental death of
Mr. Brocket; and the Duke of Grafton, then in
power, at the request of Mr. Stonehewer, immediately bestowed it upon Gray.*   In 1769, on the
death of the Duke of Newcastle,† the Duke of
Grafton was elected to the chancellorship of the
University.   His installation took place in the
summer; and Gray wrote his fine Ode that was
set to music on the occasion: " He thought it
better that Gratitude should sing, than Expectation." ‡   He told Dr. Beattie, " that he considered himself bound in gratitude to the Duke of
Grafton, to write this Ode; and that he foresaw

---

* The professorship became vacant on Sunday, and the
Duke of Grafton wrote to Gray on the following Wednesday:
see Walpole's Letters, vol. v. p. 137, and Pursuits of Literature, p. 51, and H. Walpole's Letter to Conway, Aug. 9,
1768.

† The Duke of Newcastle died in Lincoln's Inn Fields,
the 17th of November 1768, in the 77th year of his age.

‡ Pope told Lord Halifax he would be troublesome ' out of
gratitude, not expectation.' v. Johnson's Life of Pope, p. 94.

the abuse that would be thrown on him for it, but
did not think it worth his while to avoid it." He
did not appear to set much value on the poem,
for he says, "it cannot last above a single day,
or if its existence be prolonged beyond that period, it must be by means of newspaper parodies,
and witless criticism." Posterity however has
more correctly estimated this beautiful production, than the author; it is a very splendid creation raised on an apparently barren subject. *

When this ceremony was past, he went on a
tour to the Lakes of Cumberland and Westmoreland. His friend Dr. Wharton, who was to be
his companion on the journey, was seized with
the return of an asthmatic attack on the first
day, and went home. To this accident we are
indebted for a most elegant and lively journal
of his tour, intended for his friend's amusement.
The style in which these letters are written, is
evidently the production of a person thoroughly
accustomed to the contemplation of his subject;
it is peculiarly clear, simple and elegant; and
abounds with those picturesque descriptions,
which, though they can never enable language

* "Gray," says a writer of very superior talent and taste,
"has finely glanced at the bright point in Henry's character
— 'The Majestic Lord' — in that beautiful stanza where he
has made the founders of Cambridge pass before our eyes, like
shadows over a magic glass" See Hallam's Constitut. History, vol. i. p. 49.

totally to supply, can at least make it much assist, the local powers of the pencil. "He that
reads his epistolary narrative (says Dr. Johnson) wishes, that to travel, and to tell his travels, had been more of his employment: but it
is by staying at home, that we must obtain the
ability of travelling with intelligence and improvement."

In April 1770 he complains much of a depression of spirits, talks of an intended tour into
Wales in the summer, and of meeting his friend
Dr. Wharton at Mr. Mason's. In July, however,
he was still at Cambridge, and wrote to Dr.
Beattie, complaining of illness and pain in his
head; and in this letter, he sent him some criticisms on the first book of the Minstrel, which
have since been published.* His tour took place
in the autumn: but not a single letter is preserved in Mr. Mason's book on this journey, to
any of his correspondents. He wrote no journal,
and travelled with Mr. Nicholls,† of Blundeston,
in Suffolk, a gentleman of much accomplishment,

* See Forbes's Life of Beattie, vol. i. p. 197, 4to. letter xlv.
† The taste of Mr. Nicholls enabled him to adorn, in the
midst of a flat and unvaried county, and on the bleak eastern
shore of England, a little valley, near Lowestoff, with beauties
of no ordinary kind. Οὐ γάρ τι καλὸς χῶρος, ὀυδ' ἐφίμερος,
ὀυδ' ἐράτος, ὃιος ἀμφὶ Ζίριος ῥοαῖς. v. Archilochi, Fr. p. 63.
ed Liebel. "La villa (says Mr. Mathias) del Sig. Nicholls,
detta *Blundeston*, alla spiaggia Orientale della contéa de *Suffolk*, due miglia lontana dal mare, disposta, ed ornata da lui

and who was admitted, more than any other person, into intimate and unreserved friendship with Gray. He was I believe the Octavius of the Pursuits of Literature. The sketch of his life was written by Mr. Mathias, in 1809, in the Gent. Mag. and subsequently enlarged. The letters of Gray to Mr. Nicholls, which Mr. Dawson Turner possesses, fully prove the truth of Mr. Mathias's belief — 'that with the single exception of Mr. West, Gray was more affectionately attached to him than to any other person.'

In May 1771 he wrote to Dr. Wharton, just sketching the outlines of his Tour in Wales and some of the adjacent Counties. This is the last letter that remains in Mr. Mason's Collection. He there complains of an incurable cough, of spirits habitually low, and of the uneasiness which the thought of the duties of his professorship gave him, which, after having held nearly three years, Mr. Mason says he had now a determined resolution to resign. He mentions also different plans of amusement and travel, that he had pro-

con singolare fantasia, e con giudizio squisito. Il Sig. Gray, de' Lirici Britanni Sovrano, vide già con ammirazione, e molto ancora attendea dal genio del disegnatore." See a note in the first volume of ' Aggiunta ai Componimenti Lirici,' &c. p. ii. and xi. But alas ! instead of the " i mobili cristalli d'un limpidissimo lago," are we not reminded of

"—— Questi valli
Circondati di stagnanti fiumi
Quando cade dal ciel, più lenta pioggia — "

jected; but which unfortunately were not to be accomplished. Within a few days after the date of this last letter, he removed to London, where his health more and more declined. His physician, Dr. Gisborne, advised freer air, and he went to Kensington. There he in some degree revived, and returned to Cambridge, intending to go from that place to Old Park, near Durham, the residence of his friend Dr. Wharton.* In the spring of 1769 or 1770, his friend Mr. Robinson saw Gray for the last time, in his lodgings in Jermyn Street. He was then ill, and in a state of apparent decay, and low spirits. He expressed regret that he had done so little in literature; and began to lament, that at last, when he had become easy in his circumstances, he had lost his health. But in this he checked himself, feeling that it was wrong to repine at the decrees of Providence. On the 24th of July, while at dinner in the College hall, he was seized with an attack of the gout † in his stomach. The violence of the disease resisted all the powers of medicine: on the 29th he was seized with convulsions, which returned more violently on the 30th; and he expired in the even-

* See H. Stevenson's Works, vol. ii. p. 210.

† In a letter from Paris, August 11, 1771, H. Walpole says, on hearing the report of Gray's death, — " He called on me, but two or three days before I came hither: he complained of being ill, and talked of the gout in his stomach; but I expected his death no more than my own."

ing of that day, in the fifty-fifth year of his age;
sensible almost to the last: aware of his danger,
and expressing, says his friend Dr. Brown, no
visible concern at the thought of his approaching
death. The care of his funeral devolved on one
of his executors, Dr. Brown, the president of
Pembroke-hall; who saw him buried, as he desired in his will, by the side of his mother, in the
church-yard of Stoke. His other executor and
friend Mr. Mason was at that time absent in a
distant part of Yorkshire, and when Dr. Brown
wrote to him during Gray's short illness, he says,
" as I felt strongly at the time what Tacitus has
so well expressed on a similar occasion, I may
with propriety use his words: ' Mihi, præter
acerbitatem amici erepti, auget mœstitiam, quod
adsidere valetudini, fovere deficientem, satiari
vultu, complexu non contigit.' " *

Such was the life of Gray, who, however few

* In 1778 Mason erected a monument for Gray in Westminster Abbey, with the following inscription, which seems to
have this defect, that it is as much applicable to a monument
to Milton, as to Gray:

" No more the Grecian muse unrivall'd reigns,
     To Britain let the nations homage pay;
She felt a Homer's fire in Milton's strains,
     A Pindar's rapture in the lyre of Gray."

See Mason's Works, vol. i. p. 141. On Penn's Cenotaph to
Gray, see Repton's Inquiry into the Changes of Taste in Landscape Gardening, p. 71; see Roberts's Epistle to C. Anstey on
the English Poets, p. 110, on the death of Gray.

his works,* must still hold a very distinguished
rank among the English poets, for the excellence
of his compositions, and for the splendour of his
genius.   Though the events of his life which I
have briefly sketched, are of common occurrence,
and offer nothing in themselves to excite great
interest in the reader; yet there is surely some
pleasure in contemplating the progress of a virtuous and enlightened mind, early withdrawn from
public life to the stillness of the academic cloister;
and confining its pleasures and prospects within
the serenity of a studious retirement.   Nor is it,
I think, without some feelings of admiration, that
we reflect on the history of a life so constantly
and unremittingly devoted to the pursuit of knowledge, and the general improvement of the mind,
for its own sake, and as a final purpose.   Motives,
which have no honourable connection with literature, are yet often instrumental in increasing it.
The pursuit of wealth, of station, or of rank in a
profession, is the constant and common incentive
to mental exertion; and is dignified, perhaps not
improperly, by the name of honest ambition.
Even among those of a nobler nature, the desire
of being distinguished in their own, and after-
ages, for the endowments of their mind, and the

* "Gray joins to the sublimity of Milton the elegance and
harmony of Pope; and nothing is wanting, to render him, perhaps, *the first poet in the English language, but to have written a
little more.*" — A. Smith's Theory of Moral Sentiments, vol. i.
p. 255.

energies of their genius, acts as a perpetual spur
towards the increase of their exertions. Much of
this feeling does not appear to have existed in the
mind of Gray. To him, study seemed to bring all
the reward he asked, in its own gratification; and
his progress in learning was constant; even in
the absence of those quickening motives, which, in
almost all cases, are necessary to preserve men,
either from weariness in the toil of original composition, or from indolence in the acquisition, and
arrangement, of the materials of collected knowledge.   That the publications of Gray, however,
were so few, is to be attributed, I think, to several
causes: — to the natural modesty and reserved-
ness of his disposition; to the situation of life in
which he was placed, without any profession or
public duty that might lead his thoughts and studies in a particular direction; to his habit of submitting nothing to publication, without bestowing
on it that polish and correctness, which demands
long and patient attention, and which indeed seems
incompatible with works of any magnitude or
number; to the extent and variety of his research; and to the great temptations to read,* in
a place which afforded a ready and almost boundless supply of materials to satisfy him in any
branch of knowledge; and which would constantly
induce him, to make fresh accessions to his in-

* Mr. Mason says, that Gray often mentioned to him, that
reading was much more agreeable to him than writing.

formation, and to open new channels of inquiry.
" I shall be happy (says Mr. Mason in a letter to
Dr. Beattie) to know that the remaining books of
your 'Minstrel' are likewise to be published soon.
The next best thing, after instructing the world
profitably, is to amuse it innocently. England
has lost that man (Gray) who, of all others in
it, was best qualified for both these purposes;
but who, from early chagrin and disappointment,
had imbibed a disinclination to employ his talents
beyond the sphere of self-satisfaction and improvement."

Of Gray's person, his biographer has given no
account: and Lord Orford* has but just mentioned it. The earliest picture of him, is that
which was taken when he was fifteen years of
age, by Richardson. It is now in the possession
of Mr. Robinson of Cambridge, and by his permis-
sion has been engraved. Another portrait was
painted by Eckardt, and engraved in the Works
of Lord Orford.† It is at Strawberry-Hill, and
the design was taken from the Portrait of a Mu-
sician, by Vandyck, at the Duke of Grafton's.
This print was intended to be prefixed to Bentley's edition of Gray's Odes, with a motto from
Lucan, (x. 296).

" Nec licuit populis parvum te, Nile, videre: " ‡

---

* See Walpoliana, vol. i. p. 95.

† See Walpole's Works, vol. ii. p.431, 436; and vol. v. p.352.

‡ Dr. Warton, in his Notes on Pope (vol. i. p. 282), re-

but Gray's extreme repugnance to the proposal, obliged his friends to drop it after the engraving was commenced. The print which Mr. Mason placed before his edition of the Life of Gray in quarto, was from a picture by Wilson, drawn after the death of Gray, from his own and Mr. Mason's recollection; and which is now in the possession of Pembroke-College, by the bequest of Mr. Stonehewer. The engraving, however, has not preserved the character of the countenance, and is, on the whole, an unfavourable likeness. It is from this same picture, I understand, that the print prefixed to Mr. Mathias's edition is taken. To the edition of the Life in octavo, is prefixed a better resemblance, etched by W. Doughty,* from a drawing by Mr. Mason: and from this outline, two other portraits have proceeded: one by a Mr. Sharpe of Cambridge; and the other, which is now extremely rare, by the late Mr. Henshaw, a pupil of Bartolozzi's.† In this latter print, a very correct and

---

marks that Fontenelle had applied the very same line to Newton: and he adds: — "A motto to Mr. Gray's few, but exquisite poems might be from Lucretius, lib. iv. ver. 181 and 907:

"'Suavidicis potius quam multis versibus edam,
Parvus ut est cycni melior canor——'"

* See an account of this *picture*, and of W. Doughty, in Northcote's Life of Reynolds, p. 232.

† Dr. Turner, the late Master of Pembroke-Hall, and

spirited likeness is preserved. A portrait of Gray, bearing a resemblance to Mr. Mason's etching,* and painted by Vandergutch, I have seen in the library of Lord Harcourt, at Nuneham.

The Political opinions of Gray, H. Walpole says he never rightly understood: "sometimes he seemed inclined to the side of authority, and sometimes to that of the people." † Mr. Mason has mentioned nothing concerning any singularity in his sentiments about Religion; and there is, I believe, no passage in his published Letters, either to support, or absolutely to oppose, the assertion made on this subject in the Walpoliana.‡ I must confess myself disinclined to believe it, in any degree, upon the authority of a few words, apparently used in conversation, and which afterwards appeared, without proof or comment, in an anonymous publication. The personal friends of Gray, who could have cleared up this point, are, I believe, all dead: but I cannot find, that, in the place where he so constantly resided, or among those who have enjoyed the best opportunities of

Dean of Norwich, had two profile shades of Gray, taken with an instrument for that purpose, by a Mr. Mapletoft, formerly a fellow of that college, one of which conveys a strong resemblance.

* See Gent. Mag. May, 1814, p. 427.

† See Walpoliana, vol. i. p. 29, published by Mr. Pinkerton.

‡ Ibid. vol. i. p. 95.

hearing about his opinions, the slightest suspi-
cions existed, which could at all confirm the assertion of Walpole. It is a consideration of no
small weight, that these supposed opinions of
Gray have been delivered on the authority of two
writers, neither of them, I believe, favourable to
the cause of Christianity.*, I shall merely mention, that in a letter to Mr. Mason,† speaking of
Rousseau's ' Lettres de la Montagne,' he says :
" It is a weak attempt to separate *miracles* from
the *morality* of the Gospel; the latter he would
think, he believes was sent from God, and the former he very explicitly takes for an imposture."
In a letter to H. Walpole,‡ he gives an account
of some manuscript writings of Middleton against
Waterland, on the doctrine of the Trinity; but he
expresses an approbation of no other part of them
than of the style. He tells Dr. Wharton,§ —
" Though I do not approve the spirit of his (Middleton's) books ; methinks 'tis pity the world
should lose so rare a thing as a good writer."
Whenever Gray writes to his friends on religious
subjects, it is with uncommon seriousness, warmth,
and piety. Even Walpole calls him " a violent
enemy of atheists, such as he took Voltaire and

* See Johnson's Life of Browne, vol. xii. p. 305: he there
speaks the language of wisdom, religion, and humanity.
† See Mason's Memoirs, vol. iv. p. 95.
‡ See Walpole's Works, vol. v. p. 391.
§ See Mason's Memoirs, vol. iii. p. 124.

Hume to be." His sentiments on Shaftesbury and Bolingbroke are well known: and Mr. Mason [*] has very properly pointed out to the attention of his readers, the scorn and contempt with which he invariably mentions the works of those writers who endeavoured to disseminate the baneful doctrines of infidelity.

— " In conversation, H. Walpole [†] mentions, that Gray was so circumspect in his usual language, that it seemed unnatural, though it was only pure English." In a letter to G. Montagu he says, " I agree with you most absolutely in your opinion about Gray: he is the worst company in the world. From a melancholy turn, from living reclusely, and from a little too much dignity, he never converses easily ; all his words are measured and chosen and formed into sentences. His writings are admirable, he himself is not agreeable :" and in another letter, " My Lady Ailesbury has been much diverted, and so will you too. *Gray* is in their neighbourhood. My Lady Carlisle says, *he is extremely like me in his manner.* They went a party to dine on a cold loaf, and passed the day. Lady A. protests he never opened his lips but once, and then only said, ' Yes, my Lady, I believe so.' "[‡] Dr. Beat-

[*] See Mason's Memoirs, vol. iv. p. 210: and Walpoliana, vol. i. p. 95; and Mathias's Observations, p. 34–6.

[†] See Walpole's Thoughts on Comedy, p. 332.

[‡] See Letters to G. Montagu, p. 53, 199.

tie writes,* " Gray's letters very much resemble
what his conversation was. He had none of the
airs of either a scholar or a poet; and though on
those and all other subjects he spoke to me with
the utmost freedom, and without any reserve, he
was, in general company, much more silent than
one could have wished." And in a letter to Sir
William Forbes, he says,—" I am sorry you did
not see Mr. Gray on his return: you would have
been much pleased with him. Setting aside his
merit as a poet, which, however, in my opinion, is
greater than any of his contemporaries can boast,
in this or any other nation; I found him possest
of the most exact taste, the soundest judgment,
and the most extensive learning. He is happy
in a singular facility of expression. His conversation abounds in original observations, delivered
with no appearance of sententious formality, and
seeming to arise spontaneously, without study or
premeditation. I passed two very agreeable days
with him at Glammis, and found him as easy in
his manners, and as communicative and frank,
as I could have wished." †

" From my friend, the Rev. Mr. Sparrow, of

* See Beattie's Letters to Sir W. Forbes, in the 'Life of
Dr. Beattie,' vol. ii. 4to. p. 321.

† " I once met Gray the Poet, when I was a boy, at old
Mrs. Hamilton Campbell's, in Sackville Street, Piccadilly. He
talked with great reserve, and seeming difficulty." — Claver-
ing's Autobiog. in Metropolitan Mag., No. xiii. p. 157, 1832.

Pembroke College, who died at Walthamstow,"
(says Mr. Cradock,) " I obtained at times many
specimens of Gray's peculiar humour. Gray's
satire on Lord Holland's seat at Kingsgate, was
at first denied to be his. When stories were told
of Gray by those who knew him, they were
thought so unlike, that several were imputed to
Dr. Johnson, nay, were even printed among the
Johnsonia, which Mr. Boswell says, the Doctor
was much offended at. I can give one strong instance: Dr. Johnson is made to reply to some
impudent man, ' that in that face the north-west
wind would have the worst of it.' Now, the truth
was this: some friends of mine were educated at
Christ's Hospital, and went from thence to Pembroke Hall, in Cambridge, where Gray then
resided; one of them was rather a favourite of
Gray, but to another he had taken a particular dislike. Standing by the fire in the Hall,
the offensive gentleman, who was then curate of
Newmarket, thus addressed the celebrated poet:
' Mr. Gray, I have just rode from Newmarket,
and never was so cut in my life, the north-west
wind was full in my face.' Gray, turning to the
Rev. Mr. Sparrow, said, ' I think in that face the
north-west wind would have the worst of it.' This
I had from Mr. Sparrow. Again, it was the custom at Cambridge, when a book was ordered at a
coffee-house, that four subscribers' names should
be previously signed. The young men, knowing

that Mr. Pigot wished to be particularly thought
to be the intimate of Gray, and Mr. Gray equally
wished not to be considered as the intimate of Mr.
Pigot, so contrived it, that Gray expressed his
anger, that wherever he wrote his name, the next
was erased, and Mr. Pigot's inserted in its stead;
and, according to his *peculiar humour*, he said to
my friend, 'That man's name wherever I go,
piget, he *Pigot's* me.' This was true, but could
not then be credited."*

To record the trifling and minute peculiarities
of manners, unless they reflect considerable light
upon the character which is delineated, does not
seem to be a necessary part of the duty of a biographer. The little and singular habits of behaviour which are gradually formed in the seclusion
of a studious life, are not always viewed in a just
light, and without prejudice, by our contemporaries; and at a distance of time they are necessarily represented without those nice but discri-
minating touches that belong to them; and are
stripped of that connection of circumstances, with
which they can alone be painted with justness and
precision. Some few observations, however, of
this nature, made by the friends of Gray, I have
placed in this edition, without presuming myself
to make any remarks on their correctness: but I
have great pleasure in adding a slight sketch of
his character, drawn by a contemporary poet, the

* See Cradock's Memoirs, vol. iv. p. 226.

late translator of Æschylus.* — "If there is a writer (says Mr. Potter) who more than others has a
claim to be exempted from his [Dr. Johnson's]
petulance, Mr. Gray has that claim. His own polished manners restrained him from ever giving
offence to any good man; his warm and cheerful
benevolence endeared him to all his friends;
though he lived long in a college, he lived not
sullenly there, but in a liberal intercourse with the
wisest and most virtuous men of his time. He
was perhaps the most learned man of the age, but
his mind never contracted the rust of pedantry.
He had too good an understanding to neglect that
urbanity which renders society pleasing: his conversation was instructing, elegant, and agreeable.
Superior knowledge, an exquisite taste in the fine
arts, and, above all, purity of morals, and an unaffected reverence for religion, made this excellent
person an ornament to society, and an honour to
human nature."

Soon after the death of Gray, a sketch of his
character was drawn up by the Rev. Mr. Temple.†

---

* See Inquiry into some Passages in Dr. Johnson's Lives
of the Poets, particularly his Observations on Lyric Poetry,
and the Odes of Gray; by R. Potter, 4to. 1783.

† William Johnson Temple, LL.B., of Trinity-Hall, Cambridge, 1766, formerly rector of Mamhead, Devon, to which
he was presented by the Earl of Lisburne; and exchanged it
for St. Gluvias. He published an Essay on the Clergy, their
Studies, Recreations, Doctrines, Influence, &c., 1774, 8vo. See
Annual Register, 1796, p. 64. He also published 'Historical

This account has been adopted both by Mr. Mason and Dr. Johnson: it was considered by the former to be an impartial summary of its character, and it seems therefore not improper to introduce it into this narrative; though I must confess that, in my own opinion, it appears to be defective in several material points; nor is it sketched in that masterly and decisive manner, that leaves a fuller likeness scarcely to be desired. Its prominent defect however is, that it has thrown into the back-ground the peculiar and distinguishing features of the mind of Gray;—I mean his poetical invention, and his rich and splendid imagination; —while it is too exclusively confined in detailing the produce of his studies, and the extent of his acquired knowledge. Nor is any mention made in this portrait of his mental character, of that talent of *humour** which he possessed in a very

and Political Memoirs,' 8vo.; and ' On the Abuses of Unrestrained Power, an Historical Essay,' 1778, 8vo. He died August 8, 1796. This character of Gray originally appeared in the London Magazine for March 1772. " I never saw Mr. Gray, but my old and most intimate friend the Rev. Mr. Temple knew him well; he knew his foibles, but admired his genius, and esteemed his virtues. I know not if you was acquainted with Mr. Gray. He was so abstracted and singular a man, that I can suppose you and him never to have met." Boswell to Garrick, v. Garrick's Corresp. i. 435 ; see also Polwhele's Traditions and Recollections, vol. i. p. 327, where is a Letter by Mr. Temple.

* See some observations on this subject in Mason's Memoirs of Gray, vol. iii. p. 127.

considerable degree; and which was displayed,
both in his conversation and correspondence.
Lord Orford used to assert, "that Gray never
wrote any thing easily, but things of humour;"
and added, "that humour was his natural and
original turn." Mr. Hey mentions Gray as excelling in delicate and well-bred ridicule.* A late
writer (Dr. Campbell) has remarked "the trans-
cendant excellence of Shakspeare in the province
of *humour*, as well as in the *pathetic*;"† and I
have elsewhere had occasion to observe, how
strongly the bent of Gray's mind inclined towards
this latter quality of composition; and with what
distinguishing features it appears in his poetry.
The examples of these two eminent writers whom
I have mentioned, appears sufficiently to strengthen the excellent observation made by Mr. D.
Stewart, in a note to his Philosophical Essays
(p. 584): "that a talent for the *pathetic*, and a
talent for *humour*, are generally united in the
same person: *wit*," he observes, "is more nearly
allied to a taste for the *sublime*."

To return, however, to the observations of Mr.
Temple: — "Perhaps (he writes) Mr. Gray was
the most learned man in Europe: he was equally
acquainted with the elegant and profound parts of
science, and that, not superficially, but thoroughly.

* See Hey's Lectures, vol. i. p. 455 ; see Mason on Gray's
Humour, vol. iii. p. 127, of his Memoirs.
† See ' Philosophy of Rhetoric,' vol. i. p. 57.

He knew every branch of history both natural and civil; had read all the original historians of England, France, and Italy; and was a great antiquarian. Criticism, metaphysics, morals, politics,* made a principal part of his study. Voyages and Travels of all sorts were his favourite amusements; and he had a fine taste in painting, prints, architecture, and gardening.† With such a fund of knowledge, his conversation must have been

* How comprehensive the account is, which Mr. Temple gives of the studies of Gray, which embraced criticism, metaphysics, morals, and politics, may be seen by comparing it with the following passage of Hume, as quoted by Mr. D. Stewart in his Life of Reid, p. lviii. "In these four sciences, of logic, (which is here meant, says Mr. Stewart, as that science which explains the principles and operations of our reasoning faculty, and the nature of our ideas,) morals, criticism, and politics, is comprehended almost every thing which it can any way import us to be acquainted with; or which can tend to the improvement or ornament of the human mind."

† Mr. Mason says that Gray disclaimed any skill in gardening, and held it in little estimation ; declaring himself to be only charmed with the bolder features of unadorned nature. See also in Mason's English Garden, book iii. 25, the speech which he puts into the mouth of Gray, as agreeable to his sentiments :

"——Sovereign queen ! ——
Behold, and tremble, while thou view'st her state
Throned on the heights of Skiddaw: call thy art
To build her such a throne ; that art will feel
How vain her best pretensions ! trace her march
Amid the purple crags of Borrow-dale ;
And try like those, to pile thy range of rock,
In rude tumultuous chaos ! "

equally instructing and entertaining. But he was also a good man, a man of virtue and humanity. There is no character without some speck, some imperfection; and I think the greatest defect in his, was an affectation in delicacy* or rather effeminacy, and a visible fastidiousness or contempt and disdain of his inferiors in science. He also had in some degree that weakness which disgusted Voltaire so much in Congreve. Though he seemed to value others chiefly according to the progress they had made in knowledge, yet he could not bear to be considered merely as a man of letters: and though without birth, or fortune, or station, his desire was to be looked upon as a private independent gentleman, who read for his amusement. Perhaps it may be said, What signifies so much knowledge, when it produced so little? Is it worth taking so much pains, to leave no memorials but a few poems? But let it be considered, that Mr.

* Shenstone, in his Essays, (p. 248,) remarks " the *delicacy* of Gray's manners: " and the editor of the Censura Literaria says, " I have learned from several who knew him intimately, that the sensibility of Gray was even morbid; and often very fastidious, and troublesome to his friends. He seemed frequently overwhelmed by the ordinary intercourse, and ordinary affairs of life. Coarse manners, and vulgar, or unrefined sentiments overset him." Vol. v. p. 406. — But Mr. Mason says, " it was rather an affectation in delicacy and effeminacy, than the things themselves: and he chose to put on this appearance chiefly before persons whom he did not wish to please." See Memoirs, vol. iv. p. 237; see Censura Literaria, vol. vii. p. 396.

Gray was to others at least innocently employed;
to himself, certainly beneficially. His time passed
agreeably; he was every day making some new
acquisition in science. His mind was enlarged,
his heart softened, his virtue strengthened. The
world and mankind were shown to him without a
mask; and he was taught to consider every thing
as trifling, and unworthy the attention of a wise
man, except the pursuit of knowledge, and practice of virtue, in that state wherein God has
placed us."

To this account Mr. Mason has added more
particularly, from the information of Mr. Tyson,*
of Bene't College, that Gray's skill in zoology
was extremely accurate. He had not only con-
centrated in his Linnæus, all that other writers
had said, but had altered the style of the Swedish
naturalist, to classical and elegant Latin. From
modern writers he had also illustrated many difficult passages in the zoological treatises of Aristotle. His account of English Insects was more
perfect than any that had then appeared; and it
has lately been mentioned,† "as a circumstance

* This appears by a note in Nichols's Literary Anecdotes,
vol. vii. For an account of Tyson, see Brydges' Restituta,
vol. iv. p. 236–9. I presume that he was the author of "Illu-
minated MSS. in the Library of Christ. Coll. Camb. 1770, 4to."

† See Shaw's Zoological Lectures, vol. i. p. 3. In the
library of the late Rev. George Ashby, of Barrow, was a copy
of Linnæus, 12th edit. 1766, interleaved, in 3 vols. 4to. with
MS. notes and additions by Gray; with drawings of shells,

not generally known, that he translated the Lin-
næan Genera, or Characters of Insects, into elegant Latin hexameters; some specimens of which
have been preserved by his friends, though they
were never intended for publication." Sir J. Mackintosh very justly observes, in a letter which he
addressed to the Bishop of Landaff: — " In the
beautiful scenery of Bolton Abbey, where I have
been since I began this note, I was struck by the
recollection of a sort of merit of Gray, which is
not generally observed — that he was the *first* dis-
coverer of the beauties of nature in England, and
has marked out the course of every picturesque
journey that can be made in it." *

Botany, which he studied in early life, under
the direction of his uncle, Mr. Antrobus, formed
also the amusement and pursuit of his later years.
He made frequent experiments on flowers, to
mark the mode and progress of their vegetation.
" For many of the latter years of his life (says
Mr. Cole), Gray dedicated his hours to the study
of Botany; in which he was eminently conspi-

&c. Another copy of Linnæus, in the same library, included
a few Ornithological papers in the handwriting of Gray, which
I now possess ; and which serve as an additional proof of the
accuracy and minuteness with which he prosecuted that branch
of his studies in natural history. — Since this note was originally written, extracts from these works have been published in the edition of Mr. Mathias. See vol. ii. 548 to
580.

    * See Life of Sir J. Mackintosh, vol. ii. p. 427.

cuous. He had Linnæus's Works interleaved, always before him, when I have accidentally called
upon him." His knowledge of architecture has
been mentioned before. Mr. Mason says, that
while Gray was abroad, he studied the Roman
proportions both in ancient ruins, and in the works
of Palladio. In his later years, he applied himself to Gothic and Saxon architecture, with such
industry and sagacity, that he could, at first sight,
pronounce on the precise time when any particular part of our cathedrals was erected. For this
purpose he trusted less to written accounts and
books, than to the internal evidence of the build-
ings themselves. He invented also several terms
of art, the better to explain his meaning on this
subject. Of heraldry, to which he applied as a
preparatory science, he was a complete master,
and left behind him many curious genealogical
papers. " After what I have said of Gray, (I
use the words of the Rev. Mr. Cole,) in respect
to the beauty and elegance of his poetical compositions, it will hardly be believed, that he condescended to look into the study of antiquities.
Yet he told me that he was deeply read in Dug-
dale, Hearne, Spelman, and others of that class;
and that he took as much delight in that study,
as ever he did in any other. Indeed, I myself
saw many specimens of his industry in his collections from various manuscripts in the British
Museum. His collections related chiefly to Eng-

lish history little known, or falsified by our historians, and some pedigrees."* His taste in music was excellent, and formed on the study of the great Italian masters who flourished about the time of Pergolesi,† as Marcello, Leo, and Palestrina; he himself performed upon the harpsichord. And it is said that he sung to his own accompaniment on that instrument, with great taste, and feeling.‡ Vocal music, and that only, was what he chiefly regarded. Gray acquired also great facility and accuracy in the knowledge of painting. When he was in Italy, he drew up a paper containing several subjects proper for painting, which he had never seen executed:

* " You know how out of humor Gray has been about our diverting ourselves with pedigrees, which is at least as wise as making a serious point of haranguing against the study. * * Well, Gray has set himself to compute, and has found out that there must go a million of ancestors in twenty generations, to every body's composition." Walpole's Lett. to G. Montagu, p. 70.

† Gray was not partial to the music of Handel: but Mr. Price (from whom I derive this information) adds, " that he used to speak with wonder of that Chorus in the Oratorio of Jephtha, beginning, — ' No more to Ammon's God and King.' " — See ' Essays on the Picturesque,' vol. ii. p. 191, note ; ed. 1794, and Cradock's Memoirs, vol. i. p. 125. Mr. R. Nares says, — ' The Oratorio of the Messiah is as perfect a composition of the kind, as the faculties of human nature are capable of producing.'

‡ Cole, in his MSS. notes, says " Gray latterly played on the pianoforte, and sang to *him*, but not without solicitation." MS. Note of Bennet, Bishop of Cloyne.

and affixed the names * of different masters to each piece, to show which of their pencils he thought would be most proper to treat it. A curious List of Painters, from the Revival of the Art, to the Beginning of the last Century, was also formed by him, with great accuracy and attention. It was published for the first time, in Mr. Malone's edition of the Works of Sir Joshua Reynolds; † and has been lately reprinted among the collected productions of Mr. Mason. In his Anecdotes of Painting, H. Walpole owns himself much indebted to Gray, for information both in architecture and painting.‡ " He condescended to correct (he says) what he never would have condescended to write:" again, "I am come to put my Anecdotes of Painting into the Press. You are one of the few that I expect will be entertained with it. It has warmed Gray's coldness so much, that he is violent about it." And to him was owing the discovery of a valuable artist in the reign of Queen Elizabeth, whose name was Theodore Haveus, for some time employed at Caius-College,‖ at Cambridge; who was at once an

* See Mason's Memoirs, vol. iv. p. 98.

† See Sir J. Reynolds's Works, vol. iii. p. 293 ; and Mr. Mason's Works, vol. iii. p. 227.

‡ See Walpole's Anecdotes of Painting, p. 99 and 141 ; and Letters to G. Montagu, p. 226.

‖ " In Caius-College, is a good portrait on board of Dr. Keys (not in profile), undoubtedly original, and dated 1563, ætatis suæ 53; with Latin verses and mottos : and in the same

architect, sculptor, and painter; and who possessed that diversity, as well as depth of talent in
the arts, which appeared in such extraordinary
splendour at the revival of literature, but of which,
I believe, we have no instance recorded in the
history of ancient times.*

To the papers of Gray, the late Mr. Pennant
owned himself much indebted for many corrections and observations on the antiquities of London.† Indeed, the variety and extreme accuracy
of his studies, even considering the leisure which

room hangs an old picture (bad at first, and now almost effaced
by cleaning), of a man in a slashed doublet, dark curled hair,
and beard, looking like a foreigner, and holding a pair of
compasses, and by his side a polyedron, composed of twelve
pentagons.   This is undoubtedly *Theodore Haveus* himself,
who, from all these circumstances, seems to have been an
architect, sculptor, and painter ; and having worked many
years for Dr. Caius and the College, in gratitude left behind
him his own picture." Walpole's Anecdotes of Painting, p.
143, 4to.

    * Raphael, Leonardo da Vinci, and Julio Romano were
architects and I believe sculptors, as well as painters; but it
was reserved for the genius of Michael Angelo, to add to the
most profound knowledge of those arts, the mind and the
expression of the poet.   When Dr. Warton, in his Essay on
Pope (vol. i. p. 157), said that he could not recollect any
painters that were good poets, except Salvator Rosa, and
Charles Vermander, of Mulbrac, in Flanders ; he surely did
not mean to except the poetry of this most extraordinary man.
Pliny, in his Natural History, mentions the names of some
ancient artists who were philosophers : see lib. xxxv. c. 10, 11.

    † See Pennant's ' London,' p. 62, 4to.   Mr. Pennant had
the use of an interleaved copy of ' London and its Environs,'

he possessed, is not a little surprising; and though
he published little or nothing, his reputation for
extensive learning was thoroughly established.
Retinuit famam, sine experimento. " Excepting
pure mathematics (says Mr. Mason), and the studies dependent on that science, there was hardly
any part of human learning in which he had not
acquired a competent skill; in most of them, a
consummate mastery." He followed most impli-
citly the rule, which he so often inculcated to his
friends,* that happiness consists in employment.
" To find one's self business (he writes) I am
persuaded is the great art of life. I am never so
angry as when I hear my acquaintance wishing
they had been bred to some poking profession, or
employed in some office of drudgery; as if it were
pleasanter to be at the command of other people,
than at one's own; and as if they could not go,
unless they were wound up: yet I know and feel
what they mean by this complaint; it proves that
some spirit, something of genius (more than com-

with notes by Mr. Gray, which is in Lord Harcourt's possession. The Witch of Woky, a Poem by Dr. Harrington, was
published in Percy's Reliques ; it was given to the Public
with a note — that it had been altered by the celebrated *Gray,*
author of the Churchyard Elegy. See Annual Biog. and
Obituary, 1817, p. 409.

* See Walpole's Works, vol. v. p. 398, Lett. XI. And
Mason's Memoirs, vol. iv. p. 17, Lett. XXV.; and p. 53, Lett.
XXXVI., to Dr. Wharton.

mon) is required to teach a man how to employ himself."

With regard to Classical learning, there seems every reason to suppose that he was a profound, as well as an elegant scholar. He thought once, it is said, of publishing an edition of Strabo, and left behind him many copious notes, and curious geographical disquisitions, particularly with respect to Persia and India. He made a selection from the Anthologia Græca, inserting critical emendations and additional epigrams, besides a copious index.* On Plato (Mr. Mason says) he bestowed indefatigable pains; leaving a quantity of critical and explanatory notes on almost every part of his works. These notes have now been published † in the edition of Mr. Mathias, and they are fully sufficient to shew the respect and attention with which he studied the writings of that great philosopher. They relate chiefly to antiquity and history; whether he attended much

---

* A Transcript of this work on the Anthologia by Mr. Mathias, was in the possession of Mr. Heber, at the sale of whose Library it was purchased by Mr. Pickering. There is very little original matter in it, consisting of a few translations in Latin verse : but the Selection of the Epigrammata is made with Gray's judgment and fine taste.

† Some notes on the Ιων of Plato, by Thomas Gray, were published in the ' Musæi Oxoniensis Literarii Conspectus,' Fasc. ii. p. 39—48 ; a publication which was conducted by the present Bishop of St. David's, and which consists of three numbers. " Grayii (says the editor) poetæ celeberrimi, ob-

to verbal criticism, either in the Greek or Latin language, does not appear. I should be inclined to think, that he read the ancient writers, not so much as a critic, but with the more extended, and ampler views of the historian and the philosopher; and all that was in any way connected with the fine arts, with the poetry, the philosophy, and the history of Greece and Rome, he studied with attention; and some of the authors whom he perused, could only be relished by one, who possessed an intimate and copious knowledge of the language in which they wrote. How far Mr. Mathias may have consulted the reputation of Gray, in the extracts which he has lately made from the manuscripts at Pembroke, the voice of the public will decide. In the meanwhile, I cannot but observe, that so far as regards the observations on English metre, the remarks on

servationes in Platonis Ionem, pro liberalitate suâ, mihi describendas benignissime permisit poeta celeberrimus, Gulielmus Mason. Excerptæ sunt e spisso volumine Grayii observationum ineditarum in universa Platonis Opera, in Strabonem, et Geographos antiquos, in vetustissimos Poetas Anglicos, in Ecclesias Cathedrales Angliæ, &c. scriptarum magna eruditione, summa diligentia, raro ingenio et judicio acri, ita ut poeta ille cultissimus in vatum eruditorum numero, unà cum Miltono, merito censeri queat. Observationes in Ionem quanquam paucæ sint, doctrinæ ubertatem produnt, et judicii acumen. Ex his, quidem nonnullæ de rebus haud obscuris dictæ videantur; pauci tamen homines de aliqua re admoneri dedignabuntur, quam sui gratia notatu dignam putavit Grayius."

Lydgate, the excellent and highly entertaining
analysis of the Aves of Aristophanes, and the
English and Latin translations, there surely can
be but one sentiment of approbation and gratitude. I confess that, if I had been placed in the
situation of the editor, I should have hesitated
most, as to the propriety of publishing the notes
on Aristophanes, and the geographical disquisitions on India.

It is not, I believe, generally known, that Gray
assisted Ross * (the editor of the Epistolæ Fami-
liares of Cicero, with English notes) in an anonymous pamphlet † which he published against the
Criticisms of Markland, on some of the Epistles

* See the Selections from the Gentleman's Magazine, vol.
iv. p. 392. In the miscellaneous Tracts of Bowyer, 4to. are
many letters of Markland, shewing great contempt for a person, whose name is not mentioned. — This was *Ross*. See p.
573, 574, 576, &c. The letters at p. 575, 518, dated June 20,
1749, and June 14th, 1756, which speak in severe terms of a
book then published, relate, I believe, to Hurd's Horace.

† The title of this pamphlet is, ' A Dissertation in which
the Defence of P. Sylla, ascribed to M. Tullius Cicero, is
clearly proved to be spurious, after the manner of Mr. Markland ; with some introductory Remarks on other Writings of
the Ancients, never before suspected.' It is written in a
sarcastic style, against Markland ; but with a display of
learning very inferior to that of the excellent scholar against
whom it was directed, and in a disposition very dissimilar to
the candour and fairness which accompanied the writings of
Markland. In a MS. note in the first leaf of his copy of Markland, Gray writes : — " This book is written in an ingenious
way, but the irony not quite transparent."

and Orations of Cicero. Gray's own copy of
Markland's Treatise is now before me. The
notes which he has written in it, display a
familiar knowledge of the structure of the Latin
language, and answer some of the objections of
that ingenious critic; who had not then learnt
the caution, in verbal criticism and conjectural
emendation, which he well knew how to value,
when an editor of Euripides.*

* In 1741, Orator Tunstall (with some assistance from
Markland) published his doubts of the authenticity of the
letters between Cicero and Brutus (which Middleton had considered as genuine in his Life of Cicero), in a Latin Dissertation. This Middleton called, " a frivolous, captious,
disingenuous piece of criticism ;" answered it in English, and
published the disputed epistles with a translation. Upon this,
Orator Tunstall, in 1744, published his ' Observations on the
Epistles, representing several evident marks of forgery in
them, in answer to the late pretences of the Rev. Dr. Conyers
Middleton.' Markland, in 1745, published his arguments on
the same side of the question, adding a Dissertation on four
Orations ascribed to Cicero, viz. 1. Ad Quirites post reditum.
2. Post reditum in Senatu. 3. Pro Domo suà, ad Pontifices.
4. De Haruspicum Responsis. This called forth the pamphlet
from *Ross*, I believe, in the following year, but the book has
no date. This controversy was continued by a ' Dissertation,
in which the Observations of a late Pamphlet on the Writings
of the Ancients, after the Manner of Mr. Markland, are
clearly answered ; those Passages in Tully corrected, on
which some of the Objections are founded ; with Amendments
of a few Pieces of Criticism in Mr. Markland's Epistola Critica. London, 1746, 8vo.' Gesner published some Strictures
on Markland in the Comm. Acad. Reg. Götting. t. iii. 223—
284 : which Wolf wonders Markland did not answer; as he
had *blown his pipes louder* than Tunstall. Saxius mistakes

In the Latin poems of Gray,* some errors have
been pointed out in the notes. One or two of
them are evidently mistakes arising from haste;
and the others do not at all derogate from the
reputation which he has acquired for his classical
attainments, and the elegance and purity of his
compositions. Salmasius discovered some mistakes in quantity, among the poems of Milton,
when they first appeared; and Vavassor† detected many inaccuracies in metre and grammar,
in the poetical volume published by Beza. The
Latin poems of Buchanan, beautiful and classical
as they are in their spirit and language, are not
without defects both of grammar and of prosody.
Indeed some faults ‡ of this kind are certainly not
inexcusable. when composing in a language not

Ross's pamphlet for a serious one; and says that he attacks
Cicero's Oration pro Sulla " Harduininâ pæne licentiâ."

* In the Gentleman's Magazine, 1801, vol. lxxi. p. 591,
is a letter from a Mr. Edmund C. Mason, Sheffield, relating
an anecdote of Gray, and containing a Latin poem, which he
says is the production of the poet; and a Greek translation
of it, by West. This gentleman, however, has not given any
account of the authenticity of his manuscript.

† See Scaligeriana; art.: Barclay and Beza. See Irvine's
Lives of the Scottish Poets, v. i. p. 164.

‡ Mr. Mason says, " A learned and ingenious person, to
whom I communicated the Latin poems after they were printed
off, was of opinion that they contain some few expressions not
warranted by any good authority; and that there are one or
two false quantities to be found in them. I had once an intention to cancel the pages, and correct the passages objected
to, according to my friend's criticisms; but, on second

our own. Gray's Latin poetry, however, appears
to me to be peculiarly forcible and correct; and
formed attentively after the best models — Virgil
and Lucretius. Dr. Johnson, who was a good
judge of the purity of Latin composition (although
he did not always himself compose with that classical exactness which may be desired), allowed,
" that it were reasonable to wish Gray had prosecuted his design of excelling in Latin poetry;
for though there is at present some embarrass-
ment in his phrase, and some harshness in his
lyric numbers, his copiousness of language is such
as very few possess; and his lines, even when imperfect, discover a writer·whom practice would
have made skilful." If Gray, however, should
need any further defence, it must be observed,
that his Latin poems were never intended by him
for publication, if we except the two that he wrote
at College; that they were found by his executors
among his own papers, or those of his friends,
and that they did not receive his last correc
tions.*

thoughts, I deemed it best to let them stand exactly as I
found them in the manuscripts. The accurate classical reader
will perhaps be best pleased with finding out the faulty passages himself; and his candour will easily make the proper
allowances for any little mistakes in verses, which, he will
consider, never had the *author's last hand*." Memoirs, vol. iv
p. 234.

    * The ode written at the Grande Chartreuse perhaps ought
also to be excepted.

I have never understood that his knowledge of modern languages extended beyond the French and Italian: these, however, he studied when he was abroad with considerable diligence, and cultivated afterwards, in the leisure which he enjoyed at home. Indeed his acquaintance with the beautiful works of the Tuscan bards, has contributed, in no small degree, to enrich and adorn many passages of his English poetry : —

"Dum vagus, Ausonias nunc per umbras,
    Nunc Britannica per vireta lusit."

It remains now only to speak of an intended publication in English literature, mentioned by Gray in an advertisement to the Imitation of the Welsh Odes, and which was an 'History of English Poetry.' It appears that Warburton had communicated to Mason a paper of Pope's, containing the first sketch of a plan for a work of that nature, and which was printed in the Life of Pope by Ruffhead, and subsequently in many other works.

"Milton (says Dryden in the preface to his Fables) was the poetical son of Spenser, and Mr. Waller of Fairfax; for we have our lineal descents and clans as well as other families." Upon this principle, Pope * drew up his little catalogue

* Pope observed to Spence that " Michael Drayton was one of the imitators of Spenser, and Fairfax another. Milton, in his first pieces, is an evident follower of Spenser too, in his famous Allegro and Penseroso, and some others. Carew (a

of the English poets;* and Gray was so much
pleased with the method of arrangement which
Pope had struck out, that on Mr. Mason's agree-
ing to assist him, he examined and considerably
enlarged the plan.   He meant in the introduction
to ascertain the Origin of Rhyme; to give specimens of the Provençal Scaldic, British, and Saxon poetry: and when the different sources of
English poetry were ascertained, the history was

---

bad Waller), Waller himself and Lord Lansdown are all of
one school ; as Sir John Suckling, Sir John Minnes, and Prior
are of another.   Crashaw is a coarse sort of Cowley; he was
a follower too of Petrarch and Marino, but most of Marino.
He and Cowley were good friends ; and the latter has a good
copy of verses on his death.   About this pitch were Stanley
(the author of the Opinions of Philosophers) ; Randolph,
though rather superior ; and Sylvester, though rather of a
lower form.   Cartwright and Bishop Corbet are of this class
of poets ; and Ruggle, the author of Counter-Scuffle, might
be admitted among them.   Herbert is lower than Crashaw,
Sir John Beaumont higher, and Donne a good deal so." [Spence's
Anecdotes, quoted in] Malone's Dryden, vol. iv. p. 589.

   * I have placed Pope's Catalogue of the Poets in the
Appendix D. (with Gray's Letter on the same subject), with
some observations upon it.   It is singular that this sketch of
Pope's should have been so often printed, without any of the
editors, except Mr. Malone, pointing out its mistakes and
inaccuracies.   It disagrees also, in many points, with the
account which he gave to Spence; printed in the preceding
note.   I must observe, that this catalogue is printed by Mr.
Mathias, in a far more correct manner, than that in which it
usually appears.   It is published by him from Gray's own
handwriting ; and many of the inaccuracies pointed out by
Mr. Malone, are only the blunders of printers and transcribers

to commence with the school of Chaucer. Mr.
Mason collected but few materials for this purpose; but Gray, besides writing his imitations of
Norse and Welsh poetry, made many curious
and elaborate disquisitions into the origin of
rhyme, and the variety of metre to be found in
the ancient poets. He transcribed many passages from Lydgate, from the manuscripts which
he found at Cambridge, remarking the beauties
and defects of this immediate scholar of Chaucer.*

About this time, however, T. Warton was engaged in a work of the same nature: and Gray,
fatigued with the extent of his plan, relinquished
his undertaking, and sent a copy of his design
to Warton; of whose abilities, from his observations on Spenser, Mr. Mason says, he entertained
a high opinion. It is well known, that Warton
did not adopt this plan; and gave his reasons for
his departure from it, in the preface to his history. Gray died some years before Warton's
publication appeared; † but Mr. Mason mentions
it with praise, in a note in the fourth volume of
his Memoirs of Gray, where he calls it, " a work,
which, as the author proceeds in it through more
enlightened periods, will undoubtedly give the

---

* See Mathias' Edition of Gray, vol. ii. p. 1 to p. 80.

† Gray died in July, 1771, and Warton's first volume appeared in 1774.

world as high an idea of his critical taste, as the present specimen does of his indefatigable researches into antiquity."

Sir James Mackintosh has given a sketch of Gray's poetical character with his usual temperance of judgment, and delicacy of taste, which may with propriety be introduced, as our narrative is drawing to a close. " Gray (he writes, after some observations on the merits of Goldsmith) was a Poet of a far higher order, and of an almost opposite kind of merit. Of all English Poets he was the most finished artist. He attained the highest degree of splendour of which poetical style seems to be capable. If Virgil and his scholar Racine may be allowed to have united somewhat more ease with their elegance, no other poet approaches Gray in this kind of excellence. The degree of poetical invention diffused over such a style, the balance of taste and of fancy necessary to produce it, and the art with which the offensive boldness of imagery is polished away, are not indeed always perceptible to the common reader, nor do they convey to any mind the same species of gratification, which is felt from the perusal of those poems, which seem to be the unpremeditated effusions of enthusiasm. But to the eye of the critic, and more especially to the artist, they afford a new kind of pleasure, not incompatible with a distinct perception of the art employed, and somewhat similar to the grand emotions ex-

cited by the reflection on the skill and toil exerted
in the construction of a magnificent palace. They
can only be classed among the secondary pleasures of poetry, but they never can exist without
a great degree of its higher excellencies. Almost
all his poetry was lyrical — that species which,
issuing from a mind in the highest state of excite-
ment, requires an intensity of feeling which, for a
long composition, the genius of no poet could support. Those who complained of its brevity and
rapidity, only confessed their own inability to follow the movements of poetical inspiration.*   Of
the two grand attributes of the Ode, Dryden had
displayed the enthusiasm, Gray exhibited the
magnificence. He is also the only modern English writer whose Latin verses deserve general
notice, but we must lament that such difficult
trifles had diverted his genius from its natural objects. In his Letters he has shewn the descriptive powers of a poet, and in new combinations of
generally familiar words, which he seems to have

---

* In another place, the same writer observes : "The obscurity of the Ode on the ' Progress of Poetry,' arises from
the variety of the subjects, the rapidity of the transitions, the
boldness of the imagery, and the splendour of the language;
to those who are capable of that intense attention, which the
higher order of poetry requires, and which poetical sensibility
always produces, there is no obscurity. In the ' Bard ' some
of these causes of obscurity are lessened ; it is more impas-
sioned and less magnificent, but it has more brevity and abrupt-
ness. It is a lyric drama, and this structure is a new source
of obscurity."

caught from Madame de Sevigné, (though it must be said he was somewhat quaint) he was eminently happy. It may be added, that he deserves the comparatively trifling praise of having been the most learned poet* since Milton." †

In the short, and I am afraid, imperfect account which I have now given of the life and character of Gray, I may be permitted, before I close the narrative, to express my own sincere admiration of that splendid genius, that exquisite taste, that profound and extensive erudition, those numerous accomplishments, and those real and unassuming merits, which will preserve for him a very eminent reputation, exclusively of that which he so justly enjoys in his rank among the English poets. His life, indeed, did not abound with change of incident, or variety of situation; it was not blessed with the happiness of domestic endearments, nor spent in the bosom of social intercourse; but it was constantly and contentedly

---

* Gray and Mason first detected the imposition of *Chatterton*. See Archæological Epistle to Dean Milles, Stanza xi. It appears that Gray did not admire Hudibras. " Mr. Gray,' says Warburton, " has certainly a true taste. I should have read Hudibras with as much indifference as perhaps he did, were it not for a fondness of the transactions of those times, against which it is a satire." — Warburton's Letters, xxxi. p. 290. He appears highly to have praised some of W. Whitehead's poems. See Mason's Life of Whitehead, p. 40, &c., and he *approved* H. Walpole's Tragedy of the Mysterious Mother. See Lett. to G. Montagu, p. 406.

† See Life of Sir J. Mackintosh, vol. ii. p. 172.

employed in the improvement of the various talents with which he was so highly gifted; in a sedulous cultivation both of the moral and intellectual powers; in the study of wisdom, and in the practice of virtue.

To present his poetry to the public, more correctly than it has yet appeared, has been the design of this edition. And I am willing to hope, that I have made no unacceptable present to the literary world, in enabling them for the first time to read the genuine correspondence of Gray, in an enlarged as well as authentic form. Assuredly, to some, his letters will not be less interesting than his poetry;* and they will be read by all who are desirous of estimating, not only the variety of his learning, and the richness and playfulness of his fancy, but the excellence of his private character, the genuine goodness of his heart, his sound and serious views of life, and his warm and zealous affection towards his friends. †

* ' I have been reading Gray's Works,' says Cowper, ' and think him sublime. . . . . I once thought Swift's Letters the best that could be written, but I like Gray's better. His humour, or his wit, or whatever it is to be called, is never ill-natured or offensive, and yet I think equally poignant with the Dean's.' Hayley's Ed. 4to. vol. ii. p. 231.

† [The letters here referred to are contained in the Aldine edition of Gray's Works.]

APPENDIX.

APPENDIX A.

THE LAST WILL AND TESTAMENT OF
THOMAS GRAY.

Extracted from the Registry of the Prerogative Court of Canterbury.

In the Name of God. *Amen.* I Thomas Gray of Pembroke-Hall in the University of Cambridge, being of sound mind and in good health of body, yet ignorant how long these blessings may be indulged me, do make this my Last Will and Testament in manner and form following, First, I do desire that my body may be deposited in the vault, made by my late dear mother in the churchyard of Stoke-Pogeis, near Slough in Buckinghamshire, by her remains, in a coffin of seasoned oak, neither lined nor covered, and (unless it be very inconvenient) I could wish that one of my executors may see me laid in the grave, and distribute among such honest and industrious poor persons in the said parish as he thinks fit, the sum of ten pounds in charity. —Next, I give to George Williamson, esq. my second cousin by the father's side, now of Calcutta in Bengal, the sum of five hundred pounds reduced Bank annuities, now standing in my name. I give to Anna Lady Goring, also my second cousin by the father's side, of the county of Sussex, five hundred pounds reduced Bank annuities, and a pair of large blue and white old Japan china jars. *Item,* I give to Mary Antrobus of Cambridge, spinster, my second cousin by the mother's side, all that my freehold estate and house in the parish of St. Michael, Cornhill, London, now let at the yearly rent of sixty-five pounds, and in the occupation of Mr. Nortgeth perfumer, provided that she pay, out of the said rent, by half-yearly payments, Mrs. Jane Olliffe, my aunt, of Cambridge, widow, the sum of twenty pounds *per annum* during her natural life ; and after the decease of the said Jane Olliffe I give the said estate to the said Mary Antrobus, to have and to hold to her heirs and assigns for ever. Further; I bequeath to the said Mary Antrobus the sum of six hundred pounds new South-sea annuities, now standing in the joint names of Jane Olliffe and Thomas Gray, but charged with the payment of five pounds *per annum* to Graves Stokely of Stoke-Pogeis, in the county of Bucks, which sum of six hundred pounds, after the decease of the said annuitant, does (by the will of Anna Rogers my late aunt) belong solely and entirely to me, together with all overplus of interest in the mean-time accruing. Further, if at the time of my decease there shall be any arrear of salary due to me from his Majesty's Treasury, I give all such arrears to the said Mary Antrobus. *Item,* I give to Mrs. Dorothy Comyns of Cambridge, my other second cousin by the mother's side, the sums of six hundred pounds old South-sea annuities, of three hundred pounds four *per cent.* Bank annuities consolidated, and of two hundred pounds three *per cent.* Bank annuities consolidated, all now standing in my name. I give to Richard Stonehewer, esq. one of his Majesty's Commissioners of Excise, the sum of five hundred pounds reduced Bank annuities, and I beg his acceptance of one of my diamond rings. I give to Dr. Thomas Wharton, of Old Park in the Bishoprick of Durham, five hundred pounds reduced Bank annuities, and desire him also to accept of one of my diamond rings. I give to my servant, Stephen Hempstead, the sum of fifty pounds reduced Bank annuities, and if he continues in my service to the time of my death I also give him all my wearing-apparel and linen. I give to my two cousins above-mentioned, Mary Antrobus and Dorothy Comyns, all my plate, watches, rings, china-ware, bed-linen and table-linen, and the furniture of my chambers, at Cambridge, not otherwise bequeathed, to be equally and amicably shared between them. I give to the Reverend William Mason, precentor of York, all my books, manuscripts, coins, music printed or written, and papers of all kinds, to preserve or destroy at his own discretion. And after my just debts and the expenses of my funeral are discharged, all the residue of my personal estate, whatsoever, I do hereby give and bequeath to the said Reverend William Mason, and to the Reverend Mr. James Browne, President of Pembroke-Hall, Cambridge, to be equally divided between them, desiring them to apply the sum of two hundred pounds to an use of charity concerning which I have already informed them. And I do hereby constitute and appoint them, the said William Mason and James Browne, to be joint executors of this my Last Will and Testament. And if any relation of mine, or other legatee, shall go about to molest or commence any suit against my said executors in the execution of their office, I do, as far as the law will permit me, hereby revoke and make void all such bequests or legacies as I had given to that person or persons, and give it to be divided between my said executors and residuary legatees, whose integrity and kindness I have so long experienced, and who can best judge of my true intention and meaning. In witness whereof I have hereunto set my hand and seal this 2d day of July, 1770.

TH0. GRAY.

Signed, sealed, published, and declared by the said Thomas Gray, the testator, as and for his Last Will and Testament, in the presence of us, who in his presence and at his request, and in the presence of each other, have signed our names as witnesses hereto.   RICHARD BAKER.
THOMAS WILSON.
JOSEPH TURNER.

Proved at London the 12th of August, 1771, before the Worshipful Andrew Coltre Ducarel, Doctor of Laws and Surrogate, by the oaths of the Reverend William Mason, Clerk, Master of Arts, and the Reverend James Browne,* Clerk, Master of Arts, the executors to whom administration was granted, having been first sworn duly to administer.

JOHN STEVENS.
HENRY STEVENS.   } *Deputy Registers*
GEO. GOSTLING, *jun.*

---

* Mr. Gray used to go with his friend Browne to a reading-room in the evening. Browne, who was a very punctual man, just before the hour of going, used to get up, walk about the room, and make a bustle with his gown, &c. " Now," says Gray, " Browne is going to *strike.*"

Appendix B.

THE following curious paper I owe to the kindness of Sir
Egerton Brydges and his friend Mr. Haslewood. It was
discovered in a volume of manuscript law cases, purchased by
the latter gentleman at the sale of the late Isaac Reed's
books. It is a case submitted by the mother of Gray to the
opinion of an eminent civilian in 1735; and it proves, that
to the great and single exertions of this admirable woman,
Gray was indebted for his education, and consequently for
the happiness of his life. The sorrow and the mournful
affection with which he dwelt on his mother's memory, serves
to shew the deep sense he retained of what she suffered, as
well as what she did for him. Those who have read the
Memoirs of Kirke White in Mr. Southey's Narrative, will
recognise the similarity of the situation in which the two
poets were placed, in their entrance into life; and they will
see, that if maternal love and courage had not stept in, in
both cases, their genius and talents would have been lost in the
ignorance, or stifled by the selfishness, of those about them.

CASE.

" Philip Gray, before his marriage with his wife, (then
Dorothy Antrobus, and who was then partner with her sister
Mary Antrobus,) entered into articles of agreement with the
said Dorothy, and Mary, and their brother Robert Antrobus,
that the said Dorothy's stock in trade (which was then 240*l.*)
should be employed by the said Mary in the said trade, and
that the same, and all profits arising thereby, should be for
the sole benefit of the said Dorothy, notwithstanding her
intended coverture, and her sole receipts alone a sufficient
discharge to the said Mary and her brother Robert Antrobus,
who was made trustee. But in case either the said Philip or
Dorothy dies, then the same to be assigned to the survivor.

" That in pursuance of the said articles, the said Mary,
with the assistance of the said Dorothy her sister, hath carried
on the said trade for near thirty years, with tolerable success
for the said Dorothy. That she hath been no charge to the
said Philip; and during all the said time, hath not only found

herself in all manner of apparel, but also for all her children, to the number of twelve, and most of the furniture of his house; and paying 40*l.* a year for his shop, *almost providing every thing for her son, whilst at Eton school, and now he is at Peter-House at Cambridge.*

" Notwithstanding which, almost ever since he hath been married, he hath used her in the most inhuman manner, by beating, kicking, punching, and with the most vile and abusive language; that she hath been in the utmost fear and danger of her life, and hath been obliged this last year to quit her bed, and lie with her sister. *This she was resolved, if possible, to bear; not to leave her shop of trade for the sake of her son, to be able to assist in the maintenance of him at the University, since his father won't.*

" There is no cause for this usage, unless it be an unhappy jealousy of all mankind in general (her own brother not excepted); but no woman deserves, or hath maintained, a more virtuous character: or it is presumed if he can make her sister leave off trade, he thinks he can then come into his wife's money, but the articles are too secure for his vile purposes.

" He daily threatens he will pursue her with all the vengeance possible, and will *ruin himself to undo her, and his only son;* in order to which he hath given warning to her sister to quit his shop, where they have carried on their trade so successfully which will be almost their ruin : but he insists she shall go at Midsummer next; and the said Dorothy, his wife, in necessity must be forced to go along with her, to some other house and shop, to be assisting to her said sister, in the said trade, for *her own and son's support.*

" But if she can be quiet, she neither expects or desires any help from him: but he is really so very vile in his nature, she hath all the reason to expect most troublesome usage from him that can be thought of.

QUESTION.

" What he can, or possibly may do to molest his wife in living with her sister, and assisting in her trade, for the purposes in the said articles; and which will be the best way for her to conduct herself in this unhappy circumstance, if he should any ways be troublesome, or endeavour to force her to live with him ? And whether the said Dorothy, in the life-time of the said Philip, may not by will, or otherwise, dispose of the interest, or produce, which hath, or may arise, or become due for the said stock as she shall think fit, it being apprehended as part of her separate estate ? "

h

ANSWER.

" If Mrs. Gray should leave her husband's house, and go to live with her sister in any other, to assist her in her trade, her husband may, and probably will call her, by process in the Ecclesiastical Court, to return home and cohabit with him, which the court will compel her to do, unless she can shew cause to the contrary. She has no other defence in that case, than to make proof, before the court, of such cruelties as may induce the judge to think she cannot live in safety with her husband: then the court will decree for a separation.

" This is a most unhappy case, and such a one, as I think, if possible, should be referred to, and made up by some common friend ; sentences of separation, by reason of cruelty only, being very rarely obtained.

" What the cruelties are which he has used towards her, and what proof she is able to make of them, I am yet a stranger to. She will, as she has hitherto done, bear what she reasonably can, without giving him any provocation to use her ill. If, nevertheless, he forces her out of doors, the most reputable place she can be in, is with her sister. If he will proceed to extremities, and go to law, she will be justified, if she stands upon her defence, rather perhaps than if she was plaintiff in the cause.

" As no power of making a will is reserved to Mrs. Gray, by her marriage settlement, and not only the original stock, but likewise the produce and interest which shall accrue, and be added to it, are settled upon the husband, if he survives his wife; it is my opinion she has no power to dispose of it by will, or otherwise.

" JOH. AUDLEY."

" Doctors' Commons,
     Feb. 9th, 1735."

Appendix C.

Miscellaneus Extracts from the Manuscript Papers of the Rev. William Cole, of Milton in Cambridgeshire, relating to Gray; now in the British Museum.

I.

On Tuesday July 30th, 1771, Mr. Essex calling on me, in his way to Ely, told me that Mr. Gray was thought to be dying of the gout in his stomach. I had not heard before that he was ill, though he had been so for many days. So I sent my servant in the evening to Pembroke-Hall, to enquire after his welfare; but he was then going off, and no message could be delivered; and he died that night. He desired to be buried early in the morning at Stoke-Pogeis;* and accordingly was put in lead, and conveyed from Cambridge on Sunday morning, with a design to rest at Hoddesdon the first night, and Salt-hill on Monday night, from whence he might be very early on Tuesday morning at Stoke. He made the master of Pembroke (his particular friend) his executor; who, with his niece Antrobus, Mr. Cummins a merchant of Cambridge, who had married her sister, and a young gentleman of Christ's-College with whom he was very intimate, went in a mourning-coach after the hearse, to see him put into his grave. He left all his books and MSS. to his particular friend Mr. Mason, with a desire that he would do with the latter what he thought proper. When he saw all was over with him, he sent an express to his friend Mr. Stonehewer, who immediately came to see him; and as Dr. Gisborne happened to be with him when the messenger came, he brought

---

* Gray's tomb is at the end of the chancel of Stoke-Pogeis church. At Strawberry-Hill there is a drawing by *Bacon* of Gray's tomb, by moonlight; given to Lord Orford, by Sir Edward Walpole. See Lord Orford's Works, vol. ii. p. 425. Not far from the churchyard is the Cenotaph erected by Mr. Penn to the memory of Gray, from a design, I believe, by the late Mr. Wyatt.

him down to Cambridge with him; which was the more lucky, as Professor Plumptre * had refused to get up, being sent to in the night. But it was too late to do any good: and indeed he had all the assistance of the faculty† besides at Cambridge. It is said, that he has left all his fortune to his two nieces at Cambridge; and just before his death, about a month, or thereabout, he had done a very generous action, for which he was much commended.

His aunt Olliffe, an old gentlewoman of Norfolk, had left that county, two or three years, to come and live at Cambridge; and dying about the time I speak of, left him and Mr. Cummins executors and residuary legatees; but Mr. Gray generously gave up his part to his nieces, one of whom Mrs. Olliffe had taken no notice of, and who wanted it sufficiently. * * * * I was told by Mr. Alderman Burleigh, the present mayor of Cambridge, that Mr. Gray's father had been an Exchange-broker, but the fortune he had acquired of about 10,000*l*. was greatly hurt by the fire in Cornhill; so that Mr. Gray, many years ago, sunk a good part of what was left, and purchased an annuity, in order to have a fuller income. I have often seen at his chambers, in his ink-stand, a neat pyramidal bloodstone seal, with these arms at the base, viz. ‡ a lion rampant, within a bordure engrailed, being those of the name of Gray, and belonged, as he told me, to his father. His mother was in the millinery way of business. His person was small, well put together, and latterly tending to plumpness. He was all his life remarkably sober and temperate. I think, I heard him say he never was across a horse's back in his life. He gave me a small print or etching of himself by Mr. Mason, which is extremely like him.

II.

I am apt to think the characters of Voiture and Mr. Gray were very similar. They were both little men, very nice and

---

* Dr. Plumptre certainly refused to get up to attend Gray in his last illness; but it was to be considered, that he was grown old, and had found it necessary to adopt this rule with all his patients. ED.

† Dr. Glynn was Gray's physician at Cambridge, and likewise a very intimate friend. ED.

‡ Sir Egerton Brydges informs me, that Gray's arms are the same as those of Lord Gray of Scotland; who claimed a relationship with him, (see Mason's Memoirs, vol. iv. lett. 55,) and as the present Earl Grey's.

exact in their persons and dress, most lively and agreeable
in conversation, except that Mr. Gray was apt to be too
satirical, and both of them full of affectation. In Gil Blas,
the print of Scipio in the arbour, beginning to tell his own
adventures to Gil Blas, Antonio, and Beatrix, was so like
the countenance of Mr. Gray, that if he sat for it, it could
not be more so. It is in a 12mo edition in four volumes,
printed at Amsterdam, chez Herman Vytwerf, 1735, in the
4th volume, p. 94. — p. m. It is ten times more like him
than his print before Mason's life of him, which is horrible,
and makes him a fury. That little one done by Mr. Mason
is like him; and placid Mr. Tyson spoilt the other by altei-
ing it.

III.

It must have been about the year 1770, that Dr. Farmer
and Mr. Gray ever met, to be acquainted together, as about
that time I met them at Mr. Oldham's chambers, in Peter-
House, to dinner. Before, they had been shy of each other:
and though Mr. Farmer was then esteemed one of the most
ingenious men in the University, yet Mr. Gray's singular
niceness in the choice of his acquaintance made him appear
fastidious to a great degree, to all who were not acquainted
with his manner. Indeed, there did not seem to be any pro-
bability of any great intimacy from the style and manner of
each of them. The one a cheerful, companionable, hearty,
open, downright man, of no great regard to dress or common
forms of behaviour : the other, of a most fastidious and
recluse distance of carriage, rather averse to sociability, but
of the graver turn; nice, and elegant in his person, dress,
and behaviour, even to a degree of finicalness and effeminacy.
So that nothing but their extensive learning and abilities
could ever have coalesced two such different men, and both of
great value in their own line and walk. They were ever
after great friends; and Dr. Farmer, and all of his acquaintance, had soon after too much reason to lament his loss, and
the shortness of their acquaintance.

IV.

Two Latin Epitaphs in the Church of Burnham, in Buckinghamshire, supposed to be from the pen of Mr. Gray (published from Cole's MSS. in the European Magazine, July
1704.)

Huic Loco prope adsunt Cineres
ROBERTI ANTROBUS.
Vir fuit, si quis unquam fuit, Amicorum amans,
Et Amicis amandus.
Ita Ingenio et Doctrinâ valuit,
Ut suis Honori fuerit, et aliis Commodo.
Si Mores respicis, probus et humanus.
Si Animum, semper sibi constans.
Si Fortunam, plura meruit quam tulit.
In Memoriam defuncti posuit
Hoc Marmor
Frater $\left\{ \begin{array}{l} \text{amantissimus} \\ \text{mœstissimus} \end{array} \right\}$ J. Rogers, A.D. 1731.

M.S.
Jonathani Rogers,
Qui Juris inter Negotia diu versatus,
Opibus modicis laudabili Industriâ partis,
Extremos Vitæ Annos
Sibi, Amicis, Deo dicavit.
Humanitati ejus nihil Otium detraxit,
Nihil Integritati Negotia.
Quænam bonæ Spei justior Causa,
Quam perpetua Morum Innocentia
Animus erga Deum reverenter affectus,
Erga omnes Homines benevole ?
Vixit Ann. lxv. Ob. Stoke in Com. Bucks.
A.D. MDCCXLII. Octob. xxxi.
Anna, Conjux mœstissima,
per Annos xxxii.
Nullâ unquam intercedente
Querimoniâ
Omnium Curarum Particeps,
Hoc Marmor
(Sub quo et suos Cineres juxta condi destinat)
Pietatis Officium heu ! ultimum,
P. C.

V.

From the Information of Sir Egerton Brydges, K.J.M P.

Among the friends of Gray, was the Rev. William Robinson, (third brother of Mrs. Montagu,) of Denton Court, near Canterbury, and rector of Burfield, Berks. He was educated at Westminster, and at St. John's College, Cambridge, where he formed a particular intimacy with Gray, who twice* visited him at Denton. He died Dec. 1803, aged about seventy-five. Mr. Robinson was an admirable classical scholar, to whose taste Gray paid great deference. He did not consider Mr. Mason as equal to the task of writing Gray's Life; and on that account when Mason (from his knowledge of Mr. R.'s intimacy with Gray) communicated his intention to him, Mr. Robinson declined returning him an answer, which produced a coolness between them which was never afterwards made up. Mr. Robinson, however, owned that Mason had executed his task better than he had expected. The 'Lines on Lord Holland's House at Kingsgate,' were written when on a visit to Mr. Robinson, and found in the drawer of Gray's dressing table after he was gone. They were restored to him; for he had no other copy, and had forgotten them. What was the real ground of the quarrel between Gray and Walpole when abroad, I do not know; but have reason to believe that it was of too deep a nature ever to be eradicated from Gray's bosom; which I gather from certain expressions half dropped to Mr. Robinson. Mr. R. thought Gray not only a great poet, but an exemplary, amiable, and virtuous man. Gray's poem on 'Lord Holland' first appeared in the Gentleman's Magazine, vol. xlvii. p. 624, and vol. xlviii. p. 88; that on 'Jemmy Twitcher,' in vol. lii. p. 39.

When he went to court to kiss the king's hand† for his place, he felt a mixture of shyness and pride, which he expressed to one of his intimate friends in terms of strong ill-humour.

VI.

The pleasantest morning that I passed at Cambridge, was in company with Mr. Gray, and some critics, at the rehearsal of the music for his ode, previous to its grand performance at the Senate House: and I thought that as he had so many directions to give, and such nice distinctions to make, it was as well he had to deal with the pliant Dr. Randall, rather than with some of the able composers in the metropolis. Mr. Gray was not at that time much more comfortable than the Chancellor himself; for the press was teeming with abuse,

---

* See the beautiful description of Kentish scenery, written on this tour, in Gray's Letters by Mason.

† ' What if for nothing once you kist
Against the grain, a monarch's fist.'
Swift's Misc. vol. v. p. 162.

and a very satirical parody was then preparing, which soon afterwards appeared. His own delicious ode must always be admired, yet this envenomed shaft was so pointedly levelled at him, though he affected in his letter to Mason to disregard it, that with his fine feelings he was not only annoyed, but very seriously hurt by it. — v. Cradock's Mem. p. 107–8.

From time to time I had treasured up many bon-mots of Gray communicated by Mr. Tyson, and by the former fellow-collegian of Gray, the Rev. Mr. Sparrow, of Walthamstow, who was always attentive to his witty effusions. Some few of these have been printed incorrectly, and freely bestowed on others in the Johnsoniana. Johnson was highly displeased, that any should be attributed to him, as mentioned by Mr. Davies. When he was publishing his life of Gray, I gave him several anecdotes, but he was very anxious as soon as possible to get to the end of his labours. Not long since I received a very kind message from the Rev. Mr. Bright, Skeffington Hall, Leicestershire, to inform me that he had wished to deposit with me all the remaining documents and papers of Gray, as bequeathed to him by Mr. Stonehewer, but that he found that they all had been carried off to Rome inadvertently by a learned Editor. If recovered they should certainly be consigned to me. — Id. p. 1834.

Appendix D.

(See page xxix. *.)

'The curfew tolls the knell of parting day,'

Dr. Warton would read "The curfew tolls! — the knell of parting day." The curfew-*bell* is the general expression of the old poets; the word 'toll' is not the appropriate verb; it was not a slow bell tolling for the dead; hence,

'Curfew was *ronge* — lyghts were set up in haste.'

And Shakespeare, 'None since the curfew *rung*,' — and 'the curfew bell hath *rung*, 'tis three o'clock.' But there is another error; a confusion of time. The curfew tolls, and the ploughman returns from work. Now the ploughman returns two or three hours before the curfew rings; and 'the glimmering landscape' has long ceased to *fade* before the curfew. 'The *parting day*' is also incorrect; the day had long finished. But if the word 'curfew' is taken simply for the 'evening-bell,' then also is the time incorrect; and a *knell* is not tolled for the *parting*, but for the *parted*.

'And leaves the world to *darkness* and to me.'
'Now *fades* the *glimmering* landscape on the sight.'

Here the incidents, instead of being progressive, fall back, and make the picture confused and inharmonious; especially, as it appears soon after, that it was not *dark;* for 'The moping owl *does* * to the *moon* complain.'

'Molest her *ancient* solitary reign.'

This line would have been better without *ancient;* but Gray

---

* The expletives 'does,' and 'do,' and 'did,' were, we considered, discarded from English poetry, by Pope's taste and skill ; who proved that he could construct his musical lines without them. They have lately come to life again (or rather, appear only to have been banished, and not destroyed,) in our modern tragedies, of which Mr. Maturin's *Bertram* affords a good specimen, as pointed out by Mr. Coleridge.

'The Lord and his small train *do* stand appall'd.
With torch and bell from their high battlements,
The monks *do* summon,' &c.

had the 'antiqua regna' of the Latin poets in his mind, and the 'deserta regna.' Besides, to '*molest a reign*,' is a very ungraceful and most unusual expression ; and only endured for the rhyme's sake.

'Where *heaves* the turf in many a mouldering *heap*.'

This is redundant.

'For them no more the *blazing* hearth shall *burn*.'

If the hearth *blazes*, of course it must *burn* ; but 'blazing hearth' Gray had from Thomson, and 'burn' was added for the rhyme, 'return.'

'No more shall rouse them from their lowly bed.'

Here the epithet *lowly*, as applied to *bed*, occasions an ambiguity, as to whether the poet meant the bed on which they sleep, or the grave in which they are laid, which is in poetry called a *low* or *lowly bed*. Of course the former is designed; *but Mr. Lloyd, in his Latin translation, mistook it for the latter.* There can be no greater fault in composition than a doubtful meaning, — vitanda in primis ambiguitas.

'Or busy housewife *ply* her evening *care*.'

To *ply a care*, is an expression that is not proper to our language, and was probably formed for the rhyme — 'share.'

> 'Their furrow oft the *stubborn glebe* has broke;
> How jocund did they drive their *team afield;*
> How bent the woods beneath their *sturdy stroke*.'

This stanza is made up of various pieces inlaid. 'Stubborn glebe,' is from Gay ; 'drive afield,' from Milton ; 'sturdy stroke,' from Spenser. Such is too much the *system* of Gray's compositions, and *therefore* such the cause of his imperfections. Purity of language, accuracy of thought, and even similarity of rhyme — all give way to the introduction of certain poetical expressions ; in fact, the beautiful jewel, when brought, does not fit into the new setting, or socket. Such is the difference between the flower *stuck* into the ground, and those that grow from it.

> 'Their homely joys and destiny *obscure;*
> The short and simple annals of the *poor*.'

A very imperfect rhyme, such as Swift would not have allowed, and ought not to have appeared in such a poem, where the finishing is supposed to be high, and the expression said to be select.

' And all that beauty, all that wealth *e'er gave*.'

This expression simply means ' beauty and wealth,' and is much weakened by the addition *e'er gave*, which was necessary for the rhyme ' grave.'

' Nor you, ye proud, *impute to these the fault.*'

A prosaic and colloquial line.

' Can Honour's voice *provoke* the silent dust ? '

An unusually bold expression, to say the least. Pope has,

' But when our country's cause *provokes* to arms.'

Again,

> ' Perhaps in this neglected spot *is* laid
> Some heart once pregnant with celestial fire;
> *Hands* that the rod of empire might have sway'd,' &c.

Incorrect in the syntax: — 'Some hands *is* laid.'

' Hands that the *rod of empire* might have sway'd.'

The rod of empire ' is rather a semi-burlesque expression, than a serious one, and degrades the image. Tickell has a better: —

' Proud names, that once the *reins* of empire held.'

But then the rhyme ' sway'd ' would not have done. We see, while writing this, that ' reins ' was in the original MS., and undoubtedly dispossessed of its place for the sake of the verb.

> ' But knowledge to *their* eyes her ample page,
> Rich with the spoils of time, did ne'er unroll,' &c.

It is necessary to go back six stanzas to find the subject to which the relative *their* refers; i. e.

' The short and simple annals of the POOR.'

' *Rich with the spoils of time*, did ne'er unroll.'

This fine expression is taken from Sir Thomas **Browne's** Religio Medici — ' Rich with the spoils of Nature.'

' Chill Penury repress'd their noble rage.'

The use of the word ' rage ' for desire, if not introduced by Pope, was too much used by him.

' So just thy skill, so regular *thy rage;*'

And,

> ' Be justly warm'd by your own *native rage.*'

> ' Some village Hampden, *that* with dauntless breast.

It should be ' who,' instead of ' that.'

> ' To scatter plenty o'er a smiling land.'

This is from Tickell —

> ' To scatter blessings on the British land.'

' From insult to protect.' ' Sculpture deck'd,' is not an allowable rhyme; and what is the force or meaning of the word *still* erected nigh ? '

> ' Their lot forbade, — nor circumscrib'd alone
>   Their growing virtues, but their crimes confin'd —
> Forbade to wade through slaughter to a throne,
>   Or shut the gates of mercy on mankind;
>
> The struggling pangs of conscious truth to hide,
>   To quench the blushes of ingenuous shame,
> Or heap the shrine of luxury and pride
>   With incense kindled at the muse's flame.'

Who does not feel how flat and superfluous is the *latter* stanza, after the fine concluding couplet of the *former?* The two stanzas ought to have been remodelled; part of the second thrown into the first, and then the whole should conclude with the *greatest crime,* the grandest imagery, and the finished picture, —

> ' Forbade to wade through slaughter to a throne,
>   Or shut the gates of mercy on mankind.'

There should the description close; all after that must be weak and superfluous.

> ' Far from the madding crowd's ignoble strife,
>   Their sober wishes never learn'd to stray.'

There is an ambiguity in this couplet, which indeed gives a sense exactly contrary to that intended; to avoid which, one must break the grammatical construction. The first line is from Drummond: — ' Far from the madding worldling's hoarse discords.'

> ' Left the *warm precincts* of the cheerful day.

' Precincts,' a lifeless and prosaic word; and unsuited to the epithet ' warm.' How superior is Tasso —

> ' E lascio mesta l'*aure* suave della vita.'

‘ And *many* a holy text around she strews,
 That *teach* the rustic moralist to die.’

This is ungrammatical. ‘ Many a holy text that *teaches*,’ it ought to be.

‘ On some fond breast the parting soul relies,
 Some *pious drops* the *closing eye* requires,
E’en from the tomb the *voice of Nature* cries,
 E’en in our ashes live their wonted fires.’

‘ Pious drops ’ is from Ovid — ‘ piæ lacrymæ; ’ ‘ Closing eye,’ is from Pope’s Elegy; ‘ Voice of Nature,’ from the Anthologia; and the last line from Chaucer —

‘ Yet in our ashes cold is fire yreken.’

From so many different quarries are the stones brought to form this elaborate mosaic pavement. From this stanza the style of composition drops into a *lower key;* the language is plainer, and is not in harmony with the splendid and elaborate diction of the former part. Mr. Mason says it has a Doric delicacy.

‘ There at the foot of yonder nodding *beech*,
 His listless limbs at noontide would he *stretch*.’

Such imperfect rhymes are not allowable in short and finished poems. And so, in the following stanza, ‘ we saw him *borne* ’ — ‘ beneath yon aged *thorn*.’ And in the xx and xxi stanzas, there are four lines in the rhymes of similar sound, as ‘ nigh,’ ‘ sigh,’ ‘ supply,’ ‘ die.’

‘ Now drooping *woful-wan*, like one forlorn.’

‘ Woful-wan ’ is not a legitimate compound, and must be divided into two separate words, for such they are, when released from the *handcuffs* of the hyphen. Hurd has wrongly given ‘ lazy-pacing,’ and ‘ barren-spirited,’ and ‘ high-sighted,’ as compound epithets, in his notes on Horace’s Art of Poetry !

‘ Nor up the lawn, nor at the wood was he.’

A very bald, flat, prosaic line.

‘ Fair *Science* frown’d not on his humble birth.’

Such personifications are not in the taste of our old and best writers, but grow up in modern times. Dodsley’s Specimens are full of them. So little did the printer know about it, that he has not even printed *science* with a capital letter. **Horace** is correct, as well as beautifully poetical: —

‘ Quem tu, *Melpomene*, semel
 Nascentem placido lumine videris.’

‘ *Or* draw his frailties from their dread abode.’
It should be ‘ Nor.’

————

ADDITIONAL NOTES.

‘ ’Twas on a lofty vase’s side,
    Where China’s gayest art had dy’d
      The azure flowers that blow.’
         Ode on the Death of a favourite Cat.

So Lady M. Montagu, in one of her *Town Eclogues,* written
in 1715:

‘ Where the *tall jar* erects its stately pride,
    With antic shapes in *China’s azure dy’d.*’
         Friday — The Toilette. **D.**

‘ Save where the beetle wheels his droning flight.’
         Elegy.

So Lady M. Montagu

‘ She said, and slowly leaves the realms of night,
    While the curs’d phantoms praise her *droning flight.*’
         The Court of Dullness. **D.**

‘ Till the sad Nine, in Greece’s evil hour,
    Left their Parnassus,’ &c.   *Progress of Poesy.*

Compare Gabriel Harvey:

‘ It is not long, since the goodlyest graces of the most noble
commonwealthes upon earth, Eloquence in speech, and Civility
in manners, arriued in these remote parts of the world: it was
a happy reuolution of the heauens, and worthy to be chro-
nicled in an English Liuy, when Tiberis flowed into the
Thames; Athens removed to London; pure Italy and fine
Greece planted themselues in rich England; Apollo with his
delicate troupe of Muses forsooke his old mountaines and
riuers, and frequented a new Parnassus, and an other Helicon,
nothinge inferiour to the olde, when they were most solemnely
haunted of diuine wittes, that taught Rhetorique to speake
with applause, and Poetry to sing with admiration.’ *Pierce’s
Supererogation,* 1593, p. 15.   **D.**

‘ Amazement, in his van, with Flight combin’d,
    And Sorrow’s faded form, and Solitude behind.’
         The Bard, St. ii. 1.

So Swift:

‘ On he went, and in his van Confusion and Amaze, while
Horror and Affright brought up the Rear.’
         Battle of the Books. **D**

Appendix E.

Memorabilia—from Mr. Bray's notes. See Mrs. Bray's Description of Devonshire, in letters to R. Southey, esq., vol. iii. p. 311.

Jan. 27, 1807. In a conversation which I had with Mr. Mathias on Italian literature, he informed me that *Gray*, though so great a poet himself, and an admirer of the poets of Italy, was unacquainted with the works of Guidi, Menzini, Filicaia, &c., and indeed of almost all, that are contained in his ' Componomenti Lirici.' He had once in his possession the commonplace book of Gray, and it contained very copious extracts from the Commentary of Crescembini. He told me that he could gratify me with a sight of Gray's hand writing, and fetched from his library a fac-simile, being a kind of commentary in English on Pindar and Aristophanes. It was written remarkably neat and plain, but rather stiff, and bearing evident marks of being written slowly. It had a great resemblance to the Italian mode of writing, every part of the letters being nearly of an equal thickness. He wrote always with a crow-quill.

Observing no obliterations or erasures, and indeed only one or two interlineations, I remarked that it must have been a fair copy, and wondered how he could have taken so much pains, unless he had intended it for publication. But Mr. Mathias assured me, that Gray was so averse to publication, that had not a surreptitious copy of his ' Elegy in a Country Church-yard ' appeared, he never would have published it; and even when he did, it was without his name. The reason that he was so correct, was that he never committed any thing to paper till he had most maturely considered it before hand.

Mr. Mathias explained to me how he was so well acquainted with these particulars respecting Gray, by informing me that he was most intimate with Mr. Nichols, the familiar friend and executor of Gray, who had lent him the MSS. On my lamenting that they were never made public, he said that it was not for want of his most earnest solicitation, but that Mr. Nichols was an old man, and wished even to conceal that he was in possession of any such precious reliques, lest he should be plagued with requests to have them copied, or at least to shew them. He therefore in a manner enjoined me to secrecy, and I consequently commit the pleasant memoranda to paper, merely for my own satisfaction, that, on occasional inspection, the pleasure I received from this conversation may be more firmly brought to my recollection. For the same reason, and as these MSS. are never likely to be made public, I shall enter more at large upon the consideration of them; at least as much as a cursory inspection during a morning call would permit.

As Gray always affixed the date to everything he wrote, which, as Mr. Mathias assured me, was the custom of Petrarch, it seems that he wrote his remarks on Pindar at rather an early age. I think the date was 1747. It is very closely written : the Greek characters are remarkably neat. He begins with the date of the composition, and takes into his consideration almost every thing connected with it, both chronologically and historically. The notes of the Scholiasts do not escape him, and he is so minute as to direct his attention to almost every expression. He appears to have reconciled many apparent incongruities, and to have elucidated many difficulties. I the more lament these valuable annotations remain unpublished, as they would prove that, in the opinion of so great a man, the English language is in every respect adequate to express everything that criticism the most erudite can require. It presented to my eye a most gratifying novelty, to see the union of Greek and English, and to find that they harmonized together as well as Greek and Latin.

The remarks on the plays of Aristophanes were so minute, not only expressing where they were written and acted, but when they were revived, that, as Mr. Mathias justly observed, 'one would think he was reading the account of some modern comedy, instead of the dramatic composition of about two thousand years old.' Gray also left behind him very copious remarks upon Plato, which had also formerly been in Mr. Mathias's hands, likewise large collections respecting the customs of the ancients, &c. And so multifarious and minute were his investigations, that he directed his attention even to the Supellex, or household furniture of the ancients, collecting together all the passages of the classics that had any reference to the subject.

Mr. Mathias shewed me likewise many sheets copied by Gray from some Italian author; also, I believe, an historical composition, and a great many genealogies, of which Gray was particularly fond. On my remarking that I wished Gray had written less genealogies and more poetry, he informed me that the reason he had written so little poetry, was from the great exertion it cost him (which he made no reserve in confessing) in the labour of composition. Mr. Mathias informed me that he had seen the original copy of Gray's 'Ode on the

Progress of Poetry ! ' that there were not so many alterations
as he expected, which was evidently owing to his method of
long previous meditation, and that some of the lines were
written three or four times over; and then, what is not always
the case with an author, the best is always adopted.

He said there was nothing of which Gray had not the pro-
foundest knowledge, at least of such subjects as come under
the denomination of learning, except mathematics, of which,
as well as his friend Mason, he was completely ignorant, and
which he used frequently to lament. He was acquainted with
botany, but hardly seems to have paid it the compliment it
deserves, when he said he learnt it merely for the sake of
sparing himself the trouble of thinking."

APPENDIX F.

CLASSIFICATION OF THE POETS,

FORMED BY POPE.

(See Observ. on the English Poets, by Pope, in Spence's Anec-
dotes, ed. Malone, p. 81, 145.)

ÆRA I.

Rymer, 2d part, p. 65, 66, 67, 77. Petrarch, 78. Catal. or
Provençals. [Poets.]

1. School of Provence.
{ Chaucer's Visions.* Romaunt of the Rose.
  Pierce Plowman. Tales from Boccace.
  Gower. }

2. School of Chaucer.
{ Lydgate.
  T. Occleve.
  Walter de Mapes.
  Skelton. }

3. School of Petrarch.
{ Earl of Surrey.
  Sir Thomas Wyat.
  Sir Philip Sydney.
  G. Gascoyne. Translator of Ariosto's Co-
  medy. }

4. School of Dante.
{ Mirror of Magistrates.
  Lord Buckhurst's Induction. Gorboduck. —
  [Original of good Tragedy. — Seneca his
  Model.] }

ÆRA II.

Spenser. Col. Clout, from the School of Ariosto, and Petrarch,
translated from Tasso.

5. School of Spenser, and from Italian Sonnets.
{ W. Brown's Pastorals.
  Ph. Fletcher's Purple Island. Alabaster.
  Piscatory Eclogues.
  S. Daniel.
  Sir Walter Raleigh.
  Milton's Juvenilia. Heath. Habington. }

---

* Read. Chaucer's Romaunt of the Rose. Visions of Pierce
Plowman. [Malone.]

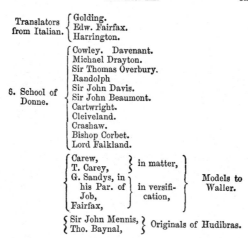

Translators from Italian.
{ Golding.
Edw. Fairfax.
Harrington. }

6. School of Donne.
{ Cowley. Davenant.
Michael Drayton.
Sir Thomas Overbury.
Randolph
Sir John Davis.
Sir John Beaumont.
Cartwright.
Cleiveland.
Crashaw.
Bishop Corbet.
Lord Falkland. }

Carew,
T. Carey,   } in matter,
G. Sandys, in
  his Par. of   in versifi-   } Models to
  Job,   cation,   Waller.
Fairfax,

Sir John Mennis, } Originals of Hudibras.
Tho. Baynal,

Here are several mistakes. The first paragraph under Æra II. viz. " Spenser, Col. Clout, from the School of Ariosto, and Petrarch, translated from Tasso," is unintelligible. We have no English poem by *Alabaster*. Golding, I believe, translated nothing from the Italian. Sir John Davies and Drayton wrote nearly as soon as Donne. Carew, and T. Carey, are the same person ; and Thomas Carew, the person meant, had published nothing when Waller wrote his first poem. There is no poet of the name of Baynal. The person meant, I suspect, was Tho. *Randal*, in which way the name of *Randolph* the poet was often written in the last century ; and Pope might not have known that *Randolph*, whom he mentioned before, and Tho. *Randal*, were the same person. [Malone.] *

To these observations by Mr. Malone, I shall add, that there does not seem to be any just ground for placing Chaucer in the

---

* Randall. — See Llewellyn's Poems, P. A. 5. *Randall.* Masters, Cartwright — See Dryden's Art of Poetry, i. 242, ' *Randall* in his Rustic Strains.' See Pref. Poems to Gayton's Chartæ Scriptæ. *Tom. Randall !* 4to. 1645. Bancroft's Essay, 4to. p. 2. *T. Randall.* See Faithf. Teate's Poems, 1699, p. 1. *Randall*, and Davenant. Marlow was spelt *Marley*, see Peele's Works, ed. Dyce, ii. 140.

school of Provence. Mr. Trywhitt says, "As to Chaucer's *language*, I have not observed, in any of his writings, a single *phrase or word*, which has the least appearance of having been fetched by him from the south of the Loire. With respect to the *manner* and *matter* of his compositions, till some clear instance of imitation be produced, I shall be slow to believe, that in either he ever copied the poets of Provence, with whose works, I apprehend, he had very little, if any, acquaintance." [Cant. Tales, pref. p. xxxv.] Even T. Warton, in his Emendations and Additions to his second volume [p. 458], says: " I have never affirmed that Chaucer imitated the Provençal bards; although it is by no means improbable that he might have known their tales." Secondly, Davenant and Drayton can never be placed in the school of *Donne*.* Drayton should be ranked with Spenser; where indeed Pope, in his conversation with Spence, placed him: and Davenant is a poet who approaches nearer to Shakspeare, in the beauty of his descriptions, the tenderness of his thoughts, the seriousness of his feeling, and the wildness of his fancy. Cartwright did not imitate Donne; † and Cleveland is a writer of a very peculiar style, which he formed for himself. " The obtrusion of *new* words on his hearers (says Dryden) is what the world has blamed in our satirist Cleveland. To express a thing hard, and unnaturally, is his new way of elocution. There is this difference between his Satires and Donne's, that the one gives us *deep* thoughts in common language, through rough cadence; the other gives us common thoughts in abstruse words." Essay on Dramatic Poesy, p. 63, 64. [See this Catalogue in Mathias's Gray, vol. ii. p. 8.]

Letter from T. Gray to Thomas Warton, in the possession of Al. Chalmers, Esq. See his Life of T. Warton, v. British Poets, vol. xviii. p. 80.

Sir, — Our friend, Dr. Hurd, having long ago desired me, in your name, to communicate any fragments or sketches of a

---

* Perhaps Pope alluded to Suckling's verses to Davenant: —

"Thou hast redeem'd us, Will: — and future Times
Shall not account unto the age's crimes
Death· of fierce Wit. Since the great Lord of it
DONNE parted hence: no man has ever writ
So near him, in his own way." ——

† Dryden first called Donne metaphysical. See Warton's Pope, vol. iv. p. 252.

design I once had to give a History of English Poetry,* you may well think me rude or negligent, when you see me hesitating for so many months, before I comply with your request; and yet, believe me, few of your friends have been better pleased than I, to find this subject (surely neither unentertaining nor unuseful) had fallen into hands so likely to do it justice. Few have felt a higher esteem for your talents, your taste, and industry. In truth, the only cause of my delay has been a sort of diffidence, that would not let me send you any thing, so short, so slight, and so imperfect as the few materials I had begun to collect, or the observations I had made on them. A sketch of the division or arrangement of the subject, however, I venture to transcribe; and would wish to know, whether it corresponds in any thing with your own plan, for I am told your first volume is in the press.

INTRODUCTION.

On the Poetry of the Gallic or Celtic nations, as far back as it can be traced. On that of the Goths, its introduction into these islands by the Saxons and Danes, and its duration. On the origin of rhyme among the Franks, the Saxons, and Provençaux. Some account of the Latin rhyming poetry, from its early origin, down to the fifteenth century.

PART I.

On the school of Provence, which rose about the year 1100, and was soon followed by the French and Italians. Their heroic poetry, or romances in verse, allegories, fabliaux, syrvientes, comedies, farces, canzoni, sonnetts, ballades, madrigals, sestines, &c. Of their imitators, the French; and of the first Italian School, commonly called the Sicilian, about the year 1200, brought to perfection by Dante, Petrarch, Boccace, and others. State of poetry in England from the Conquest, 1066, or rather from Henry the Second's time, 1154, to the reign of Edward the Third, 1327.

PART II.

On Chaucer, who first introduced the manner of the Provençaux, improved by the Italians, into our country. His charac-

---

* See a letter from Thos. Warton to Garrick, June 28, 1769, in which he says Gray had once an intention of this sort, (of writing the History of English Poetry), but he dropt it, as you may see by an Advt. to his Norway Odes. See Garrick's Corres. vol. 355.

ter, and merits at large. The different kinds in which he excelled. Gower, Occleve, Lydgate, Hawes, Gawen Douglas Lyndesay, Bellenden, Dunbar, &c.

Part III.

Second Italian School, of Ariosto, Tasso, &c., an improvement on the first, occasioned by the revival of letters, the end of the fifteenth century. The Lyric Poetry of this and the former age, introduced from Italy by Lord Surrey, Sir T, Wyat, Bryan Lord Vaulx, &c. in the beginning of the sixteenth century.

Part IV.

Spenser, his character. Subject of his poem, allegoric and romantic, of Provençal invention: but his manner of tracing it borrowed from the second Italian school. — Drayton, Fairfax, Phineas Fletcher, Golding, Phaer, &c. This school ends in Milton. A third Italian school, full of conceit, began in Queen Elizabeth's reign, continued under James, and Charles the First, by Donne, Crashaw, Cleveland ; carried to its height by Cowley, and ending perhaps in Sprat.

Part V.

School of France, introduced after the Restoration, — Waller, Dryden, Addison, Prior, and Pope, — which has continued to our own times.

You will observe that my idea was in some measure taken from a scribbled paper of Pope, of which I believe you have a copy. You will also see, I had excluded Dramatic poetry entirely; which if you had taken in, it would at least double the bulk and labour of your book.

I am, sir, with great esteem,
Your most humble and obedient servant,
THOMAS GRAY.

Pembroke Hall,
April 15, 1770.

Note. There is a most objectionable Classification of the Poets in Dr. J. Warton's Essay on Pope. v. Ded. V. 1. p. 12.

POEMS.

ODES.

I. ON THE SPRING.

[The original manuscript title given by Gray to this Ode, was 'Noontide.' It appeared for the first time in Dodsley's Collection, vol. ii. p. 271, under the title of 'Ode.' See Meleager's Ode to Spring, and Jones. Comm. Poes. Asiaticæ. p. 411. This Ode is formed on Horace's Ode ad Sestium, i. iv. Translated into Latin in Musæ Etonens. Vol. ii. p. 60.]

Lo ! where the rosy-bosom'd Hours,
   Fair Venus' train, appear,
Disclose the long-expecting flowers,
   And wake the purple year !

NOTES — Ver. 1. "The Graces, and the *rosy-bosom'd Hours.*" Milton. Comus, v. 984. *W.* Thoms. Spring, 1007.
V. 2. So Homer. Hymn. ad Vener. ii. 5:

τὴν δὲ χρυσάμπυκες ὧραι
Δέξαντ' ἀσπασίως περὶ δ' ἄμβροτα εἵματα ἕσσαν.

The *Hours* also are joined with *Venus* in the Hymn. ad Apollin. v. 194. And Hesiod places them in her train :

ἀμφι δὲ τήνγε
Ὧραι καλλίκομοι στέφον ἄνθεσιν εἰαρινοῖσι. Erg. ver. 75.

V. 3. "At that soft season when descending showers
   Call forth the greens, and *wake the rising flowers.*"
Pope. Temple of Fame, b. i. v. 1. *W.* — In some editions, "expected" is printed for "expecting." "The flowers that in its womb expecting lie." Dryden. Astræa Redux. *Rogers,*
V. 4. Apuleius. Nuptiis Cupid. et Psyc. vi. p. 427, ed. Oudendorp : "*Horæ*, rosis, et cæteris floribus *purpurabant*

The Attic warbler pours her throat,   5
Responsive to the cuckoo's note,
    The untaught harmony of spring:
While, whisp'ring pleasure as they fly,
Cool Zephyrs thro' the clear blue sky
    Their gather'd fragance fling.   10

Where'er the oak's thick branches stretch
    A broader browner shade,
Where'er the rude and moss-grown beech
    O'er-canopies the glade,
Beside some water's rushy brink   15
With me the Muse shall sit, and think

---

omnia." Also in the Pervigil. Vener. v. 13: " Ipsa gemmis *purpurantem* pingit *annum* floribus." Pope has the same expression in his Past. i. 28: " And lavish Nature paints the *purple year.*" " Gales that wake the purple year." Mallet. Zephyr.

V. 5. Martial, Epig. i. 54: " Sic ubi multisona fervet sacer *Atthide* lucus." Also in the Epitaphium Athenaidos apud Fabrettum, p. 702: " Cum te, nate, fleo, planctus dabit *Attica Aedon.*" And " *Attica* volucris." Propert. II. xvi. 6.— Ovid. Halieut. v. 110: " Attica avis vernâ sub tempestate queratus." Add Senecæ Herc. Œt. v. 200. And Milton. Par. R. iv. 245: " The *Attic bird* trills her thick-warbled notes." The expression " pours her throat" is from Pope. Essay on Man, iii. 33: " Is it for thee the linnet *pours her throat?*" So Ovid. Trist iii. 12. 8. " *Indocilique* loquax *gutture* vernat avis."

V. 7   — " The hollow Cuckoo sings
    The symphony of Spring."—
           Thoms. Spring. *Luke.*

V. 10.   — " Fresh gales and gentle airs
    Whisper'd it to the woods." Par. L. viii. 515.

v. Comus. v. 989. and P. L. iv. 327. " Cool Zephyr." *Luke.*

V. 12. Milton. Par. L. iv. 246: " The unpierc'd *shade*

(At ease reclin'd in rustic state)
How vain the ardour of the crowd,
How low, how little are the proud,
How indigent the great !   20

Still is the toiling hand of Care;
    The panting herds repose:
Yet, hark, how thro' the peopled air

Var. V. 19.   "How low, how indigent the proud,
                        How little are the great ! "

So these lines appeared in Dodsley. The variation, as
Mason informs us, was subsequently made to avoid the point
" *little* and *great*."

---

imbrown'd the noontide bowers."   " And breathes a *browner*
horror o'er the woods," Pope. Eloisa, 170. *W.* —Thomson.
Cast. of Ind. **i.** 38: " Or Autumn's varied *shades imbrown* the
walls."

V. 13. " A bank *o'ercanopied* with luscious woodbine."
Mids. N. Dr. act ii. sc. 2. *Gray.*

        " The *beech* shall yield a cool safe *canopy*."

Fletcher. Purpl. Is. i. v. 30. And T. Warton's note on Milton's Comus, v. 543.

V. 15. " The rushy-fringed bank." Comus. *Luke.*

V. 22. " Patula pecus omne sub ulmo est." Pers. Sat.
iii. 6. *W.* — But Gray seems to have imitated Pope. Past.
ii. 86:
        " The lowing *herds* to murmuring brooks retreat,
        To closer *shades the panting* flocks remove: "

    " Jam pastor umbras cum *grege languido*
        Rivumque fessus quærit." Hor. lib. III. Od. xxix. 21.

V. 23. Thomson. Autumn, 836: " Warn'd of approaching
winter, gather'd, play the *swallow-people*." And Walton.
Complete Angler, p. 260: " Now the wing'd *people* of the
sky shall sing." Add Beaumont. Psyche, st. lxxxviii. p. 46:
" Every tree *empeopled* was with birds of softest throats."
so Alciphr. Ep. p. 341. δῆμον ὅλον ὅρνεων. and Max. Tyr. See
Reiske's note, p. 82.

The busy murmur glows!
The insect-youth are on the wing,   25
Eager to taste the honied spring,
　　And float amid the liquid noon:
Some lightly o'er the current skim,
Some shew their gayly-gilded trim
　　Quick-glancing to the sun.   30

To Contemplation's sober eye
　　Such is the race of Man:
And they that creep, and they that fly,
　　Shall end where they began.
Alike the Busy and the Gay   35
But flutter thro' life's little day,
　　In Fortune's varying colors drest:

V. 24. Thus Milton. Par. R. iv. 248: " The sound of bees'
industrious murmur." Wakefield quotes Thomson. Spr. 506:
" Thro' the soft air the *busy nations* fly." And, 649: " But
restless hurry thro' the *busy air.*" Compare also Pope. T. of
Fame, 294.

V. 25. " Some to the sun their *insect-wings* unfold."
Pope. Rape of the Lock, ii. 59. *W.* This expression may
have been suggested by a line in Green's Hermitage, quoted
in Gray's Letter to Walpole: (see note at ver. 31.)

　　" From *maggot-youth* thro' change of state
　　　　They feel, like us, the turns of fate."

V. 26. See Milton, as quoted by Wakefield: Il Pen. 142,
Lycid. 140, Sams. Ag. 1066.

V. 27. " Nare per æstatem liquidam," Georg. iv. 59.
Gray. — To which, add Georg. i. 404; and Æn. v. 525; x. 272.
" There I suck the liquid air." Milton. Comus, v. 980.

V. 30. " Sporting with *quick glance,* shew to the *sun* their
wav'd coats dropp'd with gold," Par. L. vii. 410. *Gray.* — See
also Pope, Hom. Il. ii. 557; and Essay on Man, iii. 55.

V. 31. " While insects from the threshold preach," Green,
in the Grotto. Dodsley, Misc. v. p. 161. *Gray.* —Gray, in a

Brush'd by the hand of rough Mischance,
Or chill'd by Age, their airy dance
    They leave, in dust to rest,   40

Methinks I hear, in accents low,
    The sportive kind reply :
Poor moralist ! and what art thou ?
    A solitary fly !
Thy joys no glittering female meets,   45
No hive hast thou of hoarded sweets,
    No painted plumage to display :
On hasty wings thy youth is flown ;
Thy sun is set, thy spring is gone —
    We frolic while 'tis May.   50

moralizing abstract plan

---

letter to H. Walpole, says: (see Walpole's Works, vol. v.
p. 395.) " I send you a bit of a thing for two reasons; first,
because it is one of your favorite's, Mr. M. Green; and next,
because I would do justice: the *thought on which my second
Ode turns*, (The Ode to Spring, afterwards placed *first*, by
Gray,) is manifestly stole from thence. Not that I knew it
at the time, but having seen this many years before; to be
sure it imprinted itself on my memory, and forgetting the
author, I took it for my own." Then follows the quotation
from Green's Grotto. Wakefield seems to have discovered the
original of this stanza in some lines in Thomson. Summer, 342.

V. 37. " The varied colours run," Thoms. Spring. *Luke*.

V. 47.

  " From branch to branch the smaller birds with song
    Solac'd the woods, and spread their *painted wings*."

Par. L. vii. 438. *W*. And so Thomson. Spring, 582; Virg.
Georg. iii. 243; Æn. iv. 525; Claudian, xv. 3. " Pictisque
plumis." Phædri Fab. iii. v. 18.

V. 49. Πάνθ' ἅλιον ἄμμι δεδύκειν. Theocrit. Idyll. i. 102.
W. Alexis ap. Stobæum. lib. cxv.: Ἤδη γὰρ ὁ βίος ὁὑμὸς
Ἐσπέραν ἄγει. Plato has the same metaphorical expression :

II.* ON THE DEATH OF A FAVOURITE CAT,

DROWNED IN A TUB OF GOLD FISHES.

[On a favourite cat called Selima, that fell into a China Tub
with gold fishes in it, and was drowned, MS. Wharton.   Walpole, after the death of Gray, placed the China Vase on a
pedestal at Strawberry Hill, with a few lines of the Ode for
its inscription.]

'Twas on a lofty vase's side,
Where China's gayest art had dy'd
The azure flowers, that blow;

Var. V. 4. In the first edition the order of these lines was
reversed:

" The pensive Selima reclin'd,
Demurest of the tabby kind."

ἡμεῖς δ᾽ἐν δυσμαῖς τοῦ βίου, de Legib. tom. ii. p. 770, ed.
Serrani; and Aristotelis Poetica, cap. 35: καὶ τὸ γῆρας Ἑσπέραν
βίου. Add Catull. ad Lesb. c. 5. v. 5. " Nobis, cum semel
occidet brevis lux."   Twining, in his translation of the Poetics,
together with this line from Gray, has quoted Com. of Err.
(last scene): " Yet hath my *night of life* some memory," see
p. 108.   It is a phrase very common among the old English
poets. — Herrick has,

" Sunk is my sight, *set is my sun*,
And all the loom of life undone."

and " My sun begins to set," Rowley's All's lost by Lust,
p. 63, 4to. with many others.

* This Ode first appeared in Dodsley. Col. vol. ii. p. 274,
with some variations; only one of which is given by Mason.
They are all noticed in this edition, as they occur.

V. 3. This expression has been accused of redundance by

Demurest of the tabby kind,
The pensive Selima, reclin'd,   5
     Gaz'd on the lake below.

Her conscious tail her joy declar'd;
The fair round face, the snowy beard,
     The velvet of her paws,
Her coat, that with the tortoise vies,   10
Her ears of jet, and emerald eyes,
     She saw; and purr'd applause.

Still had she gaz'd; but 'midst the tide
Two angel forms were seen to glide,
     The Genii of the stream: 15

Var. V. 14. First edit. "Two beauteous forms;" a reading that appears to me preferable to the one now in the text.

Dr. Johnson and Wakefield. See Todd's Ed. of Comus, p. 139. Gray, however, could have defended it by the usage of the ancient poets. See Ovid. Metam. ix. 98: "Hunc tamen *ablati* domuit *jactura* decoris." And Statii Silv. II. v. 30: "Unius *amissi* tetigit *jactura* leonis." Ovid ad Liv. 185: "Jura *silent, mutæque tacent* sine vindice leges." In Jortin's Tracts, vol. i. p. 269, some examples of such redundant expressions are collected from the Greek and Latin poets. See on this subject also the notes of Burmann on Propertius, lib. iv El. vii. v. 69; on Ovid. Met. ii. 66, and on Poem. Lotichii, lib. i. el. 8. 27. In the Prog. of Poesy, I. i. 5. "The laughing *flowers* that round them *blow.*" "Azure flowers," v. Drummond. Mæliades. *Luke.*

V. 15. Thomson, in his Spring, v. 400, with equal beauty, speaking of fish:

     "—— in whose ample wave
The *little Naiads* love to sport at large."

Their scaly armour's Tyrian hue
Through richest purple to the view
   Betray'd a golden gleam.

The hapless nymph with wonder saw:
A whisker first, and then a claw,   20
   With many an ardent wish,
She stretch'd, in vain, to reach the prize.
What female heart can gold despise?
   What Cat's averse to fish?

Presumptuous maid! with looks intent   25
Again she stretch'd, again she bent,
   Nor knew the gulf between.
(Malignant Fate sat by, and smil'd)
The slipp'ry verge her feet beguil'd,
   She tumbled headlong in.   30

V. 17. *" Aureus* ipse; sed in foliis, quæ plurima circum
     Funduntur, violæ *sublucet purpura* nigræ."
              Virg. Georg. iv. 274. W.
  V. 18. " His shining horns diffus'd a *golden gleam,*" Pope.
Winds. For. 331. " And lucid amber casts a *golden gleam,*"
Temp. of Fame, 253.
  V. 42. This proverbial expression was a favourite among
the old English poets:

    " But all thing, which that *shineth as the gold,*
    Ne is no gold, as I have herd it told."

See Chaucer. Chanones Yemannes Tale, v. 16430. Tyrwhitt
refers to the Parabolæ of Alanus de Insulis, quoted by Leyser,
Hist. Poet. Med. Æv. 1074: " Non teneas aurum, totum quod
splendet ut aurum." Among the poems published with **Lord**

Eight times emerging from the flood,
She mew'd to ev'ry wat'ry God,
   Some speedy aid to send.
No Dolphin came, no Nereid stirr'd:
Nor cruel Tom, nor Susan heard.   85
   A fav'rite has no friend!

From hence, ye beauties, undeceiv'd,
Know, one false step is ne'er retriev'd,
   And be with caution bold.
Not all that tempts your wand'ring eyes   40
And heedless hearts is lawful prize,
   Nor all, that glisters, gold.

Var. V. 35.   " nor *Harry* heard.
         What favourite has a friend ? "   First **edit.**
   V. 40. Strikes. MS.

Surrey's, p. 226, edit. 1717: " Not every *glist'ring* gives the *gold*, that greedy folk desire." In the Paradise of Dainty Devises, "No Foe to a Flatterer," p. 60 (reprint), is this line: " But now I see all is not *gold, that glittereth in the eye.*" In England's Helicon, p. 194: " All is not *gold*, that *shineth* bright in show." Spenser. F. Queen, ii. 8. 14: " Yet *gold* all is not, that doth *golden* seem."

" Not every thinge that gives a gleame and *glitt'ring* showe, Is to be counted *gold* indeede, this proverbe well you knowe.'
      Turberville. Answer of a Woman to her Lover, st. iv

   " All as they say, that *glitters* is not *gold.*"
            Dryden. H. and Panther.

   This poem was written later than the first, third, and fourth Odes, but was arranged by Gray in this place, in his own edition.

III.* ON A DISTANT PROSPECT OF ETON COLLEGE.

'Ανθρωπος, ἱκανὴ πρόφασις εἰς τὸ δυστυχεῖν.

Menander. Incert. Fragm. ver. 382. ed. Cler. p. 245

[See Musæ Etonenses, vol. i. p. 229, and Brit. Bibliographer, vol. ii. p. 214.]

YE distant spires, ye antique towers,
   That crown the wat'ry glade,
Where grateful Science still adores
   Her Henry's † holy shade;
And ye, that from the stately brow   5
Of Windsor's heights th expanse below
Of grove, of lawn, of mead survey,

---

* This, as Mason informs us, was the *first English* production of Gray which appeared in print. It was published in folio, in 1747, and appeared again in Dodsley, Col. vol. ii. p. 267, without the name of the author. A Latin poem by him, On the Prince of Wales's Marriage, had appeared in the Cambridge Collection, in 1736, which is inserted in this edition.

V. 2.   " Haunt the watery glade." —
                 Pope. Wind. For. *Luke.*

† King Henry the Sixth, founder of the College.

V. 4. So in the Bard, ii. 3: " And spare the meek usurper's *holy head.*" And in Install. Ode, iv. 12: " The murder'd *saint.*" So Rich. III. act v. sc. 1: " *Holy* King Henry." And act iv. sc. 4: " When *holy Henry* died." This epithet has a peculiar propriety; as Henry the Sixth, though never canonized, was regarded as a *saint.* See Barrington on the Statutes, p. 416, and Douce. Illust. of Shakesp. ii. 38. " Yea and *holy Henry* lying at Windsor." Barclay. Eclog. p. 4, fol.

Whose turf, whose shade, whose flowers among
Wanders the hoary Thames along
　　His silver-winding way:　　　　　　　10

Ah, happy hills! ah, pleasing shade!
　　Ah, fields belov'd in vain!
Where once my careless childhood stray'd,
　　A stranger yet to pain!
I feel the gales that from ye blow　　　　15
A momentary bliss bestow,
　　As waving fresh their gladsome wing,
My weary soul they seem to soothe,
And, redolent of joy and youth,
　　To breathe a second spring.　　　　20

Say, father Thames, for thou hast seen

V. 5.　　　　　　　　" and now to where
　　　Majestic Windsor lifts his *princely brow.*"
　　　　　　　　　　Thoms. Sum. 1412.　*W.*
　　V. 10. " The vale of Thames *fair-winding up.*"　Thoms.
Sum. 1417.　Fenton in his Ode to Lord Gower, which was
praised by Pope and Akenside, had these two lines, iii. 1:
　　" Or if invok'd where *Thames's* fruitful tides
　　　Slow thro' the vale in *silver volumes* play."
Spenser. vol. v. p. 87: " Silver-streaming Thames."
　　V. 15. " *L'Aura* gentil che rasserena i poggi
　　　　　Destando i fior per questo ombroso bosco
　　　　　Al soavesuo spirto riconosco."　Petrarca, Son. clxi.
　　V. 19. " And bees their honey *redolent of spring.*"　Dry-
den's Fable on the Pythag. System.　*Gray.* — " And every
field is *redolent of spring,*" L. Welsted's Poems, p. 23.　It ap-
pears also in the Memoirs of Europe towards the Close of the
Eighth Century, by Mrs. Manly, 1716, vol. ii. p. 67: " The
lovely Endimion, *redolent of youth.*"　See Todd, in a note to
Sams. Agonist. (Milton, vol. iv. p. 410.)
　　V. 21. This invocation is taken from Green's Grotto: see
Dodsley. Col. vol. v. p. 159

  Full many a sprightly race
 Disporting on thy margent green,
  The paths of pleasure trace;
Who foremost now delight to cleave, 25
With pliant arm, thy glassy wave?
  The captive linnet which enthral?
What idle progeny succeed
To chase the rolling circle's speed,
  Or urge the flying ball 30

While some on earnest business bent
 Their murm'ring labours ply
'Gainst graver hours that bring constraint
 To sweeten liberty:
Some bold adventurers disdain 35
The limits of their little reign,

Var. V. 29. "To chase the hoops illusive speed." MS.

  " *Say, father Thames*, whose gentle pace
   Gives leave to view, what beauties grace
   Your flowery banks, *if you have seen.*"
Perhaps both poets thought of Cowley, vol. i. p. 117:
  " Ye fields of Cambridge, our dear Cambridge, *say,*
   Have you not seen us walking every day.*"*
Dryden. An. Mirab. St. ccxxxii. " Old *father* Thames rais'd
up his reverend head."
  V. 23. " By slow Mæander's *margent green.*" Milton. Com
232. *W.*
  V. 24. " To virtue, in the *paths of pleasure* trod." Pope.
Essay on Man, iii. 233.
  V. 26. " On the glassy wave." Todd. ed. of Comus, p. 118
  V. 27. This expression has been noticed as tautologous.
Thomson, on the *same* subject, uses somewhat redundant lan-
guage, Spring, 702:
  " Inhuman caught; and in the narrow cage
   From *liberty confined* and boundless air."

And unknown regions dare descry:
Still as they run they look behind,
They hear a voice in every wind,
    And snatch a fearful joy.   40

Gay hope is theirs by fancy fed,
    Less pleasing when possest;
The tear forgot as soon as shed,
    The sunshine of the breast:
Theirs buxom health of rosy hue,   45
Wild wit, invention ever new,
    And lively cheer, of vigour born;
The thoughtless day, the easy night,
The spirits pure, the slumbers light,
    That fly th' approach of morn.   50

V. 30. "The senator at cricket *urge the ball.*"
                                Pope. Dun. iv. 592.

V. 37. This line is taken from Cowley. Pindarique Ode to
Hobbes, **iv.** 7. p. 223: "Till *unknown regions it descries.*"

V. 40. "Magnaque post lachrymas etiamnum *gaudia pal-
lent.*" Stat. Theb. i. 620. For other expressions of this nature,
see Wakefield's note. Add Sil. Ital. xvi. 432, "lætoque pa-
vore." *Luke.*

V. 44. "Eternal *sunshine* of the spotless *mind.*" Pope.
Eloisa, ver. 209. Add Essay on Man, iv. 167, "The soul's
calm sunshine."

V. 47. "In either cheeke depeyncten *lively cheere,*" Spenser. Hobbinol's Dittie, ver. 33. *W.* See Milton. Ps. lxxxiv. 5.
"With joy and gladsome cheer." *Luke.*

V. 49. "The temperate sleeps, and *spirits light as air.*"
Pope. Im. of Horace, I. 73; Hor. Od. ii. xi. 7. "facilemque
somnum:" and Par. L. v. 3:

            "—— His *sleep*
        Was *airy light*, from *pure* digestion bred,
        And temperate vapours bland."

Alas! regardless of their doom,
   The little victims play;
No sense have they of ills to come,
   Nor care beyond to-day:
Yet see, how all around 'em wait   55
The ministers of human fate,
   And black Misfortune's baleful train!
Ah, shew them where in ambush stand,
To seize their prey, the murth'rous band!
   Ah, tell them, they are men!   60

These shall the fury Passions tear,
   The vultures of the mind,
Disdainful Anger, pallid Fear,
   And Shame that sculks behind;
Or pining Love shall waste their youth,   65
Or Jealousy, with rankling tooth,

V. 51. " E'en now, *regardless of his doom,*
     Applauding honour haunts his tomb."

Collins. Ode on the Death of Col. Ross, 4th stanza of his *first
manuscript.*

V. 55. These two lines resemble two in Broome. Ode on
Melancholy, p. 28:

    " While round, *stern ministers of fate,*
     Pain, and Disease, and Sorrow wait."

And Otway. Alcib. act v. sc. 2. p. 84: " Then enter, ye *grim
ministers of fate.*"

V. 61. " The *fury Passions* from that flood began." See
Pope. Essay on Man, iii. 167.

V. 63. " Exsanguisque Metus," Stat. Theb. vii. 49. And
from him Milton, Quint. Novemb. 148: " Exsanguisque Horror." Pers. Sat. iii. v. 115, " Timor albus."

V. 66. " But *gnawing Jealousy* out of their sight,
     Sitting alone, his bitter lips did bite."
                    Spenser. F. Q. vi. 23

That inly gnaws the secret heart;
And Envy wan, and faded Care,
Grim-visag'd comfortless Despair,
    And Sorrow's piercing dart.   70

Ambition this shall tempt to rise,
    Then whirl the wretch from high,
To bitter Scorn a sacrifice,
    And grinning Infamy.
The stings of Falsehood those shall try,   75
And hard Unkindness' alter'd eye,
    That mocks the tear it forc'd to flow;
And keen Remorse with blood defil'd,
And moody Madness laughing wild
    Amid severest woe.   80

Lo ! in the vale of years beneath
    A grisly troop are seen,

V. 68. " With praise enough for *Envy* to look *wan*."
Milton. Son. to Lawes, xiii. 6. *W.* Par. L. i. 601, " *Care*
sate on his *faded* cheek." *Luke.*

V. 69. Gray has here imitated Shakespeare. Richard III.
act i. sc. 1: " Grim-visag'd War," and Com. of Err. act v. sc.
1: " A *moody* and dull melancholy kinsman to *grim and comfortless Despair.*" Yarrington (Two Trag. in one) " Grim-
visag'd Despair." *Todd.*

V. 76. " Affected *Kindness* with an *alter'd* face," Dryden.
Hind. and Panth. part iii.

V. 79. " *Madness* laughing in his ireful *mood*," Dryden.
Pal. and Arc. (b. ii. p. 43. ed. Aik.) *Gray.* And so K. Hen.
VI. p. 1. act iv. sc. 2: " But rather *moody mad*.' And act
iii. sc. 1: " Moody fury." Chaucer. Knyghte's Tale, 1152.

V. 81. " Declin'd into the *vale of years*," Othello, act iii.
sc. 3. Compare also Virg. Æn. vi. 275.

The painful family of Death,
　　More hideous than their queen:
This racks the joints, this fires the veins,   85
That every labouring sinew strains,
　　Those in the deeper vitals rage:
Lo! Poverty, to fill the band,
That numbs the soul with icy hand,
　　And slow-consuming Age.   90

To each his suff'rings: all are men,
　　Condemn'd alike to groan;
The tender for another's pain,
　　Th' unfeeling for his own.
Yet, ah! why should they know their fate,   95

V. 83. "Hate, Fear, and Grief, the *family of Pain*," Pope.
Essay on Man, ii. 118. Dryden, State of Innoc. act v. sc. 1:
"With all the numerous *family of Death*." Claudian uses
language not dissimilar: Cons. Honor. vi. 323: "Inferno stri-
dentes agmine Morbi." And Juv. Sat. x. 218: "Circumsedit
agmine facto Morborum omne genus." Hor. Od. 1. iii. 30,
"Nova febrium terris incubuit cohors."

V. 84. See T. Warton's Milt. p. 432, 434, 511.

V. 90. "His *slow-consuming* fires." Shenstone. Love and
Honour.

V. 95. We meet with the same thought in Milton. Com. ver.
359.
　　"Peace, brother; be not over-exquisite
　　　To cast the fashion of uncertain evils;
　　　For grant they be so, while they rest unknown,
　　　What need a man forestall his date of grief?"   *W.*

V. 98. Soph. Ajax, v. 555: Ἐν τῷ Φρονεῖν γαρ μηδεν,
ἥδιστος βίος.   *W.*   See Kidd's note to Hor. Ep. xi. 2. 140.

V. 99. See Prior, (Ep. to Hon. C. Montague, st. ix.)
　　"From ignorance our comfort flows,
　　　The only wretched are the wise." — *Luke.*

Add Davenant Just Italian, p. 32, "Since knowledge is but

Since sorrow never comes too late,
  And happiness too swiftly flies?
Thought would destroy their paradise.
No more; — where ignorance is bliss,
  'Tis folly to be wise.   100

HYMN TO ADVERSITY.*

— Zῆνα —

Τὸν φρονεῖν Βροτοὺς ὁδώ-
σαντα, τῷ πάθει μαθὼν
Θέντα κυρίως ἔχειν.

ÆSCH. AGAM. ver. 181.

[This Ode, suggested by Dionysius' Ode to Nemesis. v. Ara-
tus. ed. Oxford, p. 51, translated by S. Meyrick, in Bell's
Fug. Poetry, vol. xviii. p. 161.]

DAUGHTER of Jove, relentless power,
  Thou tamer of the human breast,

---

sorrow's spy, it is not safe to know." And Dodsley. Old
Plays, xi. p. 119: —
— "Ignorance is safe;
I then slept happily; if knowledge mend me not,
Thou hast committed a most cruel sin
To wake me into judgment."

  * This Hymn first appeared in Dodsley. Col. vol. iv. together with the "Elegy in a Country Churchyard;" and not,
as Mason says, with the three foregoing Odes, which were
published in the second volume. In Mason's edition it is
called an *Ode;* but the title is now restored, as it was given
by the author. The motto from Æschylus is not in Dodsley.

  V. 1. 'Aτη, who may be called the goddess of Adversity, is

Whose iron scourge and tort'ring hour
  The bad affright, afflict the best!
Bound in thy adamantine chain,   5
The proud are taught to taste of pain,
And purple tyrants vainly groan
With pangs unfelt before, unpitied and alone.

When first thy sire to send on earth
  Virtue, his darling child, design'd,   10

---

said by Homer to be the daughter of Jupiter: Il. τ. 91.
Πρέσβα διὸς θυγάτηρ 'Ατη, ἣ πάντας ἀᾶται. Perhaps, however, Gray only alluded to the passage of Æschylus which he
quoted, and which describes Affliction as sent by Jupiter for
the benefit of man. Potter in his translation has had an eye
on Gray. See his Transl. p. 19.
  V. 2. "Then he, great *tamer* of all *human art*," Pope. Dun.
i. 163.
  V. 3. "Affliction's *iron flail*." Fletcher. Purp. Isl. ix. 28.
  Ibid. In Wakefield's note, he remarks an impropriety in the
poet joining to a material image, the "torturing hour." If
there be an impropriety in this, it must rest with Milton, from
whom Gray borrowed the verse:
              "—— when the *scourge*
Inexorably, and the *torturing hour*,
Calls us to penance."   Par. Lost, ii. 90.
But this mode of speech is authorized by ancient and modern
poets. In Virgil's description of the lightning which the Cy-
clopes wrought for Jupiter, Æn. viii. 429.
    "Tres imbris torti radios, tres nubis aquosæ
    Addiderant, rutili tres ignis, et alitis Austri:
    Fulgores nunc horrificos, *sonitumque*, *metumque*
    Miscebant," &c.
In Par. Lost, x. 297, as the original punctuation stood:
    "Bound with Gorgonian *rigor* not to move,
    And with Asphaltic *slime*." 1

---

1 This punctuation is now altered in most of the editions.
The new reading was proposed by Dr Pearce.

To thee he gave the heav'nly birth,
 And bade to form her infant mind.
Stern rugged nurse! thy rigid lore
With patience many a year she bore:
What sorrow was, thou bad'st her know, 15
And from her own she learn'd to melt at others' woe.

Scar'd at thy frown terrific, fly
 Self-pleasing Folly's idle brood,
Wild Laughter, Noise, and thoughtless Joy,
 And leave us leisure to be good. 20
Light they disperse, and with them go
The summer friend, the flatt'ring foe;

V. 5. 'Αδαμαντίνων δεσμῶν ἐν ἀῤῥήκτοις πέδαις· Æsch. Prom. vi. *W.*, from whom Milton. Par. L. i. 48: " In *adamantine chains*, and penal fire." And the expression occurs also in the Works of Spenser, Drummond, Fletcher, and Drayton. See Todd's note on Milton. " In *adamantine chains* shall Death be bound," Pope. Messiah, ver. 47; and lastly, Manil. Astron. lib. i. 921. And Boisson. on Philost. Heroic, p. 405.

V. 7. " Till some new *tyrant* lifts his *purple* hand," Pope. Two Choruses, ver. 23. Wakefield cites Horace, lib. i. od. xxxv. 12: " *Purpurei* metuunt *tyranni*." Add Tasso. Gier. Lib. c. vii. *Luke.*

V. 8. " Strange horror seize thee, *and pangs unfelt before.*" Par. L. ii. 703.

V. 13. An expression similar to this occurs in Sidney. Arcadia, vol. iii. p. 100: " Ill fortune, my awful governess."

V. 16. " Non ignara mali, miseris succurrere disco." *Luke.*

V. 20. " If we for HAPPINESS COULD LEISURE find," Hurd's Cowley, vol. i. p. 136; and the note of the editor. " And know I have not yet *the leisure to be good*," Oldham. Ode, st. v. vol. i. p. 83.

V. 22.   " ——For *men*, like butterflies,
  Shew not their mealy wings, but to the *summer*."
      Troil. and Cress. A. iii. sc. 3.

By vain Prosperity receiv'd,
To her they vow their truth, and are again believ'd.

Wisdom in sable garb array'd,   25
    Immers'd in rapt'rous thought profound,
And Melancholy, silent maid,
    With leaden eye that loves the ground,
Still on thy solemn steps attend:
Warm Charity, the gen'ral friend,   30
    With Justice, to herself severe,
And Pity, dropping soft the sadly-pleasing tear.

Oh! gently on thy suppliant's head,
    Dread goddess, lay thy chast'ning hand!
Not in thy Gorgon terrors clad,   35
    Not circled with the vengeful band

Also,   "The common people swarm like *summer flies*,
            And whither fly the gnats, but to the sun."

Henry VI. P. iii. act 2. sc. 9. "Such summer-birds are men!"
Tim. of Ath. act iii. sc. 7. But the exact expression is George
Herbert's: "fall and flow, like leaves, about me, or like *sum-
mer-friends*, flies of estates and sunshine," Temple, p. 296.
And (The W. Devil) v. Dodsley's Old Plays, vol. vi. p. 292.
"One summer she." Quarles. Sion's Elegies, xix. "Ah, sum-
mer friendship with the summer ends." Mr. Rogers quotes
Massinger's Maid of Honor, "O summer friendship." Gray
seems to have had Horace in his mind, lib. I. Od. xxxv. 25.
    V. 25.   "O'erlaid with *black*, staid *Wisdom's* hue."
                                Il Penser. 16. *W.*
    V. 28.   "With a sad *leaden* downward cast,
                Thou fix them on the earth as fast."
Il Penser. 43. *W.* "So leaden eyes." Sidney. Astroph. and
Stella, Song 7. "And stupid *eyes that ever loved the ground*,"
Dryden. Cim. and Iphig. v. 57. "Melancholy lifts her head,"
Pope. Ode on St. Cec. v. 30. "The sad companion, *dull-eyed
Melancholy*," Pericles, act i. sc. 2. And so we read "leaden

(As by the impious thou art seen)
With thund'ring voice, and threat'ning mien,
With screaming Horror's fun'ral cry,
Despair, and fell Disease, and ghastly Poverty: 40

Thy form benign, oh goddess, wear,
    Thy milder influence impart,
Thy philosophic train be there
    To soften, not to wound, my heart.
The gen'rous spark extinct revive,   45
Teach me to love and to forgive,
Exact my own defects to scan,
What others are to feel, and know myself a Man.

Contemplation " in Love's Lab. Lost, act iv. sc. 3. In Beaument. Passionate Madman, act iii. sc. 1:

> " A look that's fasten'd to the ground,
> A tongue chain'd up without a sound."

V. 31. " To Servants kind, to Friendship clear,
To *nothing but herself* severe."

Carew. Poems, p. 87. And

> " *Judge* of thyself alone, for none there were
> Could be so *just*, or could be so *severe*."

Oldham. Ode on Ben Jonson, p. 71, vol. ii. " Forgiving others, to himself severe," Dryden. Misc. vi. 322. " The Muses' friend unto himself severe," Waller. Poems, p. 149. " Candid to all, but to himself severe," E. Smith. El. on J. Philips, v. Lintot. Misc. p. 161.

Ver. 32. " Ours be the lenient, not *unpleasing tear*," Thomson. Mr. Rogers quotes Dryden. Virg. Æn. x. a " sadly-pleasing thought."

V. 35. " *Gorgoneum* turpes crinem mutavit in hydros.
Nunc quoque, ut *attonitos formidine terreat hostes*."
                    Ovid. Met. iv. 801.

> "——Horrentem colubris, *vultuque tremendam*
> Gorgoneo."——   Val. Flac. vi. 175

Milt. Par. L. ii. 611. " Medusa with Gorgonian terrors."

THE PROGRESS OF POESY.

A PINDARIC ODE.*

[Finished in 1754. Printed together with the Bard, an Ode,
    Aug. 8, 1757. MS.]

Φωνᾶντα συνετοῖσιν· ἐς
Δὲ τὸ πᾶν ἑρμηνέων
Χατίζει.   PINDAR. OL. II. V. 152.

I. 1.

AWAKE, Æolian lyre, awake,
And give to rapture all thy trembling strings.

Var. V. 1. " Awake, my lyre: my glory, wake." MS.
    V. 2. *Rapture*] Transport. MS.

---

* When the author first published this and the following
Ode, he was advised, even by his friends, to subjoin some few
explanatory notes; but had too much respect for the under-
standing of his readers to take that liberty. *Gray.*
V. 1. " Awake, my glory: awake, lute and harp."
                                David's Psalms. *Gray.*
        " Awake, awake, my lyre,
        And tell thy silent master's humble tale."
                        Cowley. Ode of David, vol. ii. p. 423.
Pindar styles his own poetry, with its musical accompani-
ments, Αἰολὶς μολπὴ, Αἰολίδες χορδαὶ, Αἰολίδων πνοαὶ αὐλῶν,
Æolian song, Æolian strings, the breath of the Æolian flute.
Gray.[1]
The   subject and simile, as usual with Pindar, are united.
The various sources of poetry, which gives life and lustre to
all it touches, are here described; its quiet majestic progress
enriching every subject (otherwise dry and barren) with a
pomp of diction and luxuriant harmony of numbers; and its

[1] This note was occasioned by a strange mistake of the
Critical Reviewers, who supposed the Ode addressed to the
" Harp of Æolus."   See Mason. Memoirs, let. 26, sec. 4; and
Crit. Rev. vol. iv. p. 167.   And the Literary Magaz. 1757,
p. 422; at p. 466 of the same work, is an Ode to Gray on his
Pindaric Odes.

From Helicon's harmonious springs
  A thousand rills their mazy progress take:
The laughing flowers, that round them blow,
Drink life and fragrance as they flow.
Now the rich stream of music winds along,
Deep, majestic, smooth, and strong,

---

more rapid and irresistible course, when swoln and hurried away by the conflict of tumultuous passions. *Gray.*

V. 3. Thomson has joined the subject and simile in a passage strongly resembling this:

    " In thy full language speaking mighty things,
      Like a clear torrent close, or else diffus'd
      A broad majestic stream, and rolling on
      Thro' all the winding harmony of sound."

Liberty, ii. 257.

And see Quinctil. Inst. xii. 10. 61. " At ille qui saxa devolvat," &c.

In Huntingford, Apology for his Monostrophics, p. 80, referred to by Wakefield, several passages of Pindar are pointed out, to which he supposes that Gray alluded, viz. Ol. ii. 62, 229. vii. 12. xii. 6.

V. 4. " The melting voice through mazes running."

Milt. L'Allegro, 142. *Luke.*

V. 5. " Albaque de viridi *riserunt lilia* prato," Petron. cap. 127. " *Ridenti* colocasia fundet *acantho*," Virg. Ecl. iv. 20; and Achilles Tatius has the expression, τὸ πέταλον τῷ ζεφύρῳ γελᾶ. See Burm. ad Ovid. v. ii. p. 1023.

V. 6. " Bibant violaria fontem," Virg. Georg. iv. ver. 32. *W.*

    " And mounting in loose robes the skies
      Shed light and fragrance as she flies."

Green. Spleen, v. 79.

V. 7. This couplet seems to have been suggested by some lines of Pope. Hor. Epist. II. ii. 171:

    " Pour the full tide of eloquence along,
      Serenely pure, and yet divinely strong."

Wakefield refers to Pope. Cecilia, 10:

    " While in more lengthened notes, and slow,
      The *deep majestic* solemn organs blow."

Dr. Berdmore of the Charter-House, in his pamphlet on Literary Resemblance, p. 16, supposes that Gray had Horace in his mind. Od. III. xxix. 32.

Thro' verdant vales, and Ceres' golden reign.
Now rolling down the steep amain,   10
Headlong, impetuous, see it pour;
The rocks and nodding groves rebellow to the roar.
                    I. 2.
   Oh! Sov'reign of the willing soul,
Parent of sweet and solemn-breathing airs,
Enchanting shell! the sullen Cares   15
   And frantic Passions hear thy soft controul.
On Thracia's hills the Lord of War

Var. V. 11. "With torrent rapture, see it pour." MS.

V. 9. Shenstone. Inscr. "Verdant vales and fountains
bright." *Luke.*
   V. 10. "Immensusque ruit profundo Pindarus ore."
                                        Hor. Od. iv. 2. 8.
   V. 12. "And *rocks* the *bellowing* voice of boiling seas
resound," Dryden. Virg. Georg. i. "Rocks rebellow to the
roar," Pope. Iliad.
   V. 13. Power of harmony to calm the turbulent sallies of
the soul. The thoughts are borrowed from the first Pythian
of Pindar. *Gray.*
   V. 14. Milton. Comus, 555, "A soft and solemn-breathing
sound." See Todd's note.
   " V. 15. "While *sullen Cares* and wither'd Age retreat,"
Eusden. Court of Venus, p. 101. "Revengeful *Cares* and *sullen*
Sorrows dwell," Dryden. Virgil. Æn. vi. 247. "*Care* shuns thy
soft approach, and *sullen* flies away," Dryden. Ceyx. vol. iv.
p 33, the same expression occurs in many other poets.
   V. 17.   " The *God of War*
            Was drawn triumphant on his iron car."
                              Dryden, vol. iii. 60. ed. Warton
And Collins in his Ode to Peace, ver. 4:
            " When War, by vultures drawn afar,
              To Britain bent his *iron car.*"
" Mavortia Thrace," Statii Ach. 1. 201, Theb. vii. 34, and
" Mars Thracen occupat," Ovid. Ar. Am. ii. ver. 588. Virg.
Æn. iii. 35. "Gradivumque patrem Geticis qui præsidet
arvis." v. Bentl. on Hor. Od. i. xxv 19.

Has curb'd the fury of his car,
And dropt his thirsty lance at thy command.
Perching on the sceptred hand   20
Of Jove, thy magic lulls the feather'd king
With ruffled plumes and flagging wing:
Quench'd in dark clouds of slumber lie
The terrors of his beak, and lightnings of his eye.

I. 3.

Thee the voice, the dance, obey,   25
Temper'd to thy warbled lay.

Var. V. 23. *Dark*] Black. MS.

V. 19. " Winn'st from his fatal grasp the spear."
Collins. Ode to Mercy, ver. 5.

In the Lusus Poetici of Jortin (Hymn to Harmony, p. 45),
published in 1722, is the following couplet, strongly resembling
Gray's, and from the same source:

" Thou mak'st the *God of War* forsake the field,
And *drop his lance*, and lay aside his shield."

See also Ovid. Fasti, iii. v. 1: " Bellice, depositis clypeo paulisper et hastà, Mars, ades." Claudiani Præf. in Rufin. lib. ii.
" Thirsty blade," Spens. F. Q. i. v. xv.

V. 20. This is a weak imitation of some beautiful lines in
the same ode. *Gray.* Pyth. i. ver. 10; and see D. Stewart.
Philos. Essays, p. 373. For an error in the imagery of this
line, see Class. Journ. No. xiii. p. 285.

V. 21.   " Every fowl of tyrant wing,
Save the *Eagle feather'd King.*"
Shakes. Pass. Pilg. xx.

V. 22. H. Walpole, in describing the famous Boccapadugli
eagle, of Greek sculpture, says: " Mr. Gray has drawn the
' flagging wing.' " See Works, vol. ii. p. 463. Philips (Past.
5.) " She hangs her flagging wings; " *Luke.* Add A. Behn
on the D. of Buckingham, v. Works, v. ii. p. 208: " Now
with their broken notes and flagging wing." See Wakef. on
Virg. Georg. iv. 137; G. Steevens quotes Ronsard, Ode xxii.
ed. 1632, fol.

V. 25. Power of harmony to produce all the graces of
motion in the body. *Gray.*

V. 26. " Tempering their sweetest notes unto thy lay,"

C

O'er Idalia's velvet-green
The rosy-crowned Loves are seen
On Cytherea's day;
With antic Sport, and blue-eyed Pleasures,   30
Frisking light in frolic measures;
Now pursuing, now retreating,
   Now in circling troops they meet:
To brisk notes in cadence beating,

Var. V. 30. *Sport*] Sports. ms.
   V. 34. *In cadence*] The cadence. ms.

Fletcher, P. Island, c. ix. s. iii. and Lycidas, 32. *Luke.*
V. 27. " At length a fair and spacious *green* he spide,
          Like calmest waters, plain; like *velvet*, soft."
                              Fairfax. Tasso, xiii. 38.
   " She rears her flowers, and spreads her *velvet-green.*"
                              Young. Love of Fame, Sat. v. p. 128.
This expression, it is well known, has met with reprehension
from Dr. Johnson; who appears by his criticism to have
supposed it first [1] introduced by Gray. It was numbered,
however, among the absurd expressions of Pope, by the authors
of the *Alexandriad,* (some of the heroes of the Dunciad,) see
p. 288. It occurs in a list of epithets and nouns which Pope
had used, and which these authors held up to ridicule.
   V. 30.   " I'll charm the air to give a sound,
             While you perform your *antic round.*"
                              Macb. act. iv. sc. 1. *W.*
   V. 31.   " In *friskful* glee, their *frolics* play,
                              Thoms. Spring. *Luke.*
   V. 32. Wakefield refers to Callimachi Hymn. Dian. 3. and
Hom. Il. Σ. 593.
   V 35.   Μαρμαρυγὰς θηεῖτο ποδῶν· θαύμαζε δὲ θυμῷ.
                              Hom. Od. Θ. ver. 265.   *Gray.*
      " Or rustling turn the *many-twinkling* leaves
      Of aspin tall."
                              Thoms. Spring, 157. *W.*

---

[1] Shakespeare has, " Make boot upon the summer's *velvet
buds,*" Hen. V. act i. sc. 2.

Glance their many-twinkling feet.   35
Slow melting strains their Queen's approach de-
    clare:
Where'er she turns, the Graces homage pay.
With arms sublime, that float upon the air,
    In gliding state she wins her easy way:
O'er her warm cheek, and rising bosom, move   40
The bloom of young Desire and purple light of
    Love.

V. 36. Compare the following stanza of a poem by Barton
Booth, in his Life, written in 1718, published 1733:
 " Now to a *slow and melting air* she moves,
    So like in air, in shape, in mien,
    She passes for the Paphian queen;
    The Graces all around her play,
    The wond'ring gazers die away;
    Whether her *easy body* bend,
    Or her faire *bosom heave* with sighs;
    Whether her *graceful arms extend,*
    Or gently fall, or slowly rise;
    Or *returning or advancing,*
    Swimming round, or sidelong glancing,
    Strange force of motion that subdues the soul."
And Apuleii. Metam. Lib. x. p. 349. ed. Delph.
   V. 37. " For wheresoe'er she turn'd her face, they bow'd."
                    Dryden. Flower and Leaf, v. 191.
   V. 39. " Incessu patuit Dea," Virg. Æn. i. 405. And see
Heyne's quotation from Eustathius. " On all sides round
environ'd, wins his way." Par. Lost, ii. 1016.
   V. 41.   Λάμπει δ' ἐπὶ πορφυρέῃσί
                 Παρείῃσι φῶς ἔρωτος.
              Phrynicus apud Athenæum.   *Gray.*
          "——*lumen*que juventæ
    Purpureum, et lætos oculis afflàrat honores."
Virg. Æn. i. 594. *W.* Add Ovid. Amor. ii. 1. 38: " *Pur-*
pureus quæ mihi dictat *Amor.*" And ix. 34: " Notaque
purpureus tela resumit *Amor.*" And Art. Amor. i. 232. Fast.
vi. 252. " purpureâ luce." Dryden. Brit. Rediviva, p. 93:
" Breath'd Honour on his eyes, and his *own purple light.*"
Pope. Hor. Od. iv. 1. " Smiling loves and young desires."
Rogers.

II. 1.

Man's feeble race what ills await!
Labour, and Penury, the racks of Pain,
Disease, and Sorrow's weeping train,
    And Death, sad refuge from the storms of fate!   ₄₅
The fond complaint, my song, disprove,
And justify the laws of Jove.
Say, has he giv'n in vain the heav'nly Muse?
Night and all her sickly dews,
Her spectres wan, and birds of boding cry,   ₅₀
He gives to range the dreary sky;

V. 42. To compensate the real and imaginary ills of life, the Muse was given to mankind by the same Providence that sends the day, by its cheerful presence, to dispel the gloom and terrors of the night. *Gray.*

V. 46. "His fond complaints," Addison. Cato, A. 1, 6.

V. 49. Wakefield refers to Milton. Hymn to the Nativity, xxvi. and Par. Reg. iv. 419. But a passage in Cowley is pointed out by his last editor, Dr. Hurd, as alluded to by Gray, vol. i. p. 195:

"Night and her ugly subjects thou dost fright,
  And Sleep, the lazy owl of night;
  Asham'd and fearful to appear,
They skreen their horrid shapes with the black hemisphere."
Thomson. Spring, "Sickly damps."

V. 50. " Love not so much the doleful knell
    And news the *boding night-birds* tell."
                    Green. Grotto, 126.

" Obscœnique Canes, *importunæque Volucres*
  Signa dabant."   Virg. Georg. i. v. 470.

" He withers at the heart, and looks as *wan*
  As the *pale spectre* of a murder'd man."
             Dryden. Pal. and Arcite. B. 1.

V. 52. " Or seen the morning's well-appointed star
    Come marching up the eastern hills afar "
                 Cowley. *Gray.*

The couplet from Cowley has been wrongly quoted by Gray, and so continued by his different editors. It occurs in Brutus, an Ode, stan. iv. p. 171. vol. 1. Hurd's ed.:

Till down the eastern cliffs afar
Hyperion's march they spy, and glitt'ring shafts
   of war.

Var. V. 52.

  " Till fierce Hyperion from afar
    Pours on their scatter'd rear, his glitt'ring shafts of war,
    Hurls *at* their *flying*,
        o'er   scatter'd
                 shadowy
    Till o'er   from far
    Hyperion hurls around his." MS.

" One would have thought 't had heard the morning crow,
   Or seen her well-appointed star
  Come marching up the eastern hills afar."

In Gray's Letter to Dr. Wharton, containing a Journal of
his Tour to the Lakes, he says: " While I was here, a little
shower fell; red *clouds came marching up the hills from the
east*," &c. Mason's ed. 4. p. 175, and Warton's Note on
Milton, p. 304.

V. 53. In Mant's edition of Warton (vol. ii. p. 41), and in
Steevens's note on Hamlet (act i. sc. 2), it is remarked that
all the English poets are guilty of the same *false quantity*,
with regard to this word, except Akenside, as quoted by
Mant, Hymn to the Naiads, 46; and the author of 'Fuimus
Troes' by Steevens. See Dodsley. Old Plays, vii. p. 500.
The assertions, however, of these learned editors are not
correct; as will appear from the following quotations:

    " That Hyperion far beyond his bed
    Doth see our lions ramp, our roses spread."
        Drummond (of Hawthornd.) Wand. Muses, p. 180.

    " Then Hyperion's son, pure fount of day,
    Did to his children the strange tale reveal."
           West. Pindar, Ol. viii. 22, p. 63.

Gray has used this word again with the same quantity:
Hymn to Ignorance, v. 12: " Thrice hath Hyperion roll'd his
annual race." [1]

V. 53. " Non radii solis, neque *lucida tela* diei," Lucret.

---

[1] The old English Poets (as Jortin remarks) did not regard
quantity. Spenser has Iöle, Pylādes, Caphäreus, Rhœtĕan,
Amphȳon. Gascoyne in his " Ultimum Vale: " " Kinde Erato,

II. 2.

In climes beyond the solar road,   54
Where shaggy forms o'er ice-built mountains roam,
The Muse has broke the twilight gloom
    To cheer the shivering native's dull abode.
And oft, beneath the od'rous shade
Of Chili's boundless forests laid,
She deigns to hear the savage youth repeat,   60

Var. V. 57. *Buried* natives, ' shivering ' in the Marg. MS.
    Chill abode, ' dull ' in the Marg. MS.

---

i. 148. vi. 39. Ausonii Mosell. 269: " *Luciferique* pavent letalia
tela diei." *W.* Add Eurip. Phœn. 171. ed. Porson.
        Εὡοις ὁμοια φλεγέθων
        βολαισῖν ὑελίοο.
V. 54. Extensive influence of poetic genius over the remotest and most uncivilized nations: its connection with liberty,
and the virtues that naturally attend on it. [See the Erse,
Norwegian, and Welsh fragments; the Lapland and American
songs.]
    " Extra anni solisque vias — " Virg. Æn. vi. 795.
" Tutta lontana dal camin del sole. Petr. Canz. 2. *Gray.*
    " Out of the *solar walk,* and heaven's high way," Dryden.
Threnod. August. st. 12. "Inter solisque vias, Arctosque
latentes," Manil. i. 450. Pope also has this expression:
" Far as the *solar walk* and milky way," Essay on Man, ch. i.
102. Stat. Sylv. iv. 3. 156. " Ultra sidera, flammeumque
solem." Ἡελίοιο κελεύθους. Dionys. Geogr. v. 17.
    V. 56. " The nymphs in *twilight shade* of tangled thickets
mourn." Milton. Hymn to Nativ. st. xx. *W.*

---

and wanton Thalïa." Turberville in the " Ventrous Lover,"
stanz. i:
" If so Leander durst, from Abȳdon to Sest,
    To swim to Hero, whom he chose his friend above the rest."
Lord Sterline in his " Third Hour," st. xiii. p. 50: " Then
Pleiades, Arcturus, Orïon, all." Id. p. 87: " Which carrying
Orion safely to the shore." But Orion has all the syllables
doubtful. See Erythræi, Ind. Virg. art. Orion. Chaucer and
Surrey have Cithëron.

In loose numbers wildly sweet,
Their feather-cinctur'd chiefs and dusky loves.
Her track, where'er the goddess roves,
Glory pursue, and gen'rous Shame,   64
Th'unconquerable Mind, and freedom's holy flame.

II. 3.

Woods, that wave o'er Delphi's steep,

V. 59. "Earth was to them a *boundless forest* wild."
        Thom. S. of Ind. c. ii. st. xiv. *Luke.*

V. 61.   "Or *sweetest* Shakespeare, fancy's child,
        Warble his native woodnotes *wild.*"

Milton. L'Alleg. 133. *W.* Hor. Od. iv. ii. 12, "Numeris-
que fertur lege solutis."

V. 62. "Girt with feather'd cincture." Par. L. ix. 1116.

V. 62. "Reap their own fruits, and woo their *sable loves.*"
Pope, Winds. For. 410. Gray's epithet, as Dr. Warton remarks, is the more correct. He has used it again: " The
dusky people drive before the gale," Frag. on Educ. and Gov.
v. 105.

V. 64. This use of the verb plural after the first substantive
is in Pindar's manner, Nem. x. 91. Pyth. 4. 318. Hom. Il. E.
774. *W.* "I cannot help remarking (says Dugald Stewart,
Philos. of the Human Mind, vol. i. p. 505, 8vo.) the effect of
the solemn and uniform flow of verse in this exquisite stanza,
in retarding the pronunciation of the reader, so as to arrest
his attention to every successive picture, till it has time to
produce its proper impression."

V. 65. Akens. Pl. of Im. i. 468: " Love's holy flame."
Luke. "The unconquerable mind," is in Hor. Od. ii. 1. 22.
" Et *cuncta* terrarum *subacta*, præter atrocem *animum* Cato-
nis."

V. 66. Progress of Poetry from Greece to Italy, and from
Italy to England. Chaucer was not unacquainted with the
writings of Dante or of Petrarch. The Earl of Surrey and
Sir Thomas Wyatt had travelled in Italy, and formed their
taste there. Spenser imitated the Italian writers ; Milton
improved on them : but this school expired soon after the Restoration, and a new one rrose on the French model, which
has subsisted ever since. *Gray.*

"With hollow shriek the *steep of Delphos* leaving."
        Milton. Hymn to Nativ. **xix.** *W.*

Isles that crown th' Ægean deep,
　　Fields, that cool Ilissus laves,
　　Or where Mæander's amber waves
In lingering lab'rinths creep,　　　　　　　　70
　　How do your tuneful echoes languish,
　　Mute, but to the voice of anguish!
Where each old poetic mountain
　　Inspiration breath'd around;
Ev'ry shade and hallow'd fountain　　　　　　75
　　Murmur'd deep a solemn sound:

Var. V. 76. "Murmur'd *a celestial sound.*" MS

V. 67. So Dionsyii Perieg. v. 4:
　　　　—— ἐν γὰρ ἐκείνῳ
Πᾶσα χθὼν, ἄτε νῆσος ἀπείριτος ἐστεφανῶται.
Ovid. Metam. v. 388: "Silva *coronat* aquas." And Seneca
Œdip. 488: "Naxos Ægæo *redimita* Ponto." And Jortin, in
Lusus Poetici, vol. i. p. 4:
　　"Cyclades sparsas ubi Naxos inter
　　　Surgit *Ægeo redimita Ponto.*"
V. 69. "There Susa by Choaspes, *amber stream*," Par. Reg.
iii. 288. "Rolls o'er Elysian flow'rs her *amber stream*," Par.
Lost, iii. 359. Callimachi Cer. 29:
　　　　—— τὸ δ', ὥστ' ἀλέκτρινον ὕδωρ
ἐξ 'μαροᾶν ἀνέθυε. *W.*
To which add Eurip. Hipp. ver. 741. "Purior electro cam-
pum petit amnis," Virg. Georg. iii. 520.
　　V. 70. "Non secus ac liquidis Phrygiis Mæandros in arvis
Ludit, et ambiguo lapsu refluitque fluitque," Ov. Met. viii.
162.
　　V. 71. In the Quarterly Review for July, 1814, p. 314,
some lines are quoted from Addison's letter from Italy, containing an idea similar to these of Gray: "Poetic fields encom-
pass me around," &c.
　　V. 73. "Like that *poetic mountain* to be hight," G. West.
Educ. C. 1. *Luke.*
　　V. 75. Virg. Ecl. i. 53, "fontes sacros." *Luke.*
　　V. 80. "Servitude that hugs her chain," Ode on the In-
stall. V. *W.*

Till the sad Nine, in Greece's evil hour,
   Left their Parnassus for the Latian plains.
Alike they scorn the pomp of tyrant Power,
   And coward Vice, that revels in her chains.   80
When Latium had her lofty spirit lost,
They sought, oh Albion! next thy sea-encircled
    coast.

III. 1.

Far from the sun and summer-gale,
In thy green lap was Nature's darling laid,
What time, where lucid Avon stray'd,   85
   To him the mighty mother did unveil
Her awful face : the dauntless child

V. 83. " Piu lontan del Ciel," Dante. Il Inferno, c. **ix.**

V. 84. " Nature's darling." Shakespeare. *Gray.* — This expression occurs in Cleveland. Poems, p. 314:

> " Here lies within this stony shade,
> *Nature's darling;* whom she made
> Her fairest model, her brief story,
> In him heaping all her glory."

Stat. Theb. iv. 786, " At puer in gremio vernæ telluris."

> "The flowery May, who from her *green lap* throws
> The yellow cowslip, and the pale primrose."
>   Milton. Son. on May Morn. *Gray.*

V. 85. Senec. Thyest. 129, " gelido flumine *lucidus Alpheos.*" *Luke.*

V. 86. " The *mighty mother,* and her son who brings
    The Smithfield muses to the ear of kings."
                 Pope. Dunc. i. 1.
" A cloud of fogs dilates her *awful face.*" Id. i. 262. **W.**
See also Virg. Georg. i. 466, by Dryden:

> " On the *green turf* thy careless limbs display,
> And celebrate the *mighty mother's* day."

V. 87. " Animosus infans," Hor. iii. 4. 20. *Luke.* Wakefield refers to Virg. Eclog. iv. 60: " Incipe, parve puer, risu cognoscere matrem." And Berdmore, in his Literary Resemblances, p. 40, to the description of the infant Hercules in

Stretch'd forth his little arms and smil'd.
"This pencil take (she said), whose colours clear
Richly paint the vernal year: 90
Thine too these golden keys, immortal Boy!
This can unlock the gates of joy;
Of horror that, and thrilling fears,
Or ope the sacred source of sympathetic tears."

III. 2.

Nor second He, that rode sublime   90

Var. V. 93. *Horror*] Terror. MS.

Milton

Theoc. Idyll. xxv. 55. But the two lines in Gray are the same as two in Sandys. Ovid, p. 78, ed. 12mo. (see Metam. iv. 515.)

"——*the child*
Stretch'd forth its little arms, and on him smil'd."

See also Catulli Ep. Jul. et Manl. c. lxi. ver. 216.
——" Parvolus
Matris e gremio suæ
Porrigens teneras manus,
Dulce rideat."

V. 89. Milton. P. L. v. 24, "How nature paints her colours." *Luke.*

V. 91. Similar, perhaps, καθαρὰν ἀνοίξαν-
τα κλῇδα φρενῶν·
Eurip. Med. 658.

" *Nature,* which favours to the few,
All art beyond, imparts,
To him presented, at his birth,
The key of human hearts." Young. Resig.

" Yet some there be, that with due steps aspire
To lay their hands upon that *golden key*
That opes the palace of eternity." Milton. Com. 13. *W.*

V. 92. See Soph. Antig. v. 803.

V. 95. Milton. P. L. vi. 771. *Gray.*

V. 97. This alludes to Milton's own picture of himself:
——" Up led by thee,
Into the Heaven of Heavens, I have presum'd
An earthly guest, and drawn empyreal air."
Par. L. vii. 12, also Eleg. v. 15.

Upon the seraph-wings of Extasy,
The secrets of th' abyss to spy.

He pass'd the flaming bounds of place and time:
The living throne, the sapphire blaze,
Where angels tremble while they gaze,   100
He saw ; but, blasted with excess of light,
Clos'd his eyes in endless night.
Behold, where Dryden's less presumptuous car
Wide o'er the fields of glory bear   104
Two coursers of ethereal race,   [pace.
With necks in thunder cloth'd, and long-resounding

V. 98. " Flammantia mœnia mundi," Lucret. i. 74. *Gray.*
See also Stat. Silv. iv. 3. 156: " Ultra sidera, flammeumque
solem." And Cicero de Finibus, ii. 31. Hor. Epist. I. xiv. 9.

V. 99. " For the spirit of the living creature was in the
wheels. And above the firmament that was over their heads,
was the likeness of a throne, as the appearance of a sapphire
stone. This was the appearance of the glory of the Lord."
Ezek. i. 20, 26, 28. *Gray.* — " Ay sang before the *saphir-
color'd* throne," Poem at a solemn Music (Milton), ver. 7.

" Guiding the fiery-wheeled throne,
    The cherub Contemplation." Il. Pens. ver. 53.
" Whereon a *sapphire throne* inlaid, with pure
    Amber, and colours of the showery arch." Par. L. vi. 758.
" He on the wings of cherub rode sublime,
    On the crystalline sky, in *sapphire thron'd.*" Ibid. ver. 771.

V. 101. " Dark with excess of bright thy skirts appear."
Milt. P. L. iii. 380. *Luke.*

V. 102. 'Οφθαλμῶν μὲν ἄμερσε· δίδου δ' ἡδεῖαν ἀοιδήν.
    Hom. Od. Θ. ver. 64. *Gray.*
" In æternam clauduntur lumina noctem," Virg. Æn. x. 746.
W. " And closed her lids, at last, in endless night." Dryden.

V. 103. See Pope. Account of Dryden, Ep. I. b. ii. ver. 267:
" Waller was smooth; but Dryden taught to join
The varying verse, the full *resounding* line,
The long majestic march, and energy divine."

V. 105. " Æthereal race " is a phrase of Pope, v. Hom.
Il. xi. 80.

III. 3.

Hark, his hands the lyre explore!
Bright-eyed Fancy, hov'ring o'er,
Scatters from her pictur'd urn
Thoughts that breathe, and words that burn.   110
But ah! 'tis heard no more——
    Oh! lyre divine, what daring spirit
    Wakes thee now? Tho' he inherit

Var. V. 108. *Bright-eyed*] Full-plumed. MS.

V. 106. " Hast thou clothed his neck with thunder?"
Job. — This verse and the foregoing are meant to express the
stately march and sounding energy of Dryden's rhymes.
Gray.
     " Currum, geminosque jugales
   Semine ab æthereo, spirantes naribus ignem."
Virg. Æn. vii. 280. *W.* " The long-resounding course."
Thomson. Winter, 775, Hymn. 85.

V. 110. " Words that weep, and tears that speak," Cowley.
Prophet, vol. i. p. 113. *Gray.* " Her words burn as fire,"
Eccles. ix. 10. *Rogers.* " Oaths are burning words," Dekker.
Satirom. p. 65, 4to.

V. 111. We have had in our language no other odes of the
sublime kind, than that of Dryden on St. Cecilia's Day; for
Cowley, who had his merit, yet wanted judgment, style, and
harmony, for such a task. That of Pope is not worthy of
so great a man. Mr. Mason, indeed, of late days, has
touched the true chords, and with a masterly hand, in some
of his choruses; above all in the last of Caractacus:
   " Hark! heard ye not yon footstep dread?" &c. *Gray.*

V. 113. So Elegy, st. xii: " Or *wake* to extasy the living
lyre." And Lucret. ii. 412:
    " Ac Musæa mele per chordas organicei quæ
   Mobilibus digitis *expergefacta* figurant."
And Callimach. Hymn. Del. 312. *W.*

V. 114. " They shape his *ample pinions* swift as darted
flame," Young. N. Thoughts.

V. 115. Διὸς πρὸς ὄρνιχα θεῖον, Olymp. ii. 159   Pindar
compares himself to that bird, and his enemies to ravens that
croak and clamour in vain below, while it pursues its flight,

Nor the pride, nor ample pinion,
  That the Theban eagle bear,   113
Sailing with supreme dominion
  Thro' the azure deep of air :
Yet oft before his infant eyes would run
  Such forms as glitter in the Muse's ray,

Var. V. 118.

    " Yet when they first were open'd on the day
      Before his visionary eyes would run." MS.

    V. 119. *Forms*] " shapes." MS.

---

regardless of their noise. *Gray.* See Spenser. F. Q. V. iv. 42:
  " Like to an eagle in his *kingly* pride
  Soaring thro' his wide empire of the aire
  To weather his brode sailes."
Cowley, (i. 166. ed. Hurd.) in his Translation of Hor. Od.
IV ii. calls Pindar " the Theban swan: "
  " Lo ! how the obsequious wind and swelling air
  The *Theban Swan* does upward bear."
Pope, Temple of Fame, 210, has copied Horace, and yoked
four swans to the car of the poet:
  " Four swans sustain a car of silver bright."
See also Berdmore, Specimens of Lit. Resemblance, p. 102.

    V. 117. Eurip. Med. 1294: ἐς αἰθέρος βάθος. " Cœli fre-
tuin," Ennius apud Non. Marcell. 3. 92. Lucret. ii. 151.
v. 277: " Aeris in magnum fertur mare." *W.* Oppian.
Κυνηγ. iii. 497:
      Ἠέρος ὑψιπόροισιν ἐπιπλωούσι κελεύθοις.
Timon of Athens, act iv. sc. 2. p. 126. ed. Steevens: " Into
this sea of air." And Cowley's Poems : " Row thro' the
trackless *ocean of the air.*"

    V. 118. See the observation of D. Stewart, Philosophy of
the Human Mind, p. 486: " that Gray, in describing the
infantine reveries of poetical genius, has fixed with exquisite
judgment on that class of our conceptions which are derived
from *visible* objects." And see also his Philosophical Essays,
p. 231. There is a passage in Sir W. Temple. Essay on
Poetry, vol. iii. p. 402, which has been supposed to have been
the origin of this passage. See Gentleman's Magazine, vol.
lxi. p. 91.

With orient hues, unborrow'd of the sun :   120
   Yet shall he mount, and keep his distant way
Beyond the limits of a vulgar fate,
Beneath the Good how far — but far above the
   Great.

Var. V. 122. " Yet never can he fear a vulgar fate." MS.

THE BARD.

A PINDARIC ODE.

[This Ode is founded on a tradition current in Wales, that
Edward the First, when he completed the conquest of that
country, ordered all the Bards that fell into his hands to be
put to death. *Gray.* (See Barrington on the Statutes,
p. 358; Jones's Relics, vol. i. p. 38; Sayer's Essays, p. 20.)

I. 1.

" RUIN seize thee, ruthless king !
  Confusion on thy banners wait ;

V. 120. Spenser. Hymn: " With much more *orient hew*."
Milt. Par. L. i. 545: " with *orient colours*." *Luke.*

V. 123. "Still show how much the *good* outshone the *great*."
K. Philips, fol. p. 133.

" I have sometimes thought (says Prof. D. Stewart,) that
in the last line of the following passage, Gray had in view the
two different effects of words already described; the effect of
some, in awakening the powers of conception and imagination;
and that of *others* in exciting associated emotions:

  " Hark, his hands the lyre explore !
    Bright-eyed Fancy, hov'ring o'er,
    Scatters from her pictur'd urn
    Thoughts that breathe, and words that burn."

V. Elem. of the Phil. of the H. Mind, vol. i. p. 507.

V. 1. Shakes. Hen. VI. 2nd part, act i. sc. 3: " See, *ruthless Queen*, a hapless father's tears." *Luke.*

Tho' fann'd by Conquest's crimson wing,
   They mock the air with idle state.
Helm, nor hauberk's twisted mail,   5
Nor e'en thy virtues, Tyrant, shall avail
   To save thy secret soul from nightly fears,
     From Cambria's curse, from Cambria's tears!"
Such were the sounds that o'er the crested pride
   Of the first Edward scatter'd wild dismay,   10
As down the steep of Snowdon's shaggy side

V. 2. "Confusion waits." K. John, IV. sc. ult. *Rogers.*

V. 3. "Where the Norweyan *banners flout* the sky,
      And *fan* our people cold." Macbeth, act i. sc. 2.

V. 4. "Mocking the air with colours idly spread."
                     King John, act v. sc. 1. *Gray.*

   V. 5. The hauberk was a texture of steel ringlets, or rings interwoven, forming a coat of mail that sat close to the body, and adapted itself to every motion. *Gray.*
             "With helm and hauberk."
                     Rob. of Gloucester, vol. i. p. 297.
"*Hauberks and helms* are hew'd with many a wound,"
Dryden. Pal. and Arcite, lib. iii. v. 1879. Fairfax, in his Trans. of Tasso, has joined these words in many places; as canto vii. 38: "Now at his *helm,* now at his *hauberk* bright." See also p. 193, 199, 299, edition 1624, folio.

   V. 7. "Within her secret mind," v. Dryden. Æn. iv.
                                    Rogers.

   V. 9.   "The crested adder's pride."
             Dryden. Indian Queen. *Gray.*

   V. 11. Snowdon was a name given by the Saxons to that mountainous tract which the Welsh themselves call Craigian-eryri: it included all the highlands of Caernarvonshire and Merionethshire, as far east as the river Conway. R. Hygden, speaking of the castle of Conway, built by King Edward the First, says, "Ad ortum amnis Conway ad clivum montis Ere-ry;" and Matthew of Westminster, (ad ann. 1283) "Apud Aberconway ad pedes montis Snowdoniæ fecit erigi castrum forte." *Gray.*
   The epithet "shaggy," applied to "Snowdon's side," is highly appropriate, as Leland says that great woods clothed

He wound with toilsome march his long array.
Stout Glo'ster stood aghast in speechless trance :
" To arms !" cried Mortimer, and couch'd his
    quiv'ring lance.

I. 2.

On a rock whose haughty brow,   15
Frowns o'er old Conway's foaming flood,
  Robed in the sable garb of woe,
With haggard eyes the poet stood;
  (Loose his beard, and hoary hair

---

the different parts of the mountain in his time: see Itin. v. 45.
Dyer. Ruins of Rome, p. 137:
                  " as Britannia's oaks
  On Merlin's mount, or *Snowdon's rugged sides,*
  Stand in the clouds."
Lycidas, 54, " Nor on the *shaggy top of* Mona high," v. Par.
L. vi. 645. " By the shaggy tops," &c. Todd's note.

V. 12. " In long array," Dryden. E. xi. *Rogers.*

V. 13. Gilbert de Clare, surnamed the Red, earl of Gloucester and Hertford, son-in-law to King Edward. *Gray.*

V. 14. Edmond de Mortimer, Lord of Wigmore. *Gray.*

They both were Lord Marchers, whose lands lay on the
borders of Wales, and probably accompanied the king in this
expedition. *Gray.*
        " Hastam quassatque trementem."
        Virg. Æn. xii. 94. *Luke.*

V. 15. Hom. Il. Υ. ver. 151: 'Επ' ὀφρύσι καλλικολώνης.
And Mosch. Id. ii. 48: 'Επ' ὀφρύος αἰγιαλοῖο. Ap. Rhod. i.
ver. 178. St. Luke, iv. 29. And Virg. Georg. i. 108: " Ecce
supercilio clivosi tramitis." *W.* " A huge aspiring rock,
whose surly brow," Daniel. Civ. Wars, p. 58.

V. 16. " Above the foamy flood," v. Dyer. R. of Rome.
                                    Luke.

V. 17. " Perpetuo *mœrore,* et *nigra veste* senescant," Juvenal.
Sat. x. 245. *W.* Also Propert. Eleg. IV. vii. 28: " *Atram*
quis *lacrymis* incaluisse *togam.*" Senec. H. Fur. 694, " *ater-
que luctus* sequitur. '

V. 19. The image was taken from a well-known picture of
Raphael, representing the Supreme Being in the vision of Eze-

Stream'd, like a meteor, to the troubled air)   20
And with a master's hand, and prophet's fire,
Struck the deep sorrows of his lyre.

" Hark, how each giant-oak, and desert cave,
Sighs to the torrent's awful voice beneath!
O'er thee, oh King! their hundred arms they
        wave,   25
Revenge on thee in hoarser murmurs breathe;
Vocal no more, since Cambria's fatal day,
To high-born Hoel's harp, or soft Llewellyn's lay.

---

kiel. There are two of these paintings, both believed to be
originals, one at Florence, the other in the Duke of Orleans'
collection at Paris. *Gray.*

V. 20. " Shone like a *meteor streaming* to the wind."
            Par. L. i. ver. 535. *W.* See Todd's note.

" The meteors of a troubled heaven."
            Shakesp. K. Henry IV. pt. i. act i. sc. 1. *Luke.*

Todd mentions a passage very similar to the one in the text:
" The circumference of his *snowy beard* like *the streaming rays
of a meteor* appeared," Persian Tales of Inatulla, vol. ii. p. 41.
This image is often used metaphorically, as Stat. Theb iii.
332. And see Manil. Astron. i. 836.

Ford, in his Perkin Warbeck, p. 25, ed. Weber:
            " —— since the *beard*
Of this *wild comet* conjur'd into France."

V. 23. " The woods and *desert caves*." Lycidas.

V. 26. " The stream that down the distant rocks *hoarse mur-
muring* fell." Thomson. *Luke.*

V. 27. See some observations on the poetical and proper use
of " vocal," as used by Gray in this place, in Huntingford.
Apolog. for the Monostr. p. 31.

V. 28. Hoel is called *high-born*, being the son of Owen Gwynedd, prince of North Wales, by Finnog, an Irish damsel. He
was one of his father's generals in his wars against the Eng
lish, Flemings, and Normans, in South Wales; and was a famous bard, as his poems that are extant testify. See Evan.
Spec. p. 26, 4to.; and Jones. Relics, vol. ii. p. 36, where he is

                        D

I. 3.

" Cold is Cadwallo's tongue,
That hush'd the stormy main: 39
Brave Urien sleeps upon his craggy bed:
Mountains, ye mourn in vain
Modred, whose magic song
Made huge Plinlimmon bow his cloud-topt head.

---

called the "*Princely* Bard   Who says that he wrote eight
pieces, five of which are translated by him in his interesting
publication. The whole are given in Mr. Owen's translation
in Mr. Southey's Madoc, vol. ii. p. 162.

V. 28. In a Poem to Llewellyn, by Einion the son of Gui-
gan, a similar epithet is given to him (p. 22): "Llewellyn is
a *tender-hearted* prince."   And in another Poem to him, by
Llywarch Brydydd y Moch (p. 32): "Llewellyn, though in
battle he killed with fury, though he burnt like an outrageous
fire, yet was a *mild prince* when the mead horns were distri-
buted." Also in an Ode to him by Llygard Gwr (p. 39), he
is called "Llewellyn the *mild*, and prosperous governor of
Gwynedd." Llewellyn's '*soft Lay*' is given by Jones in his
Relics, vol. ii. p. 64.

V. 29. *Cadwallo* and *Urien* are mentioned by Dr. Evans in
his "Dissertatio de Bardis," p. 78, among those bards of whom
no works remain. See account of *Urien's* death in Jones.
Relics, i. p. 19. He is celebrated in the Triads, "as one of
the three bulls of war." Taliessin dedicated to him upwards
of twelve poems, and wrote an elegy on his death: he was
slain by treachery in the year 560. Modred is, I suppose, the
famous "Myrddin ab Morvryn," called Merlyn the Wild; a
disciple of Taliessin, and bard to the Lord Gwenddolaw ab
Ceidiaw. He fought under King Arthur in 542 at the battle
of Camlau, and accidentally slew his own nephew. He was
reckoned a truer prophet than his predecessor, the great magi-
cian Merdhin Ambrose. See a poem of his called the "Orchard," in Jones. Relics, vol. i. p. 24. I suppose Gray altered
the name "euphoniæ gratia;" as I can nowhere find a bard
mentioned of the name of "Modred.'

V. 30. "Uttering such dulcet and harmonious breath,
       That the rude sea grew civil at her song.'
Mids. N. Dream, act ii. sc. 2.   *W.*   Add Milt. Comus, 86.

On dreary Arvon's shore they lie,　　　　35
Smear'd with gore, and ghastly pale:
Far, far aloof th' affrighted ravens sail;
　　The famish'd eagle screams, and passes by.
Dear lost companions of my tuneful art,
　　Dear as the light that visits these sad eyes,　　40

" Who with his soft pipe and smooth dittied song
　Well knows to still the wild winds when they roar,
　And *hush* the waving woods." *Luke.*

V. 34. "Cloud-capt towers," Tempest, act iv. sc. 1. *W.* —
Drayton has used this image very poetically in his Poly-Olbion,
vol. iii. p. 1126, in the speech of Skedow:
" But from my glorious height into its depth I pry,
　Great hills far under me, but as my pages lie;
　And when my *helm of clouds upon my head* I take."
So in the tragedy of Nero, 1624, p. 27: "Hebrus stood still,
Pangæa bow'd his head."

V. 35. The shores of Caernarvonshire opposite the isle of
Anglesey. *Gray.*

V. 36. "*Smear'd with gore, a ghastly stream.*" King of
France's Daughter: Percy. Reliques, iii. 164; and Macbeth,
act ii. sc. 2, "*Smear* the sleepy grooms with blood."

V. 37. This image may be found in Lucret. vi. ver. 1213.
xii. 565. Ovid. Met. vii. 550. Lucan. vi. ver. 625. Stat.
Theb. i. ver. 624. Prudent. Steph. 5, 400. It is also in
Dryden. Pal. and Arcite, ver. 1142:
" The fowl that scent afar the borders fly,
　And shun the bitter blast, and wheel about the sky."

V. 38. Camden and others observe, that eagles used an-
nually to build their aerie among the rocks of Snowdon, which
from thence (as some think) were named by the Welsh Craigian-eryri, or the crags of the eagles. At this day (I am told)
the highest point of Snowdon is called the Eagle's Nest. That
bird is certainly no stranger to this island, as the Scots, and
the people of Cumberland, Westmoreland, &c. can testify it
even has built its nest upon the peak of Derbyshire. [See
Willoughby's Ornithol. by Ray.] *Gray.* "The Tempest sees
their strength, and sighs and passes by," v. Swift's Misc.
ii. 189

V. 40. " As dear to me as are the ruddy drops
　　　　That visit my sad heart."
　　　　　　　　　Jul. Cæsar, act ii. sc. 1. *Gray.*

Dear as the ruddy drops that warm my heart,
  Ye died amidst your dying country's cries —
No more I weep.   They do not sleep,
  On yonder cliffs, a grisly band,
I see them sit, they linger yet,   45
  Avengers of their native land:
With me in dreadful harmony they join,
And weave with bloody hands the tissue of thy line.

II. 1.

  " Weave the warp, and weave the woof,
The winding sheet of Edward's race.   50

See Callimach. H. Dian. v. 211.   Theocr. Id. cap. 53.
Quint. Smyrn. x. 475. Catul. xiv. 1. Virg. Æn. iv. 31.
Otway, in his Venice Preserved, act v. p. 309, was more im-
mediately in Gray's mind:

  " Dear as the vital warmth that feeds my life,
    Dear as these eyes that weep in fondness o'er thee."

In Sydney's Arcadia, vol. ii. p. 415: " Oh, mother, said
Amphialus, speak not of doing them hurt, no more than to
mine *eyes* or my *heart*, or if I have any thing more *dear than
eyes or heart unto me*."   King Lear, act 1. sc. 2: " Dearer
than eye-sight."

  V. 42. " And greatly falling with a falling state." Pope.

  " And couldst not fall, but with thy country's fate,"
                                        Dryden.   *W.*

  V. 44. I have thought that this image was shadowed by
the poet from the following passage of Stat. xi. 420.   The
third line is almost translated:

  " Ipse quoque Ogygios monstra ad gentilia *manes*
    Tartareus rector porta jubet ira reclusa.
    Montibus insidunt patriis, tristique corona
    Infecere diem, et *vinci* sua crimina gaudent."

" For neither were ye playing on the *steep*, where your old
bards, *the famous Druids, lie*." Lycidas.

  V. 48. See the Norwegian ode (the Fatal Sisters) that
follows. *Gray.*

  V. 49. " No wool to work on, neither *weft nor warp*."
                        Swift's Misc. viii. p. 198, ed. Nich

Give ample room, and verge enough
The characters of hell to trace.
Mark the year, and mark the night,
When Severn shall re-echo with affright
The shrieks of death, thro' Berkley's roof that ring,
Shrieks of an agonizing king!   56

  She-wolf of France, with unrelenting fangs,
That tear'st the bowels of thy mangled mate,
  From thee be born, who o'er thy country hangs
The scourge of heav'n. What terrors round him
    wait!   60

V. 51. "I have a soul that like an *ample* shield
    Can take in all, and *verge enough* for more."
               Dryden. Sebastian, act i. sc. 1.
V. 55. Edward the Second, cruelly butchered in Berkley
Castle. *Gray.* See Drayton. Barons' Wars, v. lxvii.
"Berkley, whose fair seat hath been famous long,
  Let thy sad *echoes shriek a deadly sound*
  To the vast air; complain his grievous wrong,
  And keep the blood that issued from his wound."
V. 56. This line of Gray is almost in the same words as
Hume's description, vol. ii. p. 359: "The *screams* with which
the *agonizing king* filled the castle."
V. 57. Isabel of France, Edward the Second's adulterous
queen. *Gray.*
This expression is from Shakespeare's Henry VI. pt. iii.
act i. sc. 4: "*She-wolf of France,* but worse than wolves of
France." Latin writers have used the same language. Apu-
leius, speaking of the sisters of Psyche: "*Perfidæ lupulæ* ne-
farias insidias comparant." And Ausonius, ed. Tollii, p. 23:
"Et *mater* est vere *lupa.*" Plutarch in Vita Romuli, c. iv.
p. 84. ed. Reiske. ΛΟΥΠΑΣ γὰρ ἐκάλουν Ὁι ΛΑΤΙΝΟΙ τῶν
τε θηρίων τὰς λυκαίνας, καὶ τῶν γυναικῶν τὰς ἑταιρούσας, &c
V. 59. "This evening from the sun's decline arriv'd,
    Who tells of some infernal spirit seen."
             P. L. iv. 792.   *Rogers.*
V. 60. Triumphs of Edward the Third in France.   *Gray.*
    "Circumque atræ formidinis ora,
Iræque, insidiæque, Dei comitatus, aguntur."
            Virg. Æn. xii. 335.   *W.*

Amazement in his van, with flight combin'd,
And sorrow's faded form, and solitude behind.

II. 2.

" Mighty victor, mighty lord!
Low on his funeral couch he lies!
No pitying heart, no eye, afford   G.
A tear to grace his obsequies.
Is the sable warrior fled?
Thy son is gone.   He rests among the dead.
The swarm, that in thy noontide beam were born?

> Var. V. 63. *Victor*] Conqueror. MS.
> V. 64. *His*] The. MS.
> V. 65. *No, no*] What, what. MS.
> V. 69. Hover'd in thy noontide ray.   MS.

V. 61. Cowley has a couplet with similar imagery, vol. i.
p. 254:

> " He walks about the perishing nation,
> Ruin behind him stalks, and empty desolation."

And Oldham in his Ode to Homer, stan. iii.

> " Where'er he does his dreadful standard bear,
> Horror stalks in the van, and slaughter in the rear."

> " On he went, and in his van confusion and amaze,
> While horror and affright brought up the rear."   Swift.

V. 62. " Care sat on his faded cheek."   V. Milt. P. L. i.
601.

V. 64. Death of that king, abandoned by his children, and
even robbed in his last moments by his courtiers and his mistress.   *Gray.*

" Lo! there the mighty warrior lies."   Oldham. D. of Saul.

V. 65. The same *words*, with the same elliptical expression,
occur in the Instal. Ode, vi.:

> " Thy liberal *heart*, thy judging *eye*,
> The flower unheeded shall *descry*."

On this ellipsis see Jortin. Obs. on Spenser: Tracts, vol. i. p. 91.

V. 67. Edward the Black Prince, dead some time before his
father.   *Gray.*

> " Hence Edward dreadful with his *sable shield*."

> Prior. Poems, p. 210.

Gone to salute the rising morn. *70*

Fair laughs the morn, and soft the zephyr blows,

   While proudly riding o'er the azure realm

In gallant trim the gilded vessel goes;

Var. V. 70. *Morn*] Day. MS.
   V. 71. *Fair laughs, &c.*
     " Mirrors * of Saxon truth and loyalty
     Your helpless, old, expiring master view !
     They hear not: scarce religion does supply
     Her mutter'd requiems, and her holy dew.
     Yet thou, proud boy, from Pomfret's walls shalt send
     A sigh, and envy oft thy happy grandsire's end."

---

   * " Mirror of ancient faith, in early youth
     Undaunted worth, inviolable truth."
                   Dryd. S. vi. *Rogers.*

   In Peacham's ' Period of Mourning,' 1613, a similar epithet is given, but from a different reason:

     " Appeared then in armes a goodly prince
     Of *swarthy hew,* by whom there hung a launce
     Of wondrous length, preserved ever since;
     He overthrew, at Poitiers, John of Fraunce.
     A dial his device, the stile at *one* —
     And this, ' *No night, and yet my day is done.*' '

   V. 69. So in Agrippina:
      " —— around thee call
     The *gilded swarm,* that wantons in the *sunshine*
     Of thy full favour."

   V. 71. Magnificence of Richard the Second's reign. See Froissard, and other contemporary writers. *Gray.* See M. of Venice, act ii. s. 6. " How like a younker," &c. Spenser. Vision of the World's Vanity, " Looking far forth," &c. And Vision of Petrarch, c. ii. " After at sea a tall ship did appear," &c., which passages are too long for transcription.

   V. 72. " Cœruleo pollens conjunx Neptunia regno."
                 Virg. Cir. 483. *Luke.*

   V. 73. So Pope, Donne, Sat. iv. 230, who has used the same words on the same subject: " *Top-gallant* he, and she in all her *trim.*"

Youth on the prow, and Pleasure at the helm ;
Regardless of the sweeping whirlwind's sway,   75
That, hush'd in grim repose, expects his ev'ning
    prey.

II. 3.

" Fill high the sparkling bowl,
The rich repast prepare ;
Reft of a crown, he yet may share the feast:
Close by the regal chair   80

" The goodly London in her *gallant trim,*

And on her shadow *rides* in floating *gold.*"
Dryden. An. Mirab. 151.

V. 74. " Ipse gubernabit residens in puppe Cupido," Ov.
Heroid. Ep. xv. 215. And so Petrarch: " E al governo, siede
'l Signor, anzi 'l nimico mio," Son. clvi.

V. 75. So in his Fragment on Education and Government,
v. 48:
" And where the deluge burst with *sweepy sway.*"
The expression is from Dryden. See Virg. Georg. i. 483:
" And rolling onwards with a *sweepy sway.*"
And in Granada, act v. sc. 1:
" That whirls along with an impetuous *sway,*
And like chain-shot *sweeps* all things in the way.'
And Ov. Met. " Rushing onwards with a *sweepy sway.*"
And Æn. vii. " The branches bend before their *sweepy sway.*"

V. 76. " So like a lion that unheeded lay,
Dissembling sleep and watchful to betray,
With inward rage he meditates his prey."
Dryden. Sig. and Guise
" Fermenting tempest brew'd in the *grim evening sky.*"
Thomson.

V. 77. Richard the Second, as we are told by Archbishop
Scroop and the confederate Lords in their manifesto, by Thomas
of Walsingham, and all the older writers, was starved to death.
The story of his assassination by Sir Piers of Exon is of much
later date. *Gray.*
For the profusion of Richard II. see Harding. Chron. quoted
in the Preface to Mason's Hoccleve, p. 5; Daniel. Civil Wars,

Fell Thirst and Famine scowl
A baleful smile upon their baffled guest.
Heard ye the din of battle bray,
Lance to lance, and horse to horse?
Long years of havock urge their destined
    course,   85
And thro' the kindred squadrons mow their way.

Var. V. 82. *A baleful smile*] A smile of horror MS.

---

iii. 87; and Pennant. London, p. 89, 4to.   Dr. Berdmore com-
pares this passage to the following lines of Virgil, Æn. vi. 603:
           " Lucent genialibus altis
Aurea fulcra toris, *epulæque ante ora paratæ*
Regifico luxu: Furiarum maxima juxta
Adcubat, et manibus prohibet contingere mensas,
Exsurgitque facem adtollens, atque intonat ore."

V. 79. " Such is the robe that kings must wear,
      When death has *reft their crown*."
             Mallett. Will. and Marg. st. 3. *W.*

V. 80. "Regales inter mensas." Virg. Æn. i. 686. "Sate
Matilda in the regal chair." Davenport. K. John and Matilda, p. 25, 4to.

V. 82.
" He ceas'd: for both seemed highly pleas'd; and Death
Grinn'd horrible a *ghastly smile*."   Par. L. ii. 845. *W.*

So Hom. Il. E. 212: Μειδιόων βλοσυροῖσι προσώπασι.   And
other examples cited in the note of Newton to the Par. Lost.

V. 83. Ruinous wars of York and Lancaster. *Gray.*

V. 83. " Arms on armour clashing brayed."
                Milt. Par. L. vi. 209   *Luke.*

V. 84. " Harry to Harry shall, not *horse to horse*." Shakes.
Hen. IV. pt. i. act iv. sc. i. " Man to man, and horse to
horse." Massing. M. of Honor. *Rogers.*

V. 86. " Cognatasque acies," Lucan. i. 4. *W.* — And so
in Sidon. Apollin. xv. 28: " *Cognatam* portans *aciem*." In
Dryden, All for Love, act i. we find an expression similar to
the text,
        " *Mow* them out a *passage*,
And entering where the foremost *squadrons* yield."

Ye towers of Julius, London's lasting shame,
With many a foul and midnight murder fed,
　　Revere his consort's faith, his father's fame,
And spare the meek usurper's holy head.　　ᴼ
Above, below, the rose of snow,
　　Twin'd with her blushing foe, we spread:

Var. V. 87. *Ye*] Grim. ᴍꜱ.　V. 90. *Holy*] Hallow'd. ᴍꜱ.

V. 87. Henry the Sixth, George Duke of Clarence, Edward
the Fifth, Richard Duke of York, &c., believed to be mur-
dered secretly in the Tower of London. The oldest part of
that structure is vulgarly attributed to Julius Cæsar. *Gray.*

V. 89. Margaret of Anjou, a woman of heroic spirit, who
struggled hard to save her husband and her crown.
　　　　　　　　　　　　　　　　　　　　　　Gray.

Ibid. Henry the Fifth. *Gray.*

V. 90. Henry the Sixth, very near being canonized. The
line of Lancaster had no right of inheritance to the crown.
　　　　　　　　　　　　　　　　　　　　　　Gray.

V. 91. The white and red roses, devices of York and Lancaster. *Gray.*

　　　　　　" —— no, Plantagenet,
　　'Tis not for fear, but anger — that thy cheeks
　　Blush for pure shame, to counterfeit our *roses.*"
　　　　　　　　　　　　Henry VI. pt. i. act ii. sc. 4.

V. 93. The silver boar[1] was the badge of Richard the Third;
whence he was usually known in his own time by the name of
the Boar. *Gray.*

　　" Nor easier fate the *bristled boar* is lent."

---

[1] The crest or bearing of a warrior (says Scott in his notes
to the Lay of the Last Minstrel, p. 300) was often used as a
" nom de guerre." Thus Richard III. acquired his well-
known epithet, — " the Boar of York." In the violent satire
on Cardinal Wolsey, commonly but erroneously imputed to
Dr. Bull, the Duke of Buckingham is called the *Beautiful
Swan;* and the Duke of Norfolk, or Earl of Surrey, *the White
Lion.* See Dr. Nott. Surrey. i. p. 302, 304. And see the

The bristled boar in infant-gore
  Wallows beneath the thorny shade.
Now, brothers, bending o'er the accursed loom, 95
Stamp we our vengeance deep, and ratify his doom.

III. 1.

  " Edward, lo! to sudden fate
(Weave we the woof. The thread is spun.)
  Half of thy heart we consecrate.

See Mirror for Magis. p. 417. Anon. 62, 69, 80. Again,
> " At Stonie Stratford being upon my way,
>   The *bloodie bore my uncle* that did aime."

Mirror for Magis. p. 740. " The bristled baptist boar," Dryden. The Princes are called the roses:
> " Oh ! noble Edward, from whose royal blood
> Life to their infant bodies nature drew,
>   *Thy roses both are cropt e'en in the bud.*"

And p. 745, with the same allusion:
> " Why didst thou leave that *bore* in time t' ensue
> To spoil those *plants* that in thy garden grew."

See also the Battle of Flodden Field, st. 255; and Ford. Perkin Warbeck, act i. sc. 1. p. 12. ed. Weber.

V. 96.
" If Fate weave common thread, I'll change the doom,
And with new purple weave a nobler loom." Dryd. Seb.

V. 98.   " Yet rather let him live, and twine
His *woof of dayes* with some *thread* stolen from mine."

Cartwright. Poems, p. 239. 'Αγαμέμνονι πότμον ὑφαίνει.
Tryphiod. v. 409. Nonni. Dion. iv. 244.

V. 99. Eleanor of Castile died a few years after the conquest of Wales. The heroic proof she gave of her affection

---

Lay of the Last Minstrel, cant. iv. st. xxx:
> " Yet hear, quoth Howard, calmly hear,
> Nor deem my words the words of fear;
> For who, in field or foray slack,
> Saw the *Blanche Lion* e'er fall back? "

And so in Henry VI. part ii. act v. sc. 2. Warwick is called the *Bear*, from his father's badge, old Neville's crest:
> " The rampant *Bear* chained to the ragged staff "

(The web is wove.   The work is done.)   100
Stay, oh stay! nor thus forlorn
Leave me unbless'd, unpitied, here to mourn:
In yon bright track, that fires the western skies,
They melt, they vanish from my eyes.   104
But oh! what solemn scenes on Snowdon's height
  Descending slow their glittering skirts unroll?
Visions of glory, spare my aching sight!
  Ye unborn ages, crowd not on my soul!

Var. V. 101. *Thus*] Here. MS.
    V. 102. *Me unbless'd, unpitied, here*] Your despairing
        Caradoc. MS.
    V. 103. *Track*] Clouds. MS.
    V. 104. *Melt*] Sink. MS.
    V. 105. *Solemn scenes*] Scenes of Heaven. MS.
    V. 106. *Glittering*] Golden. MS.

---

for her lord is well known. The monuments of his regret and sorrow for the loss of her, are still to be seen at Northampton, Gaddington, Waltham, and other places. *Gray.*

V. 106. Milt. P. L. xi. 332. "Though but his utmost skirts of glory." *Luke.*

V. 107. From Dryden. State of Innocence, act iv. sc. 1:

"Their *glory* shoots upon my *aching sight.*"

V. 109. It was the common belief of the Welsh nation, that King Arthur was still alive in Fairyland, and would return again to reign over Britain.

V. 110. Both Merlin and Taliessin had prophesied that the Welsh should regain their sovereignty over this island; which seemed to be accomplished in the house of Tudor. *Gray.*

V. 111. "Throngs of knights and barons bold," Milton. L'Alleg. 119. *Luke.*

V. 112. "His *starry front* low rooft beneath the skies," Milton. Ode on the Passion, iii. 18. "Sideribus similes oculos," Ovid. Met. i. 499. "Heu! ubi siderei vultus," Stat. Theb. v. 613. "Sidereo læta supercilio," Claud. xv v. 58; and "Sidereos oculos," Manilius Ast. iv. 905; and, lastly, "Gli occhi sereni, et le *stellanti ciglia,*" Petr. Son clxvii. v. 9.

No more our long-lost Arthur we bewail. 109
All hail, ye genuine kings, Britannia's issue, hail!
III. 2.
" Girt with many a baron bold
Sublime their starry fronts they rear;
And gorgeous dames, and statesmen old
In bearded majesty, appear.
In the midst a form divine! 115
Her eye proclaims her of the Briton-line;

Var. V. 109, 110. *No more our long-lost, &c.*]
  " From Cambria's thousand hills a thousand strains
   Triumphant tell aloud, another *Arthur* reigns." MS.
  V. 111, 112. *Girt with, &c.*]
  " Youthful knights, and barons bold
   With dazzling helm, and horrent spear " MS.

 V. 114. It has been remarked that there is an inaccuracy
in this expression, as the Bard, whose own beard is compared
to a *meteor*, would not be struck with the dignity of the *short
curled beards of Elizabeth's days.* See Selections from Gentleman's Magazine, vol. ii. p. 237.

 V. 116. So Peacham, in his 'Period of Mourning,' p. 16,
speaking of Elizabeth:

  "Where when I saw that brow, that cheeke, that *eye*
  Hee left imprinted in *Eliza's face.*"

Wakefield quotes a stanza from Spenser. Hobbinol's Dittie, in
praise of Eliza:

  " Tell me, have ye seene her *angelike face,*
   Like Phœbe fayre !
  Her heavenly haveour, her *princely grace*
   Can you well compare ?
  The *redde rose* medled, with the *white* yfere
  In either cheek depeincten *lively chere;*
   Her modest *eye,*
   Her majestye,
  When have you seene the like but there ? "

England's Helicon, p. 13; and Spenser. ed. Todd, i. 64; and
the note of T. Warton

Her lion-port, her awe-commanding face,
Attemper'd sweet to virgin-grace.
What strings symphonious tremble in the air,
    What strains of vocal transport round her play!
    Hear from the grave, great Taliessin, hear; 121
    They breathe a soul to animate thy clay.
Bright Rapture calls, and soaring as she sings,
Waves in the eye of heav'n her many-colour'd
    wings.

Var. V. 117. *Her, her*] A, an. MS.

V. 117. Speed, relating an audience given by Queen Elizabeth to Paul Dzialinski, ambassador of Poland, says, "And thus she, lion-like rising, daunted the malapert orator no less with her stately port and majestical deporture, than with the tartnesse of her princelie cheekes." *Gray.* See Puttenham, Engl. Poesy, iii. c. 24. p. 249, quoted by Dr. Nott on Surrey, vol. i. p. 307. See Ellis's Lett. on Engl. Histy. iii. 41: a copy of this speech is in MS. Landsdowne, No. 94, art. 50.

V. 121. Taliessin, chief of the bards, flourished in the sixth century. His works are still preserved, and his memory held in high veneration among his countrymen. *Gray.* On his supposed sepulchre, see Wyndham. Tour in Wales, p. 100. See Evans. Spec. p. 18, who says, "Taliessin's poems, on account of their great antiquity, are very obscure." There is a great deal of the Druidical cabala introduced in his works, especially about the transmigration of souls. Evans says that he had fifty of Taliessin's poems, and that many spurious ones are attributed to him. At p. 56, Evans has translated one of his odes, beginning "Fair Elphin, cease to weep;" comforting his friend on his bad success in the salmon-fishery. There is a fuller account of him in Jones. Relics, vol. i. p. 18, 21. vol. ii. p. 12, 19, 31, 34, where many of his poems are translated; and Pennant's Wales, vol. ii. p. 316; and Turner's Vind. of the Ancient British Poems, p. 225, 237.

V. 123. From Congreve. Ode to Lord Godolphin, st. vi.:

    "And soars with rapture while she sings."

V. 124. "It was as glorious as the *eye of Heaven.*" Cowley. Add Warton. note to Milton, p. 87. "Interest that waves on

III. 3.

" The verse adorn again   125
    Fierce war, and faithful love,
And truth severe, by fairy fiction drest.
    In buskin'd measures move
Pale grief, and pleasing pain,
With horror, tyrant of the throbbing breast.   130
    A voice, as of the cherub-choir,
Gales from blooming Eden bear;
And distant warblings lessen on my ear,
    That lost in long futurity expire.

---

party-colour'd wings." Pope. Dunc. iv. 538. And, "Colours
that change where'er they wave their wings." Rape of the
Lock, ii. 68. Wakefield cites the Tempest, act iv. sc. 1:
"Hail, many-colour'd messenger." See Milt. Par. L. vii.
641: " Wings he wore of *many a colour'd* plume."

           " Her angel's face
    As the great *eye of Heaven* shined bright."
                          Spenser. F. Q. cant. iii.
Ovid. Met. iv. 228. " Mundi oculus." And Milton. Il
Pens. ver. 141: "Hide me from *day's* garish *eye.*" Par. Lost,
b. v. ver. 171: "Thou *sun* of this great *world*, both *eye* and
soul." Shakesp. Rich. II. act iii. sc. 2: " The searching *eye
of Heaven* is hid."

V. 126. " Fierce wars and faithful loves shall moralize my
song." Spenser. Proëme to the F. Q. *Gray.*

V. 127. " *Truth*, Wisdom, Sanctitude *severe* and *pure.*"
                          Milt. P. L. iv. 293. *Luke.*

V. 128. Shakespeare. *Gray.* " Ennobled hath the *bus-
kined* stage." Milt. Il Pens. 102.

V. 129. F. Queen, vi. c. 9. s. x. " With sweet pleasing
payne." Dryden. Virg. Ecl. iii. 171. " Pleasing pains of
love." *Luke.*

V. 130. " Imaginative woe my *throbbing breast* inspires."
                          Thomson.

V 133. The succession of poets after Milton's time.
                          Gray.

Fond impious man, think'st thou yon sanguine
    cloud,   135
  Rais'd by thy breath, has quench'd the orb of
    day?
To-morrow he repairs the golden flood,
  And warms the nations with redoubled ray.
Enough for me ; with joy I see

V. 135. This apostrophe with its imagery seems taken from
Vida:
            ——"Impie, quid furis?
  Tene putas posse illustres abscondere cœli
  Auricomi flammas, ipsumque extinguere solem?

  .   .   .   .
  Forsitan humentem nebulam proflare, brevemque
  Obsessis poteris radiis obtendere nubem.
  Erumpet lux; erumpet rutilantibus auris
  Lampas; et aurifluâ face, nubila differet omnia."
Vidæ Hymnus D. Andreæ Apostolo. v. 99. T. i. p. 335.
Steevens refers to "Fuimus Troes," act i. sc. 1:
            "Think ye the smoky mist
  Of sun-boil'd seas can stop the eagle's eye?"
but a closer coincidence is in Dekker's Play, "If this be not
a good play," &c. p. 73.
            ——"Think'st thou, base lord,
  Because the glorious sun behind black clouds
  Has awhile hid his beams, he's darken'd for ever,
  Eclips'd never more to shine?"
  V. 137. "And yet anon *repairs* his drooping head." Lycidas, 169.   "So soon *repairs her light*, trebling her new-born
raies," Fletcher. Purple Island, vi. 64.   "That never could
he hope his *waning to repaire*," Ib. st. 70.   Add Hor. Od. iv.
7. 13. "Damna tamen celeres *reparant* cœlestia lunæ." Lucret. v. 733, On the Moon, "Atque alia illius *reparari* in parte
locoque." Young. N. Thoughts, "A golden flood of endless
day." *Luke.*
  V. 141. There is a passage in the Thebaid of Statius, iii. 81,
similar to this, describing a bard who had survived his companions:
            "Sed jam nudaverat ensem
  Magnanimus vates, et nunc trucis ora tyranni,
  Nunc ferrum aspectans, nunquam tibi sanguinis hujus

The diff'rent doom our fates assign. 140
Be thine despair, and sceptred care ;
  To triumph, and to die, are mine."
He spoke, and headlong from the mountain's
    height
Deep in the roaring tide he plunged to endless
    night.*

Jus erit, aut magno feries imperdita Tydeo
Pectora. *Vado equidem exultans, ereptaque fata*
Insequor, et comites feror expectatus ad umbras.
Te superis, fratrique. ——

Compare also the conclusion of the first Olymp. of Pindar,
ver. 184, which Gray seems to have had in his mind:

    Εἴη σὲ τε τοῦτον
    Ὑψοῦ χρόνον πατεῖν, ἐμε
    Τε τοσσάδε νικαφόροις
    Ὁμιλεῖν. κ. τ. λ.

This similarity has apparently struck the author of the late
Translations, as I judge by his language: v. R. Heber. Poems,
p. 94.

V. 143. " Medias *præceps* tunc *fertur in undas*, Lucan. ix.
122. " Præceps aerii specula de montis in undas, Deferar;
extremum hoc munus morientis habeto," Virg. Ecl. viii. 58.

---

    * The original argument of this ode, as Mr. Gray had set
it down in one of the pages of his common-place book, was as
follows: " The army of Edward I., as they march through a
deep valley, (and approach Mount Snowdon, MS.) are suddenly
stopped by the appearance of a venerable figure seated on the
summit of an inaccessible rock, who, with a voice more than
human, reproaches the king with all the misery and desolation
(desolation and misery, MS.) which he had brought on his
country; foretells the misfortunes of the Norman race, and
with prophetic spirit declares, that all his cruelty shall never
extinguish the noble ardour of poetic genius in this island;
and that men snall never be wanting to celebrate true virtue
and valour in immortal strains, to expose vice and infamous
pleasure, and boldly censure tyranny and oppression. His

                     E

song ended, he precipitates himself from the mountain, and is
swallowed up by the river that rolls at its foot."

" Fine (says Mr. Mason) as the conclusion of this ode is at
present, I think it would have been still finer, if he could
have executed it according to this plan; but, unhappily for
his purpose, instances of English poets were wanting. Spenser had that enchanting flow of verse which was peculiarly
calculated to *celebrate virtue and valour;* but he chose to celebrate them, not literally, but in allegory. Shakespeare, who
had talents for every thing, was undoubtedly capable *of
exposing vice and infamous pleasure;* and the drama was a
proper vehicle for his satire; but we do not ever find that he
professedly made this his object ; nay, we know that, in one
inimitable character, he has so contrived as to make vices of
the worst kind, such as cowardice, drunkenness, dishonesty,
and lewdness, not only laughable, but almost amiable; for
with all these sins on his head, who can help liking Falstaff ?
Milton, of all our great poets, was the only one *who boldly
censured tyranny and oppression:* but he chose to deliver this
censure, not in poetry, but in prose. Dryden was a mere
court parasite to the most infamous of all courts. Pope, with
all his laudable detestation of corruption and bribery, was a
Tory; and Addison, though a Whig, and a fine writer, was
unluckily not enough of a poet for his purpose. On these
considerations Mr. Gray was necessitated to change his plan
towards the conclusion: hence we perceive, that in the last
epode he praises Spenser only *for his allegory,* Shakespeare
for his powers of moving the passions, and Milton *for his epic
excellence.* I remember the ode lay unfinished by him for a
year or two on this very account; and I hardly believe that
it would ever have had his last hand, but for the circumstance
of his hearing Parry play on the Welsh harp at a concert at
Cambridge, (see Letter xxv. sect. iv.) which he often declared
inspired him with the conclusion.

" Mr. Smith, the musical composer and worthy pupil of Mr.
Handel, had once an idea of setting this ode, and of having
it performed by way of serenata or oratorio. A common
friend of his and Mr. Gray's interested himself much in this
design, and drew out a clear analysis of the ode, that Mr.
Smith might more perfectly understand the poet's meaning.
He conversed also with Mr. Gray on the subject, who gave
him an idea for the overture, and marked also some passages
in the ode, in order to ascertain which should be recitative,
which air, what kind of air, and how accompanied. This
design was, however, not executed; and therefore I shall
only (in order to give the reader a taste of Mr. Gray's musical
feelings) insert in this place what his sentiments were concerning the overture. ' It should be so contrived as to be a

proper introduction to the ode; it might consist of two movements, the first descriptive of the horror and confusion of
battle, the last a march grave and majestic, but expressing
the exultation and insolent security of conquest. This movement should be composed entirely of wind instruments, except
the kettle-drum heard at intervals. The *da capo* of it must
be suddenly broke in upon, and put to silence by the clang
of the harp in a tumultuous rapid movement, joined with the
voice, all at once, and not ushered in by any symphony. The
harmony may be strengthened by any other stringed instrument; but the harp should every where prevail, and form the
continued running accompaniment, submitting itself to nothing
but the voice.'

" I cannot (adds Mr. Mason) quit this and the preceding
ode, without saying a word or two concerning the obscurity
which has been imputed to them, and the preference which,
in consequence, has been given to his Elegy. It seems as if
the persons, who hold this opinion, suppose that every species
of poetry ought to be equally clear and intelligible : than
which position nothing can be more repugnant to the several
specific natures of composition, and to the practice of ancient
art. Not to take Pindar and his odes for an example, (though
what I am here defending were written professedly in imitation of him,) I would ask, are all the writings of Horace, his
Epistles, Satires, and Odes, equally perspicuous ? Among
his odes, separately considered, are there not remarkable
differences of this very kind ? Is the spirit and meaning of
that which begins, 'Descende cœlo, et dic, age, tibiâ,' Ode
iv. lib. 3, so readily comprehended as ' Persicos odi, puer,
apparatus,' Ode xxxviii. lib. 1. And is the latter a finer
piece of lyrical composition on that account? Is ' Integer
vitæ, scelerisque purus,' Ode xxii. lib. 1, superior to ' Pin-
darum quisquis studet æmulari,' Ode ii. lib. 4 ; because it
may be understood at the first reading, and the latter not
without much study and reflection? Now between these odes,
thus compared, there is surely equal difference in point of
perspicuity, as between the Progress of Poesy, and the Prospect of Eton College; the Ode on the Spring, and the Bard.
' But,' say these objectors, ' the end of poetry is universally
to please. Obscurity, by taking off from our pleasure, destroys
that end.' I will grant that if the obscurity be great, constant, and insurmountable, this is certainly true; but if it be
only found in particular passages, proceeding from the nature
of the subject and the very genius of the composition, it does
not rob us of our pleasure, but superadds a new one, which
arises from conquering a difficulty; and the pleasure which
accrues from a difficult passage, when well understood, provided the passage itself be a fine one, is always more perma-

nent than that which we discover at the first glance. The
Lyric Muse, like other fine ladies, requires to be courted, and
retains her admirers the longer for not having yielded too
readily to their solicitations.   This argument, ending as it
does in a sort of simile, will, I am persuaded, not only have
its force with the intelligent readers (the ΣΥΝΕΤΟΙ), but
also with the men of fashion: as to critics of a lower class,
it may be sufficient to transcribe, for their improvement, an
unfinished remark, or rather maxim, which I found amongst
our author's papers; and which he probably wrote on occasion
of the common preference given to his Elegy.   ' The *Gout*
de comparaison (as Bruyere styles it) is the only taste of
ordinary minds.   They do not know the specific excellence
either of an author or a composition: for instance, they do
not know that Tibullus spoke the language of nature and love;
that Horace saw the vanities and follies of mankind with the
most penetrating eye, and touched them to the quick; that
Virgil ennobled even the most common images by the graces
of a glowing, melodious, and well-adapted expression : but
they do know that Virgil was a better poet than Horace, and
that Horace's Epistles do not run so well as the Elegies of
Tibullus.' "

ODE FOR MUSIC.

(IRREGULAR.)

This Ode was performed in the Senate-House at Cambridge, July 1, 1769, at the installation of His Grace Augustus Henry Fitzroy, Duke of Grafton, Chancellor of the University. (This Ode is printed with the divisions adopted by the Composer, Dr. Randall, then Professor of Music at Cambridge. On Dr. Burney's disappointment that he did not set this Ode to music, see Miss Burney's Mem. i. 212; and Cradock's Mem. i. p. 107.)

I. AIR.

" HENCE, avaunt, ('tis holy ground)
  Comus, and his midnight-crew,
And Ignorance with looks profound,
  And dreaming Sloth of pallid hue,
Mad Sedition's cry profane,   5
Servitude that hugs her chain,
Nor in these consecrated bowers
Let painted Flatt'ry hide her serpent-train in
     flowers.

CHORUS.

Nor Envy base, nor creeping Gain,

V. 1. So Callim. H. in Apoll. ver. 2: Ἑκὰς ἑκὰς ὅστις ἁλιτρὸς. Virg. Æn. vi. 258: " Procul, O procul este profani." Stat. Sylv. iii. 3: " Procul hinc, procul ite nocentes." Claud. Rap. Pros. i. 3: " Gressus removete profani."

V. 2. " Meanwhile welcome joy, and feast,
        Midnight shout, and revelry,
        Tipsy dance, and jollity." Milt. Com. 102. *W.*
  " Though he and his cursed *crew*." Milt. Com. 653.

V. 7. " Near to her close and *consecrated bower*."
                      Mids. N. Dr. act iii. sc. 2. *W.*

V. 9. " *Base Envy* withers at another's joy." Thomson. Spring. Also, " Safe pursuits and *creeping cares*." Liberty, p. iv. *Luke.*

Dare the Muse's walk to stain,   10
While bright-eyed Science watches round:
Hence, away, 'tis holy ground!"

II. RECITATIVE.

From yonder realms of empyrean day
  Bursts on my ear th' indignant lay:
There sit the sainted sage, the bard divine,   15
    The few, whom genius gave to shine
Thro' every unborn age, and undiscover'd clime.

  Rapt in celestial transport they:
  Yet hither oft a glance from high
  They send of tender sympathy   20

V. 13. " From your empyreal bowers, and from the realms
of everlasting day." G. West's Poems.

V. 15. *There sit*] Surely a better word than this, " sit," in
pronunciation and imagery could have been found.

V. 17. " *Nations unborn* your mighty name shall sound,
    And *worlds* applaud that must not yet *be found*."
          Pope. Essay on Criticism, 193.   *W.*

V. 26. " E'en mitred Rochester would *nod the head*."
Pope. Prol. to the Sat. 143.   *W.*   See Warton. Milt. p. 4.

V. 27. " To *arched* walks of twilight *groves*,
    And shadows *brown* that Sylvan loves."
          Il Penser. 133.   *W.*
And so Pope, in his Transl. of the Odyssey : " Brown with
o'erarching shades."

This stanza, supposed to be sung by Milton, is very judiciously written in the metre which he fixed upon for the stanza
of his Christmas Hymn : " 'Twas in the winter wild," &c.
Mason.

  " Nought have we here but *willow-shaded shore*,
    To tell our *Grant* his banks are left forlore."
          Hall. Sat. b. i. sat. i.

V 30. Wakefield has justly remarked that this stanza is
indebted to the following passage in the Il Pens. of Milton,
ver. 61:

To bless the place, where on their opening soul
   First the genuine ardour stole.
'Twas Milton struck the deep-ton'd shell,
And, as the choral warblings round him swell,
Meek Newton's self bends from his state sublime,
And nods his hoary head, and listens to the rhyme.

III. AIR.

  " Ye brown o'er-arching groves,
    That Contemplation loves,
Where willowy Camus lingers with delight!
    Oft at the blush of dawn   30
    I trod your level lawn,
Oft woo'd the gleam of Cynthia silver-bright

" Sweet bird, that shunn'st the noise of *folly*,
  Most musical, most *melancholy!* *

V. 31. " In long excursion skims the *level lawn.*"
                    Thomson. Spring. *Luke.*
V. 32. " With silver-bright who moon enamels."

---

  * Gaw. Douglas, in his Transl. of Virgil, Prolog. to bk. xiii.
p. 450, describes the notes of the nightingale as *merry:*

" — The *mery* nyghtyngele Philomene,
That on the thorne sat syngand fro the splene,
Quhais *myrthfull* nottis langing for to here," &c.

" Ah! far unlike the nightingale! — she sings
Unceasing thro' the balmy nights of May;
She sings from *love and joy.*" Thomson. Agamem. p. 63.

" Him will I *cheare* with chanting all this night,
And with that word she 'gan to clear her throate:
But such a *lively song*, now by this light,
Yet never hearde I such another note."
      Gascoigne. Complaynt of Phylomene.
Mr. Fox has, I think, given no authority but that of *Chaucer*,
for the *merry* notes of the nightingale; see his Letter to Lord
Grey, p. 12. But see Todd. Illust. of Gower.

In cloisters dim, far from the haunts of Folly,
With Freedom by my side, and soft-eyed Melancholy."

IV. RECITATIVE.

But hark! the portals sound, and pacing forth   35
   With solemn steps and slow,
High potentates, and dames of royal birth,
And mitred fathers in long order go:
Great Edward, with the lilies on his brow
   From haughty Gallia torn,   40
And sad Chatillon, on her bridal morn

Drummond, son. xii. *Luke.* "Their arrow that marched
hence so *silver-bright.*" K. John. *Rogers.*

   V. 33. Scared in *cloisters dim* the superstitious herd."
                        Thomson. Liberty, pt. iii. *Luke.*

   V. 34. " And sensible *soft Melancholy,*" Pope. On a certain Lady at Court, ver. 8. *W.* V. Pope. Prol. to Satires,
v. 286. *Luke.*

   V. 36. "With wand'ring *steps and slow,*" Par. Lost, b. xii.
ver. 648. *W.* — And Pope. Odys. b. x. ver. 286. Dunc. b. iv.
ver. 465, as quoted by Mr. Todd. " At every step solemn
and slow," Thomson. Summer. *Luke.*

   V. 38. "In long order stand," Dryd. Æn. iii. 533. " In
long order come," v. 133. *Rogers.*

   " Unde omnes *longo ordine* possit
Adversos legere, et venientum discere vultus."
                        Virg. Æn. vi. 754. *W.*

   V. 39. Edward the Third, who added the fleur de lys of
France to the arms of England. He founded Trinity College.
See Philips, in " Cyder," ii. 592:
         " *Great Edward* thus array'd,
   With *golden Iris* his broad shield emboss'd."

" Great Edward and thy greater son,
   He that the lilies wore, and he that won." *Denham.*

   V. 41. Mary de Valentia, countess of Pembroke, daughter
of Guy de Chatillon, comte de St. Paul in France; of whom
tradition says, that her husband Audemar de Valentia, earl

That wept her bleeding Love, and princely Clare,
And Anjou's heroine, and the paler rose,
The rival of her crown and of her woes,
  And either Henry there,   45
The murder'd saint, and the majestic lord,
  That broke the bonds of Rome.
(Their tears, their little triumphs o'er,
  Their human passions now no more,
Save Charity, that glows beyond the tomb.)   50

ACCOMPANIED.

All that on Granta's fruitful plain
Rich streams of regal bounty pour'd,

---

of Pembroke, was slain at a tournament on the day of his
nuptials. She was the foundress of Pembroke College or
Hall, under the name of Aula Mariæ de Valentia. *Gray.*
But consult a letter to Tyson from Gough in Nicholl. Lit.
Anec. viii. 604. *Luke.* Fotheringay Castle was her property.

V. 42. Elizabeth de Burg, countess of Clare, was wife of
John de Burg, son and heir of the Earl of Ulster, and daughter of Gilbert de Clare, earl of Gloucester, by Joan of Acres,
daughter of Edward the First. Hence the poet gives her the
epithet of *princely.* She founded Clare Hall. *Gray.*

V. 43. Margaret of Anjou, wife of Henry the Sixth, foundress of Queen's College. The poet has celebrated her conjugal
fidelity in "The *Bard,*" epode 2d, line 13th.
Elizabeth Widville, wife of Edward the Fourth, hence called
the paler rose, as being of the house of York. She added to
the foundation of Margaret of Anjou. *Gray.*

V. 45. Henry the Sixth and Eighth. The former the
founder of King's, the latter the greatest benefactor to Trinity
College. *Gray.*

V. 49. "One *human tear* shall drop, and be forgiven."
        Pope. Eloisa, 358. *W.*

V. 50. "Charity never faileth," St. Paul, 1 Corinth. xiii.
8. *W.*

And bade these awful fanes and turrets rise,
To hail their Fitzroy's festal morning come;
  And thus they speak in soft accord   55
  The liquid language of the skies:

V. QUARTETTO.

  " What is grandeur, what is power?
  Heavier toil, superior pain.
  What the bright reward we gain?
  The grateful memory of the good.   60
  Sweet is the breath of vernal shower,
  The bee's collected treasures sweet,
  Sweet music's melting fall, but sweeter yet
  The still small voice of gratitude."

V. 56.   " —— Cui *liquidam* Pater
           Vocem."   Hor. Od. I. xxiv. 3.   W.
And so Lucret. v. 1378: " Liquidas voces." And Ovid. Amor.
I. xiii. 8.

V. 61. Milton. Ep. on M. of Winchest. " Shot up from
vernal shower." Thomson. Spring, " With vernal showers dis-
tent." *Luke.*

V. 62. This comparison we find also in Theocr. Id. viii. 83:
Κρέσσον μελπομένῳ τεῦ ἀκουέμεν, ἢ μέλι λείχεν. And in Cal-
phurn. Eclog. iv. ver. 150. These four verses, as Wakefield
remarks, were suggested by Milton's Par. Lost, b. iv. ver.
641: " Sweet is the breath of morn," &c.: but see also Theocr.
Idyll. ϑ. ver. 33:

—— οὔτε γὰρ ὕπνος,
Οὔτ' ἔαρ ἐξαπίνας γλυκερώτερον, οὔτε μελίσσαις
Ἄνθεα, ὅσσον ἐμὶν Μῶσαι φίλαι.

" Opes congestas apium," A. Marcellini. Hist. xviii. 3.

V. 63. " And melt away, in a dying, dying fall," Pope.
Ode on St. Cecilia. *Luke.*

V. 64. " After the fire, a *still small* voice," 1 Kings, xix. 12.
And in a rejected stanza of the Elegy:

" Hark how the sacred calm that breathes around
Bids every fierce tumultuous passion cease;

VI. RECITATIVE.

Foremost and leaning from her golden cloud   65
   The venerable Marg'ret see!
" Welcome, my noble son, (she cries aloud)
   To this, thy kindred train, and me:
Pleas'd in·thy lineaments we trace
A Tudor's fire, a Beaufort's grace.   70

AIR.

Thy liberal heart, thy judging eye,
The flow'r unheeded shall descry,
And bid it round heav'n's altars shed
The fragrance of its blushing head;
Shall raise from earth the latent gem   75
To glitter on the diadem.

In *still small accents* whisp'ring from the ground
A grateful earnest of eternal peace." *W*.

   " Now in a *still small tone*
Your dying accents fall." Dryd. Œdip. act ii.

V. 65. " A voice from midst a *golden cloud* thus mild was heard." Milt. P. L. vi. 27. *Luke*.

V. 66. Countess of Richmond and Derby; the mother of Henry the Seventh, foundress of St. John's and Christ's Colleges. *Gray*.

V. 70. The Countess was a Beaufort, and married to a Tudor: hence the application of this line to the Duke of Grafton, who claims descent from both these families. *Gray*.

V. 71. " Dryden alone escaped his *judging eye*."
                           Pope. Prol. to the Sat. 246.
Also: " A face untaught to feign, a *judging eye*." Pope. Epist. to Craggs, p. 289. " A liberal heart and free from gall." Fuller. Abel Red. p. 314.

V. 72. This allusion to the *flower* and the *gem* we meet with again in the Elegy.

V. 73. " Delubra, et *aras cœlitum*," Senec. Agam. v. 392. " *Cœlo*que educitur *ara*," Sil. Ital. xv. 388. " Araque Divorum," Manil. Astr. v. 18.

VII. RECITATIVE.

" Lo! Granta waits to lead her blooming **band,**
  Not obvious, not obtrusive, she
No vulgar praise, no venal incense flings;
  Nor dares with courtly tongue refin'd   80
Profane thy inborn royalty of mind:
  She reveres herself and thee.
With modest pride to grace thy youthful brow,
The laureate wreath, that Cecil wore, she brings,
  And to thy just, thy gentle hand,   85

V. 78. " *Not obvious, not obtrusive,* but retired."
                        Par. L. viii. 504. *W.*
V. 79. " No hireling she, no *prostitute for praise.*"
             Pope. Epist. to Lord Oxford, v. 36. *W.*
V. 82. Πάντων δὲ μάλιστ' αἰσχύνεο σαυτόν, Pythag. Aur.
v. 12. *W.* — And so Galen. "De Curatione Morb. Animi: "
Σὺ δὲ σαυτὸν αἰδοῦ μάλιστα.
  V. 83. " Yielded with coy submission, *modest pride.*"
                        Par. Lost, iv. 310.
  V. 84. Lord Treasurer Burleigh was chancellor of the Uni-
versity in the reign of Queen Elizabeth. *Gray.* Milt. Son.
xvi. 9: " And Worcester's *laureate wreath.*" *Luke.*
  V. 85. Par. Lost, b. iv. 308, " gentle sway," from Horace,
" lenibus imperiis," Epist. I. xviii. 44. *W.* — But the senti-
ment, as well as expression, was taken from Dryden. Thr.
August. 284:
    " And with a *willing hand* restores
      The fasces of the main."
Add Milton. Eleg. i. 67: " Vos etiam Danaæ *fasces submittite*
nymphæ." *Luke.* " With the *submitted fasces* of the main."
Dryden. Astræa. Red.
  V. 88. See Par. Lost, vii. 559.
  V. 89. " Well knows to still the *wild waves* when *they roar.*"
Comus, v. 87. *W.* " The *wild waves* mastered him." Dryden.
An. Mirabilis.
  V. 92.   " Neque altum
    Semper urguendo, neque, dum procellas
    Cautus horrescis, nimium premendo
      Littus iniquum."

Submits the fasces of her sway,
While spirits blest above and men below
Join with glad voice the loud symphonious lay.

VIII. GRAND CHORUS.

" Thro' the wild waves as they roar,
   With watchful eye and dauntless mien,   90
    Thy steady course of honour keep,
Nor fear the rocks, nor seek the shore:
   The star of Brunswick smiles serene,
    And gilds the horrors of the deep."

Hor. Od. II. x. v. 1. *W.* " Nor let her tempt that deep, nor make the shore." Prior. Ode.

   V. 93. Pope, in his Essay on Criticism, has a similarly beautiful image, v. 645:

    " The mighty Stagyrite first left the shore,
      Spread all his sails, and durst the deeps explore;
    He steer'd securely, and discover'd far,
      Led by the light of the Mæonian star."

Young, in his " Universal Passion," Sat. vii. v. 169:

    " And outwatch every *star, for Brunswick's* sake."

THE FATAL SISTERS.

AN ODE. FROM THE NORSE TONGUE.

To be found in the Orcades of Thormodus Torfæus; Hafniæ, 1697, folio; and also in Bartholinus, p. 617, lib. iii. c. 1. 4to. (The song of the Weird Sisters, translated from the Norwegian, written about 1029. Wharton, MS.)

Vitt er orpit fyrir valfalli, &c.

In the eleventh century, *Sigurd*, earl of the Orkney Islands, went with a fleet of ships and a considerable body of troops into Ireland, to the assistance of *Sictryg with the Silken beard*, who was then making war on his father-in-law *Brian*, king of Dublin: the earl and all his forces were cut to pieces, and *Sictryg* was in danger of a total defeat; but the enemy had a greater loss by the death of *Brian* their king, who fell in the action.   On Christmas day (the day of the battle), a native of Caithness in Scotland, of the name of Darrud, saw at a distance a number of persons on horseback riding full speed towards a hill, and seeming to enter into it.   Curiosity led him to follow them, till looking through an opening in the rocks, he saw twelve gigantic figures resembling women: they were all employed about a loom; and as they wove, they sung the following dreadful song; which when they had finished, they tore the web into twelve pieces, and (each taking her portion) galloped six to the north, and as many to the south.   These were the *Valkyriur*, female divinities, Parcæ Militares, servants of *Odin* (or *Woden*) in the Gothic mythology.   Their name signifies *Choosers of the slain*. They were mounted on swift horses, with drawn swords in their hands; and in the throng of battle selected such as were destined to slaughter, and conducted them to *Valkalla*, the hall of *Odin*, or paradise of the brave; where they attended the banquet, and served the departed heroes with horns of mead and ale: their numbers are not agreed upon, some authors representing them as *six*, some as *four*.   See Magni Beronii diss. de Eddis Islandicis, p. 145, in Ælrichs. Dan. et Sued. lit. opuscula, vol. i.

Now the storm begins to lower,
(Haste, the loom of hell prepare,)
Iron sleet of arrowy shower
Hurtles in the darken'd air.

Glitt'ring lances are the loom,
Where the dusky warp we strain,
Weaving many a soldier's doom,
Orkney's woe, and Randver's bane.

Var. V. 5. Launces. MS.

V. 3.
" How quick they wheel'd, and, flying, behind them shot
Sharp *sleet of arrowy show'r*." Par. Reg. iii. 324. *Gray.*

Avianus has a similar expression: " Ausa *pharetratis imbribus*
ista loqui," Fab. xli. v. 6. " Sic et *imbrem ferreum* dicunt,
cum volunt multitudinem significare telorum," Lactant.
Epitome, c. xi. Virg. Æn. xii. 284: " Tempestas telorum ac
ferreus ingruit imber." Many other examples could be given.

Thick *storms* of bullets ran like winter's *hail*,
And shiver'd lances *dark the troubled air*."
Spanish Trag. Vid. Hawkins. Ant. Drama.

V. 4. " The noise of battle hurtled in the air."
Julius Cæsar, act ii. s. 2. *Gray.*

V. 7. In Thomson. Masque of Alfred, p. 126, the weaving
of the enchanted standard is thus described:

" ———— 'Tis the same
Wrought by the sisters of the Danish king,
Of furious Ivar, in a midnight hour,
While the sick moon, at their enchanted song
Wrapt in pale tempest, labour'd thro' the clouds.
The *demons of destruction* then, (they say,)
Were all abroad, and mixing with the *woof*
Their baleful power; the Sisters even sung,
' Shake, standard, shake, this ruin on our foes ! ' "

See the grisly texture grow!
   ('Tis of human entrails made)   10
And the weights, that play below,
   Each a gasping warrior's head.

Shafts for shuttles, dipt in gore,
   Shoot the trembling cords along.
Swords, that once a monarch bore,   15
   Keep the tissue close and strong.

Mista, black terrific maid,
   Sangrida, and Hilda, see,
Join the wayward work to aid:
   'Tis the woof of victory.   20

Ere the ruddy sun be set,
   Pikes must shiver, javelins sing,
Blade with clattering buckler meet,
   Hauberk crash, and helmet ring.

(Weave the crimson web of war)   25
   Let us go, and let us fly,

Var. V. 15. *Sword*] Blade. MS.
    V. 17. *Mista, black*] Sangrida, terrific. MS.
    V. 18. *Sangrida and*] Mista black, and. MS.
    V. 23. *Blade*] Sword. W. MS.

V. 11. Dr. Warton, in his Notes on Pope (vol. ii. p. 227), has compared this passage of Gray to some lines in the Thebais of Statius, i. 720.

V. 17. The names of the Sisters, in the original, are Hilda, Hiorthrimula, Sangrida, and Swipula.

Where our friends the conflict share,
   Where they triumph, where they die.

As the paths of fate we tread,
   Wading through th' ensanguin'd field,   30
Gondula and Geira, spread
   O'er the youthful king your shield.

We the reins to slaughter give,
   Ours to kill, and ours to spare:
Spite of danger he shall live.   35
   (Weave the crimson web of war.)

They, whom once the desert-beach
   Pent within its bleak domain,
Soon their ample sway shall stretch
   O'er the plenty of the plain.   40

Low the dauntless earl is laid,
   Gor'd with many a gaping wound:
Fate demands a nobler head;
   Soon a king shall bite the ground.

Long his loss shall Eirin weep,   45
   Ne'er again his likeness see;

Var. V. 31. *Gondula and Geira*] Gunna and Gondula. MS.
   V. 44. *Shall*] Must. MS.

   V. 40. " Insult the plenty of the vales below."
                     Essay on the Alliance, &c. *Luke.*
   V. 44. (Shall bite the ground) " Θνητοι ὀδαξ ἑλον ὀυδας."
Hom. ——
   V. 45. *Eirin*] Ireland.

Long her strains in sorrow steep;
  Strains of immortality!

Horror covers all the heath,
  Clouds of carnage blot the sun.   50
Sisters, weave the web of death;
  Sisters, cease; the work is done.

Hail the task, and hail the hands!
  Songs of joy and triumph sing!
Joy to the victorious bands;   55
  Triumph to the younger king.

Mortal, thou that hear'st the tale,
  Learn the tenour of our song.
Scotland, thro' each winding vale
  Far and wide the notes prolong.   60

Var. V. 49. Heath! MS.
  V. 50. *Blot*] Veil. MS.
  V. 50 Sun! MS.
  V. 59. *Winding*] Echoing. MS.

V. 49. This stanza, as it appears in the original, Mr. Herbert has translated without the insertion or omission of a
word:
  " 'Tis horrid now to gaze around,
    While clouds thro' heaven gore-dropping sail;
    Air must be stain'd with blood of men,
    Ere all our oracles shall fail."
                    Select Icelandic Poetry, p. 50.
  V. 59. This and the following line are not in the original.
Indeed, this poem is not so much a translation, as a loose,
though highly-spirited paraphrase; and, as Herbert observes,
inferior to the "Descent of Odin."
  V. 61. "Bear me hence on wheels of speed."
                    V. Philips. (Pind. 1. Æn. 3.)

Sisters, hence with spurs of speed:
Each her thundering faulchion wield;
Each bestride her sable steed.
Hurry, hurry to the field!

V. 61—64.

> " Sisters, hence, 'tis time to ride:
>   Now your thundering faulchion wield;
>   Now your sable steed bestride.
>   Hurry, hurry to the field." MS.

THE VEGTAM'S KIVITHA;

OR, THE DESCENT OF ODIN. * AN ODE. FROM THE

NORSE TONGUE.

[The original is to be found in Saemund's Edda, and in Bartholinus, De Causis contemnendæ Mortis; Hafniæ, 1689, quarto,
Lib. III. c. ii. p. 632. (See Warton. Hist. of E. Poetry,
vol. i. p. xii. And Warton's Pope, vol. ii. p. 70. " This
Ode, I think with Lord Orford, equal to any of Gray's."]

Upreis Odinn allda gautr, &c.

---

* This Ode is much more literally translated than the preceding. The original title I have restored from Gray's MS.
The first five stanzas of this Ode are omitted; in which Balder, one of the sons of Odin, was informed that he should soon
die. Upon his communication of his dream, the other gods,
finding it true by consulting the oracles, agreed to ward off
the approaching danger, and sent Frigga to exact an oath from
every thing not to injure Balder. She, however, overlooked
the Misletoe, with a branch of which he was afterwards slain
by Hoder, at the instigation of Lok. After the execution of
this commission, Odin, still alarmed for the life of his son,

UPROSE the king of men with speed,
And saddled straight his coal-black steed;
Down the yawning steep he rode,
That leads to Hela's drear abode.
Him the dog of darkness spied;
His shaggy throat he open'd wide,
(While from his jaws, with carnage fill'd,
Foam and human gore distill'd:)
Hoarse he bays with hideous din,
Eyes that glow, and fangs that grin;   10
And long pursues, with fruitless yell,
The father of the powerful spell.
Onward still his way he takes,
(The groaning earth beneath him shakes,

Var. V. 7. (So MS. Wh.)
V. 11. *Fruitless*] Ceaseless. MS.

---

called another council; and hearing nothing but divided
opinions among the gods, to consult the Prophetess, "he uprose with speed." Vali, or Ali, the son of Rinda, afterwards
avenged the death of Balder, by slaying Hoder, and is called
a "wondrous boy, because he killed his enemy, before he was a
day old; before he had washed his face, combed his hair, or
seen one setting-sun." See Herbert's Icelandic Translations,
p. 45; to which I am indebted for part of this note. And the
Edda of Saemund, translated by Cottle. See also the Introduction to the Descent of Frea, in Sayer. Dramatic Sketches
of H. Mythology, 1792

V. 1. "When straight uprose the king of men."
Chapman. Homer. Il. xiii. p. 43.

V. 2. Sleipner was the horse of Odin, which had eight legs.
Vide Edda. *Mason.* "And *coal black steeds* yborne of hellish
brood." Spens. F. Q. I. v. xx. *Luke.*

V. 4. Vid. Cottle's Edda. "Song of Vafthrudnes," p. 29.
Note. Niflheliar, the hell of the Gothic nations, consisted

Till full before his fearless eyes   15
The portals nine of hell arise.

Right against the eastern gate,
By the moss-grown pile he sate;
Where long of yore to sleep was laid
The dust of the prophetic maid.   20
Facing to the northern clime,
Thrice he trac'd the Runic rhyme;
Thrice pronounc'd, in accents dread,
The thrilling verse that wakes the dead:
Till from out the hollow ground   25
Slowly breath'd a sullen sound.

V. 14. *Shakes*] Quakes. MS.
V. 23. *Accents*] Murmurs. MS.

---

of nine worlds, to which were devoted all such as died of
sickness, old age, or by any other means than in battle. Over
it presided Hela, the goddess of death. *Mason.*
    Hela, in the Edda, is described with a dreadful countenance,
and her body half flesh colour, and half blue. *Gray.*

V. 5. The Edda gives this dog the name of Managarmar.
He fed upon the lives of those that were to die. *Mason.*

V. 17. "Right against the eastern gate
          When the great sun begins his state."
                              L'Alleg. v. 60.   Warton. note.

V. 22. In a little poem called the "Magic of Odin," (see
Bartholinus, p. 641,) Odin says, "If I see a man dead, and
hanging aloft on a tree, I engrave *Runic characters* so won-
derful, that the man immediately descends and converses with
me. When I see magicians travelling through the air, I
disconcert them with a single look, and force them to abandon
their enterprize."

V. 24. The original word is *Valgalldr;* from *Valr* mortuus,
and *Galldr* incantatio. *Gray.*

PROPHETESS.

What call unknown, what charms presume
To break the quiet of the tomb?
Who thus afflicts my troubled sprite,
And drags me from the realms of night?   30
Long on these mould'ring bones have beat
The winter's snow, the summer's heat,
The drenching dews, and driving rain!
Let me, let me sleep again.
Who is he, with voice unblest,   35
That calls me from the bed of rest?

ODIN.

A traveller, to thee unknown,
Is he that calls, a warrior's son.
Thou the deeds of light shalt know
Tell me what is done below,   40

Var. V. 27. *What call unknown*] What voice unknown. MS.
 V. 29. *My troubled*] A weary. MS.
 V. 35. *He*] This. MS.

V. 27. " What power art thou, who from below
            Hast made me rise."   Dryd. K. Arth. vi.

V. 33. " Till cold December comes with *driving rain.*"
                            Dryden. Virg. G. i. 301. *Luke.*

V. 34. This and the two following verses are not in the
original, and therefore Gray probably borrowed them from
the Thessalian Incantation in Lucan. Ph. vi. 820: " Sic post-
quam fata peregit, stat vultu mœstus tacito, *mortemque repos-
cit.*" See Quart. Rev. No. xxii. p. 314. " Let me, let me rest."
Pope. " Let me, let me drop my freight." Dryden. Sec.
Mag. *Rogers.* " Let me, let me freeze again to death."
Dryden. K. Arth.

V. 40. Odin was anxious about the fate of his son, Balder,
who had dreamed he was soon to die. He was killed by Odin's
other son, Hoder, who was himself slain by Vali, the son of
Odin and Rinda, consonant with this prophecy. See the Edda.

For whom yon glitt'ring board is spread.
Dress'd for whom yon golden bed?

PROPHETESS.

Mantling in the goblet see
The pure bev'rage of the bee:
O'er it hangs the shield of gold; 45
'Tis the drink of Balder bold:
Balder's head to death is giv'n.
Pain can reach the sons of heav'n!
Unwilling I my lips unclose:
Leave me, leave me to repose. 50

ODIN.

Once again my call obey:
Prophetess, arise, and say,
What dangers Odin's child await,
Who the author of his fate?

Var. V. 41. *Yon*] The. MS.
 V. 48. *Reach*] Touch. MS.
 V. 51, 52. *Once again, &c.*]
  " Prophetess, my call obey,
  Once again arise and say." MS.

V. 42. " Non movet *aurea* pompa *thori.*" Prudent. π. Σ r.
iii. v. iii. " Aurato lecto." Juv. Sat. vi.
 V. 43. "The spiced *goblets mantled* high."
       T. Warton. Works, ii. 74.
 V. 50. " Quid, oro, me post Lethæa pocula, jam Stygiis pa-
ludibus innatantem ad momentariæ vitæ reducitis officia ?
Desine jam, precor, *desine, nc me in meam quietem permitte,*"
Apul. Memor. ii. 40. quoted in the Quarterly Rev. No. xxii.
p. 314.
 V. 51. Women were looked upon by the Gothic nations as
having a peculiar insight into futurity; and some there were
that made profession of magic arts and divination. These
travelled round the country, and were received in every house
with great respect and honour. Such a woman bore the name

PROPHETESS.

In Hoder's hand the hero's doom;   55
His brother sends him to the tomb.
Now my weary lips I close:
Leave me, leave me to repose.

ODIN.

Prophetess, my spell obey:
Once again arise, and say,   60
Who th' avenger of his guilt,
By whom shall Hoder's blood be spilt?

PROPHETESS.

In the caverns of the west,
By Odin's fierce embrace comprest,

Var. V. 59, 60. *Prophetess, &c.*]
    "Once again my call obey,
      Prophetess, arise and say." MS.
    V. 61, 62. *Who th' avenger, &c.*] These verses are transposed in MS.

---

of Volva Seidkona or Spakona. The dress of Thorbiorga, one of these prophetesses, is described at large in Eirik's Rauda Sogu, (apud Bartholin. lib. i. cap. iv. p. 688.) "She had on a blue vest spangled all over with stones, a necklace of glass beads, and a cap made of the skin of a black lamb lined with white cat-skin. She leaned on a staff adorned with brass, with a round head set with stones; and was girt with an Hunland-ish belt, at which hung her pouch full of magical instruments. Her buskins were of rough calf-skin, bound on with thongs studded with knobs of brass, and her gloves of white cat-skin, the fur turned inwards," &c. They were also called *Fiolkyngi,* or *Fiolkunnug,* i. e. Multi-scia; and *Visindakona,* i. e. Oraculorum Mulier; *Nornir,* i. e. Parcæ. *Gray.*

V. 58. "When my weary lips I close
    And slumber, 'tis without repose."
          N. Tate. Poems, p. 90.

V. 66. King Harold made (according to the singular custom of his time) a solemn vow never to *clip or comb his hair,* till he should have extended his sway over the whole country.

A wond'rous boy shall Rinda bear,   65
Who ne'er shall comb his raven hair,
Nor wash his visage in the stream,
Nor see the sun's departing beam,
Till he on Hoder's corse shall smile
Flaming on the fun'ral pile.   70
Now my weary lips I close:
Leave me, leave me to repose.

ODIN.

Yet a while my call obey:
Prophetess, awake, and say,
What virgins these, in speechless woe,   75

Var. V. 65. *Wond'rous*] Giant. MS.
     V. 74. *Awake*] Arise. MS.

Herbert. Iceland Translat. p. 39. In the Dying Song of
Asbiorn, p. 52:

"Know, gentle mother, know,
Thou wilt *not comb my flowing hair*,
When summer sweets return,
In Denmark's vallies, Svanvhide fair!"

V. 75. "It is not certain," says Mr. Herbert, "what Odin
means by the question concerning the weeping virgins; but it
has been supposed that it alludes to the embassy afterwards
sent by Frigga to try to redeem Balder from the infernal
regions, and that Odin betrays his divinity by mentioning
what had not yet happened." Iceland. Translat. p. 48. —
The object of this embassy was frustrated by the perfidy of
Loke, who, having assumed (as was supposed) the shape of an
old woman, refused to join in the general petition. "I Lok
(she said) will weep with *dry eyes* the funeral of Balder. Let
all things, living or dead, weep if they will, but let Hela keep
her prey." — After this, Loke hid himself, built a house
among the mountains, and made a net. Odin, however, found
out his hiding-place, and the gods assembled to take him. He,
seeing this, burnt his net, and changed himself into a salmon.
After some trouble, Thor caught him by the *tail;* and this is
the reason why salmons, ever after, have had their tails so fine

That bend to earth their solemn brow,
That their flaxen tresses tear,
And snowy veils that float in air?
Tell me whence their sorrows rose:
Then I leave thee to repose.   80

PROPHETESS.

Ha! no traveller art thou,
King of men, I know thee now;
Mightiest of a mighty line ——

ODIN.

No boding maid of skill divine

Var. V. 77. *That, flaxen*] Who, flowing. MS.
    V. 79. Say from whence. MS.
    V. 83. The mightiest of the mighty line. MS.

---

and thin. They bound him with chains, and suspended the
serpent Skada over his head, whose venom falls upon his face
drop by drop. His wife Siguna sits by his side, catches the
drops as they fall from his face in a basin, which she empties
as often as it is filled. He will remain in chains till the end
of the world, or, as the Icelanders call it, the Twilight of the
Gods. To this the prophetess alludes in the last stanza. See
Butler. Hor. Bibl. ii. 194.

V. 76. This and the following verse are not in the Latin
translation.

V. 82. " Great Love ! I know thee now,
          Eldest of the Gods, art thou."
                              Dryden. K. Arth. *Rogers.*

V. 86. In the Latin, " mater trium gigantum: " probably
Angerbode, who from her name seems to be " no prophetess
of good; " and who bore to Loke, as the Edda says, three
children, the wolf Fenris, the great serpent of Midgard, and
Hela, all of them called giants in that system of mythology.
Mason. Sams. Agon. 1247, "I dread him not, nor all his
giant-brood. Luke.

V. 88. In the original, this and the three following lines
are represented by this couplet:

Art thou, nor prophetess of good ;   85
But mother of the giant brood !

PROPHETESS.

Hie thee hence, and boast at home,
That never shall enquirer come
To break my iron-sleep again ;
Till Lok has burst his tenfold chain ;   90
Never, till substantial night
Has reassum'd her ancient right ;
Till wrapt in flames, in ruin hurl'd,
Sinks the fabric of the world.

Var. V. 87. Hie thee, Odin, boast   MS.
     V. 90. *Has*] Have.   MS.
     V. 92. *Has reassum'd*] Reassumes her.   MS.

" Et deorum crepusculum
      Dissolventes aderint."

W. Herbert has published a translation of the introductory
lines of this poem, and also much curious information illustra-
ting several passages in the text.   See his Select Iceland.
Poetry, p. 43.   He mentions some little amplifications in Gray,
tending to convey notions of the Icelandic mythology, not
warranted by the original, as " *Coal-black* steed; " *Raven-*
hair; " " *Thrice* he trac'd the Runic rhyme; " " The portals
nine of hell; " " Foam and *human* gore."

V. 89. " χάλκεος ὕπνος," Hom.   " *Ferreus* somnus," Virg.
Æn. xii. 309.   " Iron sleep," Dryden.   And " An iron slumber shuts my sleeping eyes," Dryden. Georg. iv. 717.

V. 90. Lok is the evil being, who continues in chains till
the *twilight of the gods* approaches: when he shall break his
bonds, the human race, the stars, and sun, shall disappear; the
earth sink in the seas, and fire consume the skies: even Odin
himself and his kindred deities shall perish.   For a further
explanation of this mythology, see " Introd. à l'Hist. de Dan-
nemare par Mallet," 1755, quarto; or rather a translation of
it published in 1770, and entitled " Northern Antiquities; "
in which some mistakes in the original are judiciously corrected.   *Mason.*

THE TRIUMPHS OF OWEN.*

A FRAGMENT.   FROM THE WELSH.

[From Evans. Spec. of the Welsh Poetry, 1764, quarto, p. 25,
    where is a Prose version of this Poem, and p. 127. Owen
    succeeded his father Griffith app Cynan in the principality
    of N. Wales, A.D. 1137. This battle was fought in the
    year 1157. Jones. Relics, vol. ii. p. 36.]

Owen's praise demands my song,
Owen swift, and Owen strong;
Fairest flower of Roderic's stem,
Gwyneth's shield, and Britain's gem,
He nor heaps his brooded stores,   5
Nor on all profusely pours;
Lord of every regal art,
Liberal hand, and open heart.

Compare with this poem, "Hermode's Journey to Hell," in
Dr. Percy's Translation of Mallet's Northern Antiquities,
vol. ii. p. 149. See Beronii Diss. de Eddis Island. p. 153.
Mundi credita ἐκπύρωσις in qua solem nigrescere, tellurem in
mari submersam iri, stellas de cœlo lapsuras, ignem in vetustam
orbis molem et fabricam disævituram, v. Sibyll. Velusp. Stroph.
liii.
    * The original Welsh of the above poem was the compo-
sition of Gwalchmai the son of Melir, immediately after Prince
Owen Gwynedd had defeated the combined fleets of Iceland,
Denmark, and Norway, which had invaded his territory on
the coast of Anglesea. There is likewise another poem which
describes this famous battle, written by Prince Howel, the son
of Owen Gwynedd; a literal translation of which may be seen
in Jones. Relics, vol. ii. p. 36. In Mason's edition, and in all
the subsequent editions, it is said that Owen succeeded his

Big with hosts of mighty name,
Squadrons three against him came;　10
This the force of Eirin hiding,
Side by side as proudly riding,
On her shadow long and gay
Lochlin plows the wat'ry way;
There the Norman sails afar　15
Catch the winds and join the war:
Black and huge along they sweep,
Burdens of the angry deep.

Dauntless on his native sands
The dragon-son of Mona stands;　20
In glitt'ring arms and glory drest,
High he rears his ruby crest.
There the thund'ring strokes begin,
There the press, and there the din;

father, A.D. 1120. The date I have altered, agreeably to
the text of Mr. Jones, to A.D. 1137.

V. 4. *Gwyneth*] North Wales.

V. 8. " With open heart and bounteous hand."
Swift. Cad. and Van.

V. 10. " A battle round of *squadrons three* they shew."
Fairfax. Tasso, xviii. 96.

V. 13. " And on her shadow rides in floating gold."
. Dryden. A. Mir.　*G. Steevens.*

V. 14. *Lochlin*] Denmark.

" Watery way," Dryden. Æn. iii. 330.　*Rogers.*

V. 20. The red dragon is the device of Cadwallader, which
all his descendants bore on their banners. *Mason.*

V. 23. " It seems (says Dr. Evans, p. 26,) that the fleet
landed in some part of the frith of Menai, and that it was a
kind of mixt engagement, some fighting from the shore, others
from the ships; and probably the great slaughter was owing

Talymalfra's rocky shore   25
Echoing to the battle's roar.
Check'd by the torrent-tide of blood,
Backward Meinai rolls his flood;
While, heap'd his master's feet around,
Prostrate warriors gnaw the ground.   30
Where his glowing eye-balls turn,
Thousand banners round him burn:
Where he points his purple spear,
Hasty, hasty rout is there,
Marking with indignant eye   35
Fear to stop, and shame to fly.
There confusion, terror's child,
Conflict fierce, and ruin wild,
Agony, that pants for breath,
Despair and honourable death.   40

      *   *   *   *   *

---

to its being low water, and that they could not sail. This will
doubtless remind many of the spirited account delivered by
the noblest historian of ancient Greece, of a similar conflict
on the shore of Pylus, between the Athenians and the Spar-
tans under the gallant Brasidas. Thucyd. Bel. Pelop. lib. iv.
cap. 12."

V. 25. " Tal Moelvre." *Jones.*

V. 27. This and the three following lines are not in the
former editions, but are now added from the author's MS.

Mason.

V. 31. From this line to the conclusion, the translation is
indebted to the genius of Gray, very little of it being in the
original, which closes with a sentiment omitted by the translator: " And the glory of our Prince's wide-wasting sword
shall be celebrated in a hundred languages, to give him his
merited praise."

THE DEATH OF HOEL.

AN ODE.   SELECTED FROM THE GODODIN.*

[See S. Turner's Vindication of Ancient British Poems, p 50.
Warton's Engl. Poetry, vol. i. p. lxiii.]

HAD I but the torrent's might,
With headlong rage and wild affright
Upon Deïra's squadrons hurl'd
To rush, and sweep them from the world!

---

* Of Aneurin, styled the Monarch of the Bards. He flourished about the time of Taliessin, A.D. 570.[1] This Ode is
extracted from the Gododin. See Evans. Specimens, p. 71 and
73.   This poem is extremely difficult to be understood, being
written, if not in the Pictish, at least in a dialect of the Britons,
very different from the modern Welsh. See Evans, p. 68–75.
   "Aneurin with the flowing Muse, King of Bards, brother to
Gildas Albanius the historian, lived under Mynyddawg of
Edinburgh, a prince of the North, whose Eurdorchogion, or
warriors wearing the golden torques, three hundred and sixty-
three in number, were all slain, except Aneurin and two others,
in a battle with the Saxons at Cattraeth, on the eastern coast
of Yorkshire.   His Gododin, an heroic poem written on that
event, is perhaps the oldest and noblest production of that age."
Jones. Relics, vol. i. p. 17. — Taliessin composed a poem called
'Cunobiline's Incantation,' in emulation of excelling the Gododin of Aneurin his rival.   He accomplished his aim, in the
opinion of subsequent bards, by condensing the prolixity, without losing the ideas, of his opponent.

V. 3. The kingdom of Deïra included the counties of Yorkshire, Durham, Lancashire, Westmoreland, and Cumberland.
See Jones. Relics, vol. i. p. 17.

---

[1] Mr. Jones, in his Relics, vol. i. p. 17, says, that Aneurin
flourished about A. D. 510.

Too, too secure in youthful pride,   5
By them, my friend, my Hoel, died,
Great Cian's son: of Madoc old
He ask'd no heaps of hoarded gold;
Alone in nature's wealth array'd,
He ask'd and had the lovely maid.   10

To Cattraeth's vale in glitt'ring row
Twice two hundred warriors go:
Every warrior's manly neck
Chains of regal honour deck,
Wreath'd in many a golden link: 15
From the golden cup they drink
Nectar that the bees produce,
Or the grape's extatic juice.
Flush'd with mirth and hope they burn:
But none from Cattraeth's vale return,   20

V. 7. *Cian*] In Jones. Relics, it is spelt 'Kian.'

V. 11. In the rival poem of Taliessin mentioned before, this circumstance is thus expressed: "Three, and threescore, and three hundred heroes flocked to the variegated banners of Cattraeth ; but of those who hastened from the flowing mead-goblet, save three, returned not. Cynon and Cattraeth with hymns they commemorate, and me for my blood they mutually lament." See Jones. Relics, vol. ii. p. 14. — "The great topic perpetually recurring in the Gododin is, that the Britons lost the battle of Cattraeth, and suffered so severely, because they had drunk their mead too profusely. The passages in the Gododin are numerous on this point." See Sharon Turner's Vindication of the Anc. British Poems, p. 51.

V. 14. See Sayer's War Song, from the Gaelic, in his Poems, p. 174.

V. 17. See Fr. Goldsmith. Transl. of Grotius. Joseph Sophompancas. p. 9. " Nectar of the Bees," and Euripid Bacchæ. v. 143. ῥεῖ δὲ μελισσᾶν νέκταρι.

Save Aeron brave, and Conan strong,
(Bursting through the bloody throng,)
And I, the meanest of them all,
That live to weep and sing their fall.   24

HAVE ye seen the tusky boar,*
Or the bull, with sullen roar,
On surrounding foes advance?
So Caràdoc bore his lance.

CONAN's name,† my lay, rehearse,
Build to him the lofty verse,
Sacred tribute of the bard,
Verse, the hero's sole reward.
As the flame's devouring force;   5
As the whirlwind in its course;

V. 20. In the Latin translation: "Ex iis autem, qui *nimio potu madidi* ad bellum properabant, non evasere nisi tres."

V. 21. Properly 'Conon,' or, as in the Welsh, 'Chynon.'

V. 23. In the Latin translation: "Et egomet ipse sanguine rubens, aliter ad hoc carmen compingendum non superstes fuissem." *M.* — " Gray has given a kind of sentimental modesty to his Bard which is quite out of place." *Quarterly Review.*

* This and the following short fragment ought to have appeared among the Posthumous Pieces of Gray; but it was thought preferable to insert them in this place, with the preceding fragment from the Gododin. See Jones. Relics, vol. i. p. 17.

† In Jones. Relics, vol. i. p. 17, it is ' *Vedel's* name ; ' and in turning to the original I see ' Rhudd Fedel,' as well as in the Latin translation of Dr. Evans, p. 75.

V. 2. "He knew himself to sing, and build *the lofty rhyme.*" Milt. Lycidas   *Luke.*

As the thunder's fiery stroke,
Glancing on the shiver'd oak;
Did the sword of Conan mow
The crimson harvest of the foe.

SONNET.

ON THE DEATH OF MR. RICHARD WEST.

[See W. S. Landori Poemata, p. 186.]

In vain tò me the smiling mornings shine,
    And redd'ning Phœbus lifts his golden fire;
The birds in vain their amorous descant join,
    Or cheerful fields resume their green attire:
These ears, alas! for other notes repine,
    A different object do these eyes require:
My lonely anguish melts no heart but mine;
    And in my breast the imperfect joys expire.

V. 9. "Primosque et extremos metendo stravit humum, sine clade victor." Hor. Od. iv. 14, 31.

V. 1. Milt. P. L. v. 168, "That crown'st the *smiling morn*." *Luke.*

V. 2. Lucret. vi. 204, "Devolet in terram liquidi color *aureus ignis*." *Luke.*

V. 3. Milt. P. L. iv. 602, "She all night long her *amorous descant* sung." *Luke.*

V. 8. " And in my car the imperfect accent dies."
                        Dryden. Ovid. *Rogers.*

V. 12. Spens. B. Id. cant. iii. st. 5: " On these Cupido winged armies led, of *little loves*." *Luke.*

V. 14. A line similar to this occurs in Cibber's Alteration of Richard the Third, act ii. sc. 2:

Yet morning smiles the busy race to cheer,   9
  And new-born pleasure brings to happier men :
The fields to all their wonted tribute bear ;
  To warm their little loves the birds complain :
I fruitless mourn to him that cannot hear,
  And weep the more, because I weep in vain.

EPITAPH ON MRS. JANE CLERKE.

[See Woty's Poetical Calendar, part viii. p. 121. Nicoll's
Select Poems, vol. vii. p. 331.]

This lady, the wife of Dr. John Clerke, physician at Epsom,
died April 27, 1757; and was buried in the church of
Beckenham, Kent.

Lo ! where this silent marble weeps,
A friend, a wife, a mother sleeps:
A heart, within whose sacred cell
The peaceful virtues lov'd to dwell.

" So we must weep, because we weep in vain."

" Solon, when he wept for his son's death, on one saying to
him, 'Weeping will not help,' answered : Δὶ αὐτὸ δὲ τοῦτο
δακρύω, ὅτι οὐδὲν ἀνύττω· ' I weep for that very cause, that
weeping will not avail.' " See Diog. Laert. vol. i. p. 39. ed.
Meibomii. It is also told of Augustus. See also Fitzgeffry's
Life and Death of Sir Francis Drake, B. 99.

  " Oh ! therefore do we plaine,
And therefore weepe, because we weepe in vaine."

See also Dodsley's Old Plays, vol. x. p. 139, and Bamfylde's
Sonnets, p. 6. ed. Park.

V. 1. " This *weeping marble* had not ask'd a tear."
Pope. Epitaph on Ed. D. of Buckingham. And Winds. For.
" There o'er the martyr-king the *marble weeps*," 313. " Orat
te *flebile Saxum*." Burn. Anthol. Lat. vol. ii. p. 282.

Affection warm, and faith sincere,   5
And soft humanity were there.
In agony, in death resign'd,
She felt the wound she left behind.
Her infant image, here below,
Sits smiling on a father's woe: 10
Whom what awaits, while yet he strays
Along the lonely vale of days?
A pang, to secret sorrow dear;
A sigh; an unavailing tear;
Till time shall every grief remove,   15
With life, with memory, and with love.

Var. V 7—10. *In agony, &c.*]
　　" To hide her cares her only art,
　　　Her pleasure, pleasures to impart,
　　　In ling'ring pain, in death resign'd,
　　　Her latest agony of mind
　　　Was felt for him who could not save
　　　His all from an untimely grave." MS.

V. 6. " And *soft humanity* that from rebellion fled," Dryden. Thr. Aug. s. xii. " Bred to the rules of *soft humanity*,"
ditto All for Love, act. ii. sc. i. " Oh ! *soft humanity* in age
beloved," Pope. Epitaph ix. " The *soft* virtue of *humanity*."
A. Smith. Mor. Sent. v. i. p. 310

EPITAPH ON SIR WILLIAM WILLIAMS.*

This Epitaph was written at the request of Mr. Frederick Montagu, who intended to have inscribed it on a monument at Bellisle, at the siege of which Sir W. Williams was killed, 1761. See Mason's Memoirs, vol. i. p. 73 ; and vol. iv. p. 76; and H. Walpole's Lett. to G. Montagu, p. 244. See account of Sir W. P. Williams, in Brydges. Restituta, vol. iii. p. 53; and in Clubs of London, vol. ii. p. 13. "In the recklessness of a desponding mind, he approached too near the enemy's sentinels, and was shot through the body."

" Valiant in arms, courteous and gay in peace,
See *Williams* snatch'd to an untimely tomb."
Hall Stevenson's Poems, ii. p. 49.

HERE, foremost in the dangerous paths of fame,
Young Williams fought for England's fair re-
nown ;
His mind each Muse, each Grace adorn'd his
frame,
Nor envy dar'd to view him with a frown.

---

* Sir William Peere Williams, bart. a captain in Burgoyne's dragoons.

V. 3. Εἵνεκεν εὐεπίης πινυτόφρονος, ἦν ὁ μελιχρὸς
ἤσκησεν Μουσῶν, ἄμμιγα καὶ Χαρίτων.
Sophoc. Epit. ed. Brunck. vol. i. p. 10.

Τὸν Μώσαις φίλον ἄνδρα, τὸν οὐ Νυμφαίοιν ἀπέχθη.
Theocr. Idyll. a. 141,

I recollect also the same expression in Gregory Nazianzen's Epitaph on Euphomius. ὄυτος ὃν αἱ χάριτες μόυσαις δόσαν.

" A thousand *Graces* round her *person* play,
And all the *Muses* mark'd her *fancy's* way."
A. Hill. Poems, vol. iii. p. 60.

At Aix, his voluntary sword he drew,
  There first in blood his infant honour seal'd;
From fortune, pleasure, science, love, he flew,
  And scorn'd repose when Britain took the field

With eyes of flame, and cool undaunted breast,
  Victor he stood on Bellisle's rocky steeps — 1c
Ah, gallant youth! this marble tells the rest,
  Where melancholy friendship bends, and weeps.

ELEGY WRITTEN IN A COUNTRY CHURCH-YARD.

The manuscript variations in this poem, in the Wharton papers, agree generally with those published by Mr. Mathias,
vol. i. p. 65, in his edition of Gray's Works. See Barrington
on the Statutes, p. 154. British Bibliog. vol. iii. p. viii.

THE curfew tolls the knell of parting day,
  The lowing herd winds slowly o'er the lea,
The ploughman homeward plods his weary way,
  And leaves the world to darkness and to me.

V. 5. Sir William Williams, in the expedition to Aix, was
on board the Magnanime with Lord Howe; and was deputed
to receive the capitulation. This expression has been adopted
by Scott:
  "Since riding side by side, our hand
  First *drew the voluntary brand.*'
        Marmion, Introd. to Cant. iv
V. 1.   —— " squilla di lontano
  Che paia 'l giorno pianger, che si muore."
        Dante, Purgat. l. 8. *Gray*

Now fades the glimmering landscape on the sight,
    And all the air a solemn stillness holds,   6
Save where the beetle wheels his droning flight,
    And drowsy tinklings lull the distant folds:

Var. V. 8. And] Or. ms. M. and W.

" The curfew tolls ! — the knell of parting day."
So I read, says Dr. Warton, Notes on Pope, vol. i. p. 82.
Dryden has a line resembling this:
    " That <i>tolls the knell</i> of their <i>departed</i> sense."
See Prol. to Troilus and Cressida, ver. 22.   And not dissimilar
is Shakes. Henry IV. pt. ii. act i. sc. 2:
        —— " a sullen <i>bell</i>
Remember'd <i>knolling a departed</i> friend."
    V. 2. In the Diosem. of Aratus, this picture is drawn similar
to that of the English poet, ver. 387:

'Η δ' ὅτε μυκηθμοῖο περίπλειοι ἀγέρωνται
Ἐρχόμεναι σταθμόνδε βοές βουλύσιον ὥρην,
Σκυθραὶ λειμωνὸς πόριες καὶ βουβοσίοιο.

And so Dionys. in his Perieg. ver. 190:

Κείνοις δ' ὅυποτε τερπνὸς ἀκούεται ὁλκὸς ἀμάξης,
Οὐ δὲ βοῶν μυκηθμὸς ἐς αὔλιον ἐρχομενάων.

See also Hom. Odyss. xvii. 170, pointed out by Wakefield.
Add Petrarch, " Veggio la sera, i buoi tornare sciolte, de le
campagne e de solcate colli."
    V. 3. Spens. F. Q. b. vi. st. 7. c. 39:
    " And now she was upon the <i>weary way</i>." <i>Luke.</i>
    V. 4. A similar expression occurs in Petrarch, p. 124:
    " Quando 'l sol bagna in mar l' aurato cerco,
        E 'l aer nostro, e la mia mente imbruna."
" Has paid his debt to justice and to me." Dryd. Ovid.
                                          Rogers.
" E lascia il Mundo al Foscombra." Ariosto. <i>Rogers.</i>
    V. 7.   —— " Ere the bat hath flown
His cloister'd flight; ere, to black Hecate's summons,
The shard-borne <i>beetle with his drowsy hum</i>
Hath rung night's yawning peal." Macb. act iii. sc. 2.
And so Collins, in his Ode to Evening:
    " Or where the <i>beetle winds</i>
        His <i>small, but sullen horn;</i>

Save that from yonder ivy-mantled tow'r,
    The moping owl does to the moon complain 10
Of such as, wand'ring near her secret bow'r,
    Molest her ancient solitary reign.

Beneath those rugged elms, that yew-tree's shade,
    Where heaves the turf in many a mould'ring
      heap,
Each in his narrow cell for ever laid,   15
    The rude forefathers of the hamlet sleep.

    As oft he rises midst the twilight path,
    Against the pilgrim borne in heedless hum." *W.*

V. 10. The " ignavus bubo" of Ovid. Met. v. 550. The two following passages might supply the images in the Elegy:

    " Assiduous in his *bower* the *wailing owl*
    Plies his sad song." Thoms. Winter, 114.

And   " the *wailing owl*
      Screams solitary to the mournful *moon*."
                  Mallett. Excursion, p. 244.

V. 12. " Desertaque . regna pastorum," Virg. Georg. iii. 476. *W.*

V. 13. De Lille, in his " Jardins," has imitated these stanzas of the Elegy, cant. iv. p. 86.

V. 14. " Those graves with bending osier bound,
    That nameless *heave* the *crumbl,d* ground."
              Parnell. Night Piece, 29. *W.*

V. 15. See Hor. Od. i. iv. 17 : " Domus exilis Plutonia." The word *domus*, which answers to our poet's *cell*, is often in Latin authors put for *sepulchrum;* as may be seen by referring to Burmann's Petronius, cap. 71 ; and Markland's Statius, p. 255: the reason of which is given in Barthelemy. Travels in Italy, p. 349.

V. 17. " And e'er the *odorous breath of morn*."
                  Arcades, ver. 56.

    " In Eden, on the humid flowers that breath'd
    Their *morning incense.*" Par. L. b. ix. 192. *W.*

And so Pope. Messiah, ver. 24:

    " With all the *incense* of the *breathing* spring."

The breezy call of incense-breathing morn,
   The swallow twitt'ring from the straw-built shed,
The cock's shrill clarion, or the echoing horn,
   No more shall rouse them from their lowly bed.

For them no more the blazing hearth shall burn,
   Or busy housewife ply her evening care;   22

Var. V. 19. Or] And. <small>MS.</small> M. and W.

V. 18. " Mane jam clarum reserat fenestras,
   Jam *strepit nidis vigilax hirundo*."
Auson. ed Tollii, p. 94.

Hesiod gives the swallow a very appropriate epithet: χελι-δὼν ὀρθρογόη· Εργ. 567. Wakefield quotes Thomson. Autumn. ver. 835. " The swallow-people; — there they *twitter* cheerful." " Evandrum ex *humili tecto* lux suscitat alma, et matutini volucrum sub culmine cantus." v. Virg. Æn. viii. 455.

V. 19. " When *chanticleer* with *clarion shrill* recalls
   The tardy day." Philips. Cyder, i. 753.

Wakefield cites Par. Lost, b. vii. 443:

   " The crested *cock*, whose *clarion* sounds
   The silent hours."

And Hamlet, act i. sc. 1. L'Allegro, ver. 53. To which add Quarles. Argalus and Parthenia, p. 22:

   " I slept not, till the early *bugle-horn*
   Of *chaunticlere* had summon'd in the morn."

Thomas Kyd has also joined the two images (England's Parnassus, p. 325):

   " The cheerful *cock*, the sad night's *trumpeter*,
   Wayting upon the rising of the sunne.
   The wandering *swallow* with her broken song."

V. 21. Compare Apoll. Rhod. iv. 1062.

   " Nam jam non domus accipiet se læta, neque uxor
   Optima, nec dulces occurrent oscula nati
   Præripere."   Lucretius, iil. 907.

Horace has added to the picture an image copied by Gray:

   " Quod si pudica mulier, in partem juvet
   Domum, atque dulces liberos,
. . . . .

No children run to lisp their sire's return,
  Or climb his knees the envied kiss to share.

Oft did the harvest to their sickle yield,   25
  Their furrow oft the stubborn glebe has broke:
How jocund did they drive their team afield!
  How bow'd the woods beneath their sturdy
    stroke.

Let not ambition mock their useful toil,
  Their homely joys, and destiny obscure;   30

Var. V. 24. *Or*] Nor. MS. *W.*
V. 25. *Sickle*] Sickles. MS. *W.*

    Sacrum et vetustis exstruat lignis focum
      Lassi sub adventum viri."
See also Thomson. Winter, 311:
  " In vain for him the officious wife prepares
    The fire fair-blazing, and the vestment warm:
    In vain his little children, peeping out
    Into the mingling storm, demand their sire
    With tears of artless innocence."
  V. 24. " Interea dulces pendent circum oscula nati."
                 Virg. Georg. ii. v. 523. *W.*
So Dryden. ed. Warton, vol. ii. p. 565:
" Whose little arms about thy legs are cast,
  And climbing for a kiss prevent their mother's haste."
See also Thomson. Liberty, iii. 171, and Ovid. Heroid. Ep.
viii. 93. Hom. Il. E. 408.
  V. 26. " 'Tis mine to tame the *stubborn glebe.*"
                Gay. Fabl. p. ii. xv. *Luke.*
  V. 27. " He drove afield." Lycidas, 27. *W.* Add Dry-
den. Virg. Eclog. ii. 38. " With me to drive *afield.*" *Luke*
" To drive *afield* by morn the fattening ewes." A. Philips.
  V. 28. " But to the roote bent his *sturdie stroake,*
    And made many woundes in the waste oake."
Spenser. February. *W.* See also Dryden. Georg. iii. 639.

    " Labour him with many a *sturdy stroke.*"

Nor grandeur hear with a disdainful smile
The short and simple annals of the poor.

The boast of heraldry, the pomp of pow'r,
And all that beauty, all that wealth e'er gave,
Await alike th' inevitable hour.　　　　　　　　35
The paths of glory lead but to the grave.

Nor you, ye proud, impute to these the fault,
If memory o'er their tomb no trophies raise,

Var. V. 35. *Await*] Awaits MS. *M.* and *W.*
　　V. 37, 38. "Forgive, ye proud, th' involuntary fault,
　　　　If memory to these no trophies raise."
　　　　　　　　　　　　MS.　　*M.* and *W.*

V. 33. "Very like," says the editor, (in a note to the following passage of Cowley,) " in the expression as well as sentiment, to that fine stanza in Gray's Elegy, vol. ii. p. 213, Hurd's ed.
" ' *Beauty*, and strength, and wit, and *wealth*, and *power*,
　　Have their short flourishing *hour;*
And love to see themselves, and smile,
And joy in their pre-eminence a while:
　　E'en so in the same land
Poor weeds, rich corn, gay flowers together stand.
Alas! Death mows down all with an impartial hand.' "
Gray's stanza is, however, chiefly indebted to some verses in his friend West's Monody on Queen Caroline:
　　"Ah me! what boots us all our *boasted power*,
　　　Our golden treasure, and our *purple state;*
　　They cannot ward the *inevitable hour*,
　　　Nor stay the fearful violence of fate."
　　　　　　　　　　　Dodsley. Misc. ii. 279.
V. 36. In Kippis. Biographia Britannica, vol. iv. p. 429, in the Life of Crashaw, written by Hayley, it is said that this line is "literally translated from the Latin prose of Bartholinus in his Danish Antiquities." See Hagthorpe. Poems, p. 47. "Glory doth thousands to the grave betray."
V. 39.　　　── " the roof o' the chamber
　　With golden cherubims is *fretted.*"
　　　　　　　　　　Cymbel. act ii. sc. 4.　*W.*

Where thro' the long-drawn aisle and fretted vault
The pealing anthem swells the note of praise. 40

Can storied urn, or animated bust,
    Back to its mansion call the fleeting breath?
Can honour's voice provoke the silent dust,
    Or flatt'ry soothe the dull cold ear of death?

Perhaps in this neglected spot is laid   45
    Some heart once pregnant with celestial fire;
Hands, that the rod of empire might have sway'd,
    Or wak'd to extasy the living lyre:

Var. V. 47. *Rod*] Reins. MS.   *M.*

"This majestical roof *fretted* with golden fire."
                                Hamlet, act ii. sc. 2.
V. 40. "There let the *pealing* organ blow,
    To the full-voiced quire below,
    In service high, and *anthem* clear "
                                Il Pens. 163.   *W.*
V. 41. "Heroes in *animated marble* frown," Temple of
Fame, 73.   *W.* Add Virg. Æn. vi. 849. "*vivos* ducent de
marmore *vultus.*"   *Luke.*
V. 43. "But when our country's cause *provokes* to arms."
                                Pope. Ode.
V. 44. "And sleep in *dull cold* marble."
                                Hen. VIII. act iii. sc. 2.
V. 47. "Sunt mihi quas possint sceptra decere manus,"
Ovid. Ep. v. ver. 86. "Proud names that once *the reins of
empire* held," Tickell. Poem to E. of Warwick, ver. 37.
V. 48. "*Waken* raptures high," Par. Lost, iii. 369. And
Lucret. ii. 412: "Mobilibus digitis *expergefacta* figurant."
    "Begin the song, and strike the *living lyre.*" Cowley.
And Pope. Winds. For. 281:
            —— "where Cowley strung
    His *living harp,* and lofty Denham sung."   *W.*
V. 50. "Rich with the spoils of nature."
                                Brown. Rel. Med. p. 27.

But knowledge to their eyes her ample page
   Rich with the spoils of time did ne'er unroll; 50
Chill penury repress'd their noble rage,
   And froze the genial current of the soul.

Full many a gem of purest ray serene
   The dark unfathom'd caves of ocean bear:
Full many a flower is born to blush unseen, 55
   And waste its sweetness on the desert air.

V. 51. "So just thy skill, so regular my *rage*."
                          Pope to Jervas.

   "Be justly warn'd with your own *native rage*."
             Pope. Prol. to Cato, 43.   *W.*

And, "How hard the task ! how rare the *godlike rage*."
             Tickell. Prol. (Steele. Misc. p. 70.)

   V. 53. "That like to rich and various gems inlay
      The unadorned bosom of the deep."
                       Comus, ver. 22.

And see Young. "Ocean," st. xxiv.

"There is many a rich stone laid up in the bowells of the
earth, many a fair *pearle in the bosome of the sea*, that never
was seene, nor never shall bee." Bishop Hall. Contempla-
tions, l. vi. p. 872. See Quart. Rev. No. xxii. p. 314. ad Fr.
Barberini Poem, p. 148. Μάργαρα πόλλα βαθύς συγκρύπτει
κύμασι πόντος. and see T. Warton. Milton, p. 234.

   V. 54. Ἄφαντα κευθμῶνος βάθη. Lycophr. Cass. 1277.
                               Mathias,

   V. 55. "Like roses that in deserts bloom and die."
             Pope. Rape of the Lock, iv. 157. *W*

Also Chamberlayne. Pharonida, part ii. b. iv. p. 94:
   "Like beauteous flowers which vainly waste their scent
   Of odours in unhaunted deserts."

And Young. Univ. Passion, Sat. v. p. 128:
   " In distant wilds, by human eyes *unseen*,
   She rears her flow'rs, and spreads her *velvet green;*
   Pure gurgling rills the lonely *desert* trace,
   And *waste their music* on the savage race."

Some village-Hampden, that, with dauntless
    breast,
  The little tyrant of his fields withstood,
Some mute inglorious Milton here may rest,   59
  Some Cromwell guiltless of his country's blood.

Th' applause of list'ning senates to command,
  The threats of pain and ruin to despise,
To scatter plenty o'er a smiling land,
  And read their history in a nation's eyes,

Their lot forbade : nor circumscrib'd alone   65
  Their growing virtues, but their crimes confin'd ;

Var. V. 58. Fields] Lands, erased in MS. M.

Add Philip. Thule:
    " Like woodland flowers, which paint the *desert* glades,
      And *waste their sweets in unfrequented* shades."
For the expression " desert air," Wakefield refers to Pindar.
Ol. i. 10: Ερήμας δι αιθέρος. Also Fragm. Incert. cxvi.
" Howl'd out into the desert air." Macbeth, act iv. sc. 3.
Rogers.
  V. 58. " With open freedom *little tyrants* rag'd."
Thoms. Winter. *Luke.*
  " The tyrants of villages." Johnson. Debates, i. 268.
  V. 59. So Philips, in his animated and eloquent preface to
his Theatrum Poetarum, p. xiv. ed. Brydges: " Even the very
names of some who having perhaps been comparable to Homer
for heroic poesy, or to Euripides for tragedy, yet nevertheless
sleep inglorious in the crowd of the forgotten vulgar."
  V. 60. Edwards, the author of " The Canons of Criticism,"
here added the two following stanzas, to supply what he
deemed a defect in the poem:
  " Some lovely fair, whose unaffected charms
    Shone with attraction to herself unknown;
    Whose beauty might have bless'd a monarch's arms,
    Whose virtue cast a lustre on a throne.

Forbade to wade thro' slaughter to a throne,
And shut the gates of mercy on mankind,

The struggling pangs of conscious truth to hide,
To quench the blushes of ingenuous shame, 70
Or heap the shrine of luxury and pride
With incense kindled at the Muse's flame.

Var. V. 68. *And*] Or. MS. *M.* and *W.*
V. 71. *Shrine*] Shrines. MS. *W.*
V. 72. After this verse, in Gray's first MS. of the poem, were the four following stanzas:

> " The thoughtless world to majesty may bow,
>   Exalt the brave, and idolize success;

> " That humble beauty warm'd an honest heart,
>   And cheer'd the labours of a faithful spouse;
>   That virtue form'd for every decent part,
>   The healthful offspring that adorn'd their house."

V. 61. " Tho' *wond'ring senates* hung on all he spoke."
Pope. Mor. Essays, i. 184.

V. 63. " To scatter blessings o'er the British land."
Tickell.

" Is scattering plenty over all the land."
Behn. Epilogue.

V. 64. " For in their eyes I read a soldier's love."
Beau. and Fletch. vi. 135. *Rogers.*

V. 67. " And swam to empire thro' the purple flood."
Temple of Fame, 347. *W.*

V. 68. " The *gates of mercy* shall be all *shut* up," Hen. V. act iii. sc. 3. Also in Hen. VI. part iii. : " Open thy *gate of mercy*, gracious Lord." And so says an obscure poet:

> "His humble eyes, sighs, cries, and bruised breast,
>   *Forc'd ope the gates of mercy*, gave him rest."

Nath. Richards. Poems, Sacred and Satyrical, 12mo. 1641. p. 145. " Lætitiæ janua clausa meæ est," Ovid. Pont. ii. 7. 38.

V. 70. " Quench your blushes," Wint. Tale, act iv. sc. 3 *Rogers.*

Far from the madding crowd's ignoble strife,
   Their sober wishes never learn'd to stray;
Along the cool sequester'd vale of life   75
   They kept the noiseless tenour of their way.

  But more to innocence their safety owe,
    Than pow'r or genius e'er conspired to bless.

" And thou who, mindful of th' unhonour'd dead,
    Dost in these notes their artless tale relate,
  By night and lonely contemplation led
    To wander in the gloomy walks of fate:

" Hark ! how the sacred calm, that breathes around,
    Bids every fierce tumultuous passion cease;
  In still small accents whisp'ring from the ground,
    A grateful earnest of eternal peace.

" No more, with reason and thyself at strife,
    Give anxious cares and endless wishes room;
  But through the cool sequester'd vale of life
    Pursue the silent tenour of thy doom."

And here the poem was originally intended to conclude,
before the happy idea of the hoary-headed swain, &c. suggested itself to him.   Mason thinks the third of these rejected stanzas equal to any in the whole elegy.

V. 73. "Far from the madding wordling's hoarse discords."
Drummond.   *Rogers.*

   V. 75. "Foe to *loud* praise, and friend to learned ease,
      Content with science, *in the vale of peace.*"
                  Pope. Ep. to Fenton, 6.   *W.*
    "Mollia per placidam delectant otia vitam."
                  Manil. Astr. iv. 512.

   V. 87. "*Dias* in luminis *oras,*" Lucretius, i. 23. *W.*   "E
lascio mesta l'aure soave della vita e i giorni," Tasso G. L.
c. ix. st. xxxiii.

   V. 88. So Petrarch. Tr. l'Amore, iv. ver. ult.

   ' Che 'l piè va innanzi, e l' occhio torna indietro."

Wakefield quotes a passage in the Alcestis of Euripides,
ver. 201.

Yet ev'n these bones from insult to protect,
  Some frail memorial still erected nigh,
With uncouth rhymes and shapeless sculpture
    deck'd,
  Implores the passing tribute of a sigh.   80

Their name, their years, spelt by th'unletter'd
    Muse,
  The place of fame and elegy supply:
And many a holy text around she strews,
  That teach the rustic moralist to die.

For who, to dumb forgetfulness a prey,   85
  This pleasing anxious being e'er resign'd,
Left the warm precincts of the cheerful day,
  Nor cast one longing ling'ring look behind?

On some fond breast the parting soul relies,
  Some pious drops the closing eye requires;   90

    Var V. 82. *Elegy*] Epitaph. ms. *M.*

    V. 89. So Drayton in his "Moses," p. 1564. vol. iv. ed.
1753:
    " It is some comfort to a wretch to die,
      (If there be comfort in the way of death)
      To have some friend, or kind alliance by
      To be officious at the parting breath."
    V. 90. " piæ lacrimæ." Ovid. Trist. iv. 3. 41.
  " No friend's complaint, no *kind domestic tear*
    Pleas'd thy pale ghost, or grac'd thy mournful bier;
    By foreign hands thy dying *eyes were clos'd.*"
                          Pope. Elegy, 81.
And, " Then from his *closing eyes* thy form shall part." v. 80.
And so Solon, ver. 5, ed. Brunck.:
    Μηδ' ἐμοὶ ἀκλαυστος θάνατος μόλοι, ἀλλὰ φίλοισι
    Καλλείποιμι θανὼν ἄλγεα καὶ στοναχάς.   *W.*
                      H

E'en from the tomb the voice of nature cries,
  E'en in our ashes live their wonted fires.

For thee, who, mindful of th' unhonour'd dead,
  Dost in these lines their artless tale relate;
If chance, by lonely contemplation led,   95
  Some kindred spirit shall enquire thy fate, —

Haply some hoary-headed swain may say,
  "Oft have we seen him at the peep of dawn
Brushing with hasty steps the dews away,
  To meet the sun upon the upland lawn :   100

Var. V. 92. *E'en, live*] And, glow. ms. *M.* and *W.*
    V. 92. " Awake and faithful to her wonted fires."
                                First and second editions.

V. 91. Some lines in the Anthologia Latina, p. 600. Ep. cliii.
have a strong resemblance to those in the text:
  " Crede mihi vires aliquas natura sepulchris
    Adtribuit, tumulos vindicat umbra suos."
So also Auson. (Parentalia), ed. Tollii, p. 109:
  " Gaudent compositi cineres sua nomina dici."
  V. 92. " Ch' i veggio nel pensier, dolce mio fuoco,
            Fredda una lingua, e due begli occhi chiusi
            Rimaner doppo noi pien di faville."
                            Petr. Son. clxix.   *Gray.*
      " Yet in our ashen cold, is fire yreken."
                            Chaucer. Reve. Prol. ver. 3880
    " Quamvis in cinerem corpus mutaverit ignis,
      Sentiet officium mœsta favilla pium."
                            Ovid. Trist. iii. 3. 83.
    " Interea cave, sis nos adspernata sepultos,
      Non nihil ad verum conscia terra sapit."
                            Propert. ii. 13. 41.
  Wakefield cites Pope. Ep. to M. Blount, ver. 72:
    " By this e'en now they live, e'en now they charm,
      Their wit still sparkling, and *their flame still warm.*"
  V. 98. " The nice *morn* on the Indian steep
            From her cabin'd loophole *peep.*"
                            Comus, 140. see Todd. **note.**

" There at the foot of yonder nodding beech,
    That wreathes its old fantastic roots so high,
His listless length at noontide would he stretch,
    And pore upon the brook that babbles by. 104

Var. V. 100.
    " On the high brow of yonder hanging lawn."
After which, in his first MS., followed this stanza:
    " Him have we seen the greenwood side along,
        While o'er the heath we hied, our labour done,
    Oft as the woodlark pip'd her farewell song,
        With wistful eyes pursue the setting sun."
    " I rather wonder (says Mason) that he rejected this
stanza, as it not only has the same sort of Doric delicacy
which charms us peculiarly in this part of the poem, but also
completes the account of his whole day: whereas, this evening
scene being omitted, we have only his morning walk, and his
noon-tide repose."

V. 99. —— " From off the ground, each morn,
        We *brush* mellifluous *dews*."   Par. Lost, v. 429.
So also Arcades, ver. 50:
    " And from the boughs *brush* off the evil *dew*."
                                    Add Tempest, act i. sc. 4.
    V. 100. So Petrarch:
    " Re degli altri, superbo, altero fiume
        Che 'n contril sol, quando e ne mena il giorno."
And Tasso, in his Sonnet to Camoëns:
    " Vasco, te cui felicè ardite antenne
        Incontro al sol che ne riporta il giorno," &c.
And in another Sonnet:
    " Come *va innanzi a l' altro sol* l'aurora," &c.
    V. 100. " Ere the *high lawns* appeared
            Under the opening eyelids of the morn."
                                    Lycidas, 25. *W.*
    V. 102. Spenser. R. of Rome, s. xxviii.
    " Shewing her *wreathed rootes* and naked armes." *Luke.*
    V. 103. " His goodly length stretched on a lily bed."
                            Spens. B. Ida, c. 3. s. 2. *Luke.*
    V. 104. " Unde *loquaces lymphæ* desiliunt tuæ."
                                    Hor. Od. iii. 13. 15.
                    " He lay along
    Under an oak, whose *antique root peep'd out*

" Hard by yon wood, now smiling as in scorn,
  Mutt'ring his wayward fancies he would rove ;
Now drooping, woful-wan, like one forlorn,
  Or craz'd with care, or cross'd in hopeless love.

" One morn I miss'd him on the custom'd hill,
  Along the heath, and near his fav'rite tree ; 110
Another came ; nor yet beside the rill,
  Nor up the lawn, nor at the wood was he :

" The next, with dirges due in sad array,
  Slow through the church-way path we saw
    him borne : —   114

Var. V. 106. *He would*] Would he. MS. *M.* and *W.*
    V. 109. *On*] From. MS. *M.*

" Upon the *brook*, that brawls along this wood."
                    As You Like It, act ii. sc. 1. *W.*
V. 105. " Yet at my parting sweetly did she *smile*
    In scorn."   Shakespeare Sonnets.

—— " *smylynge halfe in scorne*
At our foly." Skelton. Prol. to the Bouge de Courte, p. 59.
" It makes me smile in scorn." App. and Virg. (Old Plays,
vol. v. p. 363.) " Laughing in scorn." Massinger. B. Lover.
Rogers. Milt. P. L. iv. 903. " Disdainfully half smiling."

V. 107. " For pale and *wanne* he was, alas ! the while
    May seeme he *lov'd* or else some *care* he tooke."
                        Spenser. January 8. *W.*

V. 109. " Simul *assueta* sidetque sub ulmo."
                    Milt. Ep. Damonis. *G. Steevens.*

V. 114. " In the *church-way paths* to glide."
                    Mids. N. Dr. act v. sc. 2. *W*

V. 115. " Tell, (for you can,) what is it to be wise."
                        Pope. Ep. iv. 260. *W*

" And steal (for you can steal) celestial fire." Young.

" Scrutare tu causas (potes enim.)" Plin. Ep. iv. 30

Approach and read (for thou can'st read) the lay
  Grav'd on the stone beneath yon aged thorn."

THE EPITAPH.*

Here rests his head upon the lap of earth,
  A youth, to fortune and to fame unknown:
Fair Science frown'd not on his humble birth,
  And Melancholy mark'd him for her own.   120

---

* " Before the Epitaph," says Mason, " Gray originally
inserted a very beautiful stanza, which was printed in some of
the first editions, but afterwards omitted, because he thought
that it was too long a parenthesis in this place. The lines,
however, are in themselves exquisitely fine, and demand pre-
servation:

" ' There scatter'd oft, the earliest of the year,
    By hands unseen are show'rs of violets found;
  The redbreast loves to build and warble there,
    And little footsteps lightly print the ground.' "

V. 117. ———" How glad would lay me down,
    As in my *mother's lap*."   Par. Lost, x. 777.

Also Spens. F. Qu. v. 7. 9:

——— " On their *mother earth's* dear *lap* did lie."

" Redditur enim terræ corpus, et ita locatum ac situm quasi
operimento matris obducetur." Cicero de Legibus, ii. 22. Lucr.
i. 291. "gremium matris terrai."
  I cannot help adding to this note, the short and pathetic
sentence of Plin. Hist. Nat. ii. 63. " Nam terra novissime
complexa gremio jam a *reliquâ naturâ abnegatos, tum maxime,
ut mater, operit.*"

V. 119. " Quem tu, Melpomene, semel
    Nascentem placido lumine videris."
                    Hor. Od. iv. 3. 1.   W.

V. 121. " *Large was his soul*, as large a soul as e'er
    Submitted to inform a body here."
                    Cowley, vol. i. p. 119.
" A passage which," says the editor, " Gray seemed to have
had his eye on."

Large was his bounty, and his soul sincere,
   Heav'n did a recompense as largely send;
He gave to mis'ry (all he had) a tear,
   He gain'd from heav'n ('twas all he wish'd) a
     friend.

No farther seek his merits to disclose,   125
   Or draw his frailties from their dread abode,
(There they alike in trembling hope repose,)
   The bosom of his Father and his God.

V. 123. "Has lacrymas memori quas ictus amore, fundo quod possum." Lucr. ii. 27. "His fame ('tis all the dead can have) shall live." Pope. Hom. xvi. 556.

V. 127. —— "paventosa speme," Petr. Son. cxiv. *Gray.* "Spe trepido," Lucan. vii. 297. *W.* And Mallet:

"With *trembling* tenderness of *hope* and fear."
                Funeral Hymn, ver. 473.

"Divided here twixt *trembling hope* and fear."
                Beaum. Psyche, c. xv. 314.

Hooker has defined 'hope' to be a "trembling expectation of things far removed," Eccl. Pol. B. I. cited in Quart. Rev. No. xxii. p. 315.

In the Gentleman's Magaz. vol. lii. p. 20, it is asserted that Gray's Elegy was taken from Collins's Ode to Evening; while in the Monthly Rev. vol. liii. p. 102, it is said to be indebted to an Elegy by Gay. I see, however, no reason for assenting to these opinions. The passages from 'Celio Magno,' produced in the Edinb. Rev. vol. v. p. 51, are very curious, and form an interesting comparison. It is well known how much the Italian poet Pignotti is indebted to the works of Gray: some passages would have been given, but the editor was unwilling to increase the number of the notes, already perhaps occupying too much space.

A LONG STORY.*

[See Mason's Memoirs, vol. iii. p. 130, and Pennant's Life, p. 23.]

Gray's Elegy in a Country Church-yard, previous to its publication, was handed about in manuscript ; and had amongst other admirers the Lady Cobham, who resided at the mansion-house at Stoke-Pogeis. The performance inducing her to wish for the author's acquaintance, her relation, Miss Speed, and Lady Schaub, then at her house, undertook to effect it. These two ladies waited upon the author at his aunt's solitary habitation, where he at that time resided; and not finding him at home, they left a card behind them. Mr. Gray, surprised at such a compliment, returned the visit. And as the beginning of this acquaintance bore some appearance of romance, he soon after gave a humorous account of it in the following copy of verses, which he entitled " A Long Story." Printed in 1753 with Mr. Bentley's designs, and repeated in a second edition. MS.

In Britain's isle, no matter where,
An ancient pile of building stands:
The Huntingdons and Hattons there
Employ'd the pow'r of fairy hands

---

* This Poem was rejected by Gray in the Collection published by himself ; and though published afterwards by Mason in his Memoirs of Gray, he placed it amongst the Letters, together with the Posthumous Pieces ; not thinking himself authorized to insert among the Poems what the author had rejected.

V. 2. The mansion-house at Stoke-Pogeis, then in the possession of Viscountess Cobham. The house formerly belonged to the earls of Huntingdon and the family of Hatton. *Mason*

Sir Edmond Coke's mansion at Stoke-Pogeis, now the seat of Mr. Penn, was the scene of Gray's Long Story. The antique chimneys have been allowed to remain as vestiges of the Poet's

To raise the ceiling's fretted height,   5
    Each panel in achievements clothing,
Rich windows that exclude the light,
    And passages that lead to nothing.

Full oft within the spacious walls,
    When he had fifty winters o'er him   10
My grave Lord-Keeper led the brawls;
    The seals and maces danc'd before him.

His bushy beard, and shoe-strings green,
    His high-crown'd hat, and satin doublet,
Mov'd the stout heart of England's queen,   15
    Though Pope and Spaniard could not trouble it.

What, in the very first beginning!
    Shame of the versifying tribe!
Your hist'ry whither are you spinning?
    Can you do nothing but describe?   20

A house there is (and that's enough)
    From whence one fatal morning issues

---

fancy, and a column with a statue of Coke marks the former
abode of its illustrious inhabitant.   D'Israeli. Cur. of Lit.
(New Ser.) i. 482.   Coke married Lady Hatton, relict of Sir
William Hatton, sister of Lord Burlington.

V. 7. " And storied windows richly dight,
        Casting a dim religious light.''   Il Pens. 159.
And Pope. Eloisa, 142:
    " Where awful arches make a noonday night,
        And the dim windows shed a solemn light.''   *W.*

V. 11. Sir Christopher Hatton, promoted by Queen Elizabeth
for his graceful person and fine dancing. *Gray.* See Hume's
England, vol. v. p. 330. Naunton's Fragmenta Regalia, and
Ocklandi Elizabetha. M i. Barrington on the Statutes, p. 405.

A brace of warriors, not in buff,
  But rustling in their silks and tissues.

The first came cap-a-pee from France,   25
  Her conqu'ring destiny fulfilling,
Whom meaner beauties eye askance,
  And vainly ape her art of killing.

The other amazon kind heav'n
  Had arm'd with spirit, wit, and satire;   30
But Cobham had the polish giv'n,
  And tipp'd her arrows with good-nature.

To celebrate her eyes, her air —
  Coarse panegyrics would but tease her;
Melissa is her "nom de guerre."   35
  Alas, who would not wish to please her!

With bonnet blue and capuchiné,
  And aprons long, they hid their armour;
And veil'd their weapons, bright and keen,
  In pity to the country farmer.   40

V. 11. Brawls were a sort of French figure-dance, then in vogue. See England's Helicon, p. 101; Browne's Poems, vol. iii. p. 149, ed. Thompson; and the note by Steevens to Love's Lab. Lost, act iii. sc. 1. And so Ben Jonson, in a Masque, vol. vi. p. 27, ed. Whalley:
> "And thence did Venus learn to *lead*
> The Idalian *brawls*."

But see more particularly Marston. Malcontent, act iv. sc. 2, where it is described:
> "We have forgot the brawl," &c.
>   See Dodsley. Old Plays, vol ii. p. 210.

Fame, in the shape of Mr. P—t,
    (By this time all the parish know it)
Had told that thereabouts there lurk'd
    A wicked imp they call a poet:

Who prowl'd the country far and near,   45
    Bewitch'd the children of the peasants,
Dried up the cows, and lam'd the deer,
    And suck'd the eggs, and kill'd the pheasants.

My lady heard their joint petition,
    Swore by her coronet and ermine,   50
She'd issue out her high commission
    To rid the manor of such vermin.

The heroines undertook the task,
    Thro' lanes unknown, o'er stiles they ventur'd,

V. 41. It has been said, that this gentleman, a neighbour and acquaintance of Gray's in the country, was much displeased with the liberty here taken with his name : yet, surely, without any great reason. *Mason.* Mr. Robert Purt was Fellow of King's Coll. Cant. 1738. A.B. 1742, A.M. 1746; was an assistant at Eton school, tutor to Lord Baltimore's son there, and afterwards to the Duke of Bridgewater; in 1749 he was presented to the rectory of Settrington in Yorkshire, which he held with Dorrington in the same county: he died in Ap. 1752 of the small pox. *Isaac Reed.*

V. 51. Henry the Fourth, in the fourth year of his reign, issued out the following *commission* against this species of *vermin:* — "And it is enacted, that no master-rimour, minstrel, or other *vagabond,* be in any wise sustained in the land of Wales, to make commoiths, or gatherings upon the people there." — " *Vagabond,*" says Ritson, "was a title to which the profession had been long accustomed."

    " Beggars they are with one consent,
    And rogues by act of parliament."
                    Pref. to Anc. Songs, p. **xi**

Rapp'd at the door, nor stay'd to ask, 55
   But bounce into the parlour enter'd.

The trembling family they daunt,
   They flirt, they sing, they laugh, they tattle,
Rummage his mother, pinch his aunt,
   And up stairs in a whirlwind rattle: 60

Each hole and cupboard they explore,
   Each creek and cranny of his chamber,
Run hurry-scurry round the floor,
   And o'er the bed and tester clamber;

Into the drawers and china pry, 65
   Papers and books, a huge imbroglio!
Under a tea-cup he might lie,
   Or creased, like dogs-ears, in a folio.

There are still stronger Scotch statutes against them, some con-
demning them and "such like fules" to lose their ears, and
others their lives. By a law of Elizabeth, the English minstrels
were pronounced "rogues, vagabonds, and sturdy beggars,"
xxxix. Eliz. c. 4. s. 2. See Ritson's Engl. Songs, 1. liii. Barrington on the Statutes, p. 360. Dodsley. Old Plays, xii. p.
361. Strutt. Sports and Pastimes, p. 182—196. Puttenham.
Art of Engl. Poesie. (1589) Lib. ii. c. 9.

V. 67. There is a very great similarity between the style
of part of this poem, and Prior. Tale of the 'Dove:' as for
instance in the following stanzas, which Gray, I think, must
have had in his mind at the time:

  "With one great peal they rap the door,
    Like footmen on a visiting day:
  Folks at her house at such an hour,
    Lord ! what will all the neighbours say?
    *   *   *   *   *
  "Her keys he takes, her door unlocks,
    Thro' wardrobe and thro' closet bounces,

On the first marching of the troops,
    The Muses, hopeless of his pardon,   70
Convey'd him underneath their hoops
    To a small closet in the garden.

So rumour says: (who will, believe.)
    But that they left the door ajar,
Where, safe and laughing in his sleeve,   75
    He heard the distant din of war.

Short was his joy.   He little knew
    The pow'r of magic was no fable;
Out of the window, whisk, they flew,
    But left a spell upon the table.   80

The words too eager to unriddle,
    The poet felt a strange disorder;
Transparent bird-lime form'd the middle,
    And chains invisible the border.

So cunning was the apparatus,   85
    The powerful pot-hooks did so move him,
That, will he, nill he, to the great house
    He went, as if the devil drove him.

Peeps into every chest and box,
    Turns all her furbelows and flounces.
    *   *   *   *   *
" I marvel much, she smiling said,
    Your poultry cannot yet be found:
Lies he in yonder slipper dead,
    Or may be in the tea-pot drown'd."

Yet on his way (no sign of grace,
   For folks in fear are apt to pray)   90
To Phœbus he preferr'd his case,
   And begg'd his aid that dreadful day.

The godhead would have back'd his quarrel;
   But with a blush, on recollection,
Own'd that his quiver and his laurel   95
   'Gainst four such eyes were no protection.

The court was sat, the culprit there,
   Forth from their gloomy mansions creeping,
The lady Janes and Joans repair,
   And from the gallery stand peeping: 100

Such as in silence of the night
   Come (sweep) along some winding entry,
(Styack has often seen the sight)
   Or at the chapel-door stand sentry:

In peaked hoods and mantles tarnish'd,   105
   Sour visages, enough to scare ye,
High dames of honour once, that garnish'd
   The drawing-room of fierce Queen Mary.

The peeress comes. The audience stare,
   And doff their hats with due submission: 110
She curtsies, as she takes her chair,
   To all the people of condition.

V. 103. *Styack*] The housekeeper.   *G*

The bard, with many an artful fib,
 Had in imagination fenc'd him,
Disprov'd the arguments of Squib,   115
 And all that Groom could urge against him.

But soon his rhetoric forsook him,
 When he the solemn hall had seen;
A sudden fit of ague shook him,
 He stood as mute as poor Macleane.   120

Yet something he was heard to mutter,
 " How in the park beneath an old tree,
(Without design to hurt the butter,
 Or any malice to the poultry,)

" He once or twice had penn'd a sonnet;   125
 Yet hop'd that he might save his bacon:
Numbers would give their oaths upon it,
 He ne'er was for a conj'rer taken."

Var. V. 116. Might. ms.

V. 115. *Squib*] Groom of the chamber. *G.*

James Squibb was the son of Dr. Arthur Squibb, the de-
scendant of an ancient and respectable family, whose pedigree
is traced in the herald's visitations of Dorsetshire, to John
Squibb of Whitchurch in that county, in the 17th Edw. IV.
1477. Dr. Squibb matriculated at Oxford in 1656, took his
degree of M.A. in November, 1662; was chaplain to Colonel
Bellasis's regiment about 1685, and died in 1697. As he was
in distressed circumstances towards the end of his life, his son,
James Squibb, was left almost destitute, and was consequently
apprenticed to an upholder in 1712. In that situation he
attracted the notice of Lord Cobham, in whose service he con-

The ghostly prudes with hagged face
   Already had condemn'd the sinner.   130
My lady rose, and with a grace —
   She smil'd, and bid him come to dinner.

"Jesu-Maria! Madam Bridget,
   Why, what can the Viscountess mean?"
(Cried the square-hoods in woful fidget)   135
   "The times are alter'd quite and clean!

"Decorum's turn'd to mere civility;
   Her air and all her manners show it.
Commend me to her affability!
   Speak to a commoner and poet!"   140

[Here five hundred stanzas are lost.]

And so God save our noble king,
   And guard us from long-winded lubbers,
That to eternity would sing,
   And keep my lady from her rubbers.

---

tinued for many years, and died at Stowe, in June, 1762. His
son, James Squibb, who settled in Saville Row, London, was
grandfather of George James Squibb, Esq. of Orchard Street,
Portman Square, who is the present representative of this
branch of the family. *Nicolas.*

V. 116. *Groom*] The steward. *G.*

V. 120. *Macleane*] A famous highwayman hanged the week
before. *G.*

See a *Sequel* to the Long Story in Hakewill's History of
Windsor, by John Penn, Esq. and a farther Sequel to that, by
the late Laureate, H. J. Pye, Esq.

POSTHUMOUS POEMS AND
FRAGMENTS.

ODE ON THE PLEASURE ARISING FROM
VICISSITUDE.

Left unfinished by Gray. With additions by Mason, distinguished by inverted commas. (I have read something
that Mason has done in finishing a half-written ode of Gray.
I find he will never get the better of that glare of colouring,
' that dazzling blaze of song,' an expression of his own, and
ridiculous enough, which disfigures half his writings. V.
Langhorne's Lett. to H. More, i. 23.) See Musæ Etonenses,
ii. p. 176.

> Now the golden morn aloft
> Waves her dew-bespangled wing,

V. 1. Sophocl. Antig. v. 103, χρυσέας ἁμέρας βλέφαρον;
and Dyer. Fleece, lib. iii. " Grey dawn appears, the *golden
morn* ascends." *Luke.*

V. 3. " Vermeil cheek," see Milton. Comus, v. 749. *Luke.*

V. 4. " Rorifera mulcens aura, Zephyrus vernas evocat
herbas." Senec. Hipp. i. 11. *Luke.*

V. 8. " Half rob'd appears the hawthorn hedge,
        Or to the distant eye displays
        Weakly green its budding sprays."
                        Warton. First of April, i. 180.
See Mant's note on the passage. Add Buchan. Psalm xxiii.
p. 36. " Quæ *Veris teneri* pingit amœnitas."

V. 9. —— " Hinc *nova proles,*
        Artubus infirmis teneras lasciva per herbas
        Ludit."   Lucret. i. 260.

With vermeil cheek and whisper soft
  She wooes the tardy spring:
Till April starts, and calls around   5
  The sleeping fragrance from the ground;
And lightly o'er the living scene,
Scatters his freshest, tenderest green.

New-born flocks, in rustic dance,
  Frisking ply their feeble feet;   10
Forgetful of their wintry trance,
  The birds his presence greet:
But chief, the sky-lark warbles high
His trembling thrilling extasy;
And, lessening from the dazzled sight,   15
Melts into air and liquid light.

Rise, my soul! on wings of fire,
  Rise the rapt'rous choir among;

    " O'er the broad downs a novel race,
    Frisk the *lambs with faltering pace.*"
                       T. Warton, i. 185.

V. 17. Mason informs us, that he has heard Gray say, that Gresset's " Epitre à ma Sœur" gave him the first idea of this ode; and whoever, he says, compares it with the French poem, will find some *slight* traits of resemblance, but chiefly in the author's seventh stanza. The following lines seem to have been in Gray's remembrance at this place:

    " Mon âme, trop long tems flétrie
    Va de nouveau s' épanouir;
    Et loin de toute rêverie
      Voltiger avec le Zéphire,
    Occupé tout entier du soin du plaisir d'être," &c

Lucret. v. 282, " liquidi fons luminis." Milt. P. L. vii. 362, " drink the *liquid light.*" *Luke.*

I

Hark ! 'tis nature strikes the lyre,
   And leads the gen'ral song: 20
' Warm let the lyric transport flow,
Warm as the ray that bids it glow ;
And animates the vernal grove
With health, with harmony, and love.

Yesterday the sullen year   25
   Saw the snowy whirlwind fly ;
Mute was the music of the air,
   The herd stood drooping by :
Their raptures.now that wildly flow,
No yesterday nor morrow know ;   30
'Tis man alone that joy descries
With forward and reverted eyes.

Smiles on past misfortune's brow
   Soft reflection's hand can trace;
And o'er the cheek of sorrow throw   35
   A melancholy grace ;

V. 25. Milt. Son. xx. 3. " Help waste a *sullen* day."
                                             Luke.

V. 31. " Sure he that made us with such large discourse
      Looking before and after."   Hamlet, act iv. sc. 4,
   " Imperat, *ante videt*, perpendit, præcavit, infit."
                    Prudent. p. 374. ed. Delph.

V. 41. " Where *Pleasure's roses* void of serpents grow."
           Thomson. C. of Ind. c. ii. st. lvii.   *Luke.*

V. 43. Dr. Warton refers to Pope. Essay on Man, ii. 270:

   " See some strange comfort every state attend,
     And pride bestow'd on all, a common friend:
     See some fit passion every age supply:
     Hope travels on, nor quits us till we die "

While hope prolongs our happier hour,
Or deepest shades, that dimly lower
And blacken round our weary way,
Gilds with a gleam of distant day.   40

Still, where rosy pleasure leads,
    See a kindred grief pursue;
Behind the steps that misery treads,
    Approaching comfort view:
The hues of bliss more brightly glow,   45
Chastis'd by sabler tints of woe;
And blended form, with artful strife,
The strength and harmony of life.

See the wretch, that long has tost
    On the thorny bed of pain,   50

See Casimir Od.:
            " Alterno redeunt choro
        Risus et gemitus, et madidis prope
            Sicci cum lacrymis joci
        Nascuntur mediis gaudia luctibus."——

V. 45. " Here sweet, or strong, may every colour flow;
        Here let the pencil warm, the colours glow;
        Of light and shade provoke the noble strife,
        And wake each striking feature into life."
                        Brown. Essay on Satire, ii. 358.

V. 49. " O ! jours de la convalescence !
            Jours d'une pure volupté:
        C'est une nouvelle naissance,
            Un rayon d'immortalité.
    Quel feu ! tous les plaisirs ont volé dans mon âme,
    J'adore avec transport le céleste flambeau;
    Tout m'intéresse, tout m' enflâme —
        Pour moi, l'univers est nouveau.
        .   .   .   .
    Les plus simples objects; le chante d'un Fauvette,

At length repair his vigour lost,
    And breathe and walk again :
The meanest floweret of the vale,
The simplest note that swells the gale,
The common sun, the air, the skies,   55
To him are opening paradise.

Humble quiet builds her cell,
    Near the source whence pleasure flows ;
She eyes the clear crystalline well,
    And tastes it as it goes.   60
' While' far below the ' madding' crowd
' Rush headlong to the dangerous flood,'
Where broad and turbulent it sweeps,
' And' perish in the boundless deeps.

Mark where indolence and pride,   65
    ' Sooth'd by flattery's tinkling sound,'
Go, softly rolling, side by side,
    Their dull but daily round :

Le matin d'un beau jour, la verdure des bois,
    La fraicheur d'une violette ;
Milles spectacles, qu'autrefois
    On voyoit avec nonchalance,
Transportent aujourd'hui, présentent·des appas
    Inconnus à l' indifférence,
Et que la foule ne voit pas."   Gresset. tom. i. p. 145.

V. 55. " Communemque prius, ceu lumina solis." Ovid.
Met. i. 135. " Nec *solem proprium* natura, nec aëra fecit."
Ovid. Met. vi. 350. " Ne *lucem*, quoque hanc quæ *communis
est*." Cicero. "Sol omnibus lucet." Pet. Arb. c. 100. "Communis cunctis viventibus aura." Prudent. Sym. ii. 86. "The
common benefit of vital air." Dryden.

' To these, if Hebe's self should bring
The purest cup from pleasure's spring,   70
Say, can they taste the flavour high
Of sober, simple, genuine joy?

' Mark ambition's march sublime
    Up to power's meridian height;
While pale-eyed envy sees him climb,   75
    And sickens at the sight.
Phantoms of danger, death, and dread,
Float hourly round ambition's head;
While spleen, within his rival's breast,
Sits brooding on her scorpion nest.   80

' Happier he, the peasant, far,
    From the pangs of passion free,
That breathes the keen yet wholesome air
    Of rugged penury.
He, when his morning task is done,   85
Can slumber in the noontide sun;
And hie him home, at evening's close,
To sweet repast, and calm repose.

V. 56. " Balm from *open'd Paradise*." v. Fairfax. Tasso,
iv. 75. *Luke*. " And Paradise was open'd in the wild." Pope.
" And *paradise* was *open'd* in his face." Dryden. Absalom, ed.
Derrick, vol. i. p. 116.

V. 59. So Milton accents the word:
" On the crystálline sky, in sapphire thron'd."
                         Par. Lost, b. vi. ver. 772.

V. 65. " Tout s'émousse dans l'habitude;
        L'amour s'endort sans volupté;
        Las des mêmes plaisirs, las de leur multitude,
        Le sentiment n'est plus flatté."

' He, unconscious whence the bliss,
   Feels, and owns in carols rude,   90
That all the circling joys are his,
   Of dear Vicissitude.
From toil he wins his spirits light,
From busy day the peaceful night;
Rich, from the very want of wealth,   95
In heaven's best treasures, peace and health.'

TRANSLATION OF A PASSAGE FROM
STATIUS. *

THEB. LIB. VI. VER. 704—724.

THIRD in the labours of the disc came on,
With sturdy step and slow, Hippomedon;
Artful and strong he pois'd the well-known weight
By Phlegyas warn'd, and fir'd by Mnestheus' fate,
That to avoid, and this to emulate.   5
His vigorous arm he tried before he flung,
Brac'd all his nerves, and every sinew strung;
Then, with a tempest's whirl, and wary eye,
Pursu'd his cast, and hurl'd the orb on high;

---

* This translation, written at the age of twenty, which
Gray sent to West, consisted of about a hundred and ten lines.
Mason selected twenty-seven lines, which he published, as
Gray's first attempt at English verse; and to show how much
he had imbibed of Dryden's spirited manner at that early
period of his life.

The orb on high tenacious of its course,   10
True to the mighty arm that gave it force,
Far overleaps all bound, and joys to see
Its ancient lord secure of victory.
The theatre's green height and woody wall
Tremble ere it precipitates its fall;   15
The ponderous mass sinks in the cleaving ground,
While vales and woods and echoing hills rebound.
As when from Ætna's smoking summit broke,
The eyeless Cyclops heav'd the craggy rock;
Where Ocean frets beneath the dashing oar,   20
And parting surges round the vessel roar;
'Twas there he aim'd the meditated harm,
And scarce Ulysses scap'd his giant arm.
A tiger's pride the victor bore away,
With native spots and artful labour gay,   25
A shining border round the margin roll'd,
And calm'd the terrors of his claws in gold.

Cambridge, May 8, 1736.

V. 12. v. Milt. P. L. iv. 181, "At one slight bound high overleap'd all bound." *Luke.*

V. 14. v. Milt. P. L. iv. 140, "As the ranks ascend shade above shade, a woody theatre of stateliest view." *Luke.*

THE FRAGMENT OF A TRAGEDY,

DESIGNED BY MR. GRAY ON THE SUBJECT OF THE DEATH

OF AGRIPPINA.*

" THE Britannicus of Racine, I know, was one of Gray's most
favourite plays; and the admirable manner in which I have
heard him say that he saw it represented at Paris, seems to
have led him to choose the death of Agrippina for his first and
only effort in the drama.   The execution of it also, as far as
it goes, is so very much in Racine's taste, that I suspect, if
that great poet had been born an Englishman, he would have
written precisely in the same style and manner. However, as
there is at present in this nation a general prejudice against
declamatory plays, I agree with a learned friend, who perused
the manuscript, that this fragment will be little relished by
the many; yet the admirable strokes of nature and character
with which it abounds, and the majesty of its diction, prevent
me from withholding from the few, who I expect will relish it,
so great a curiosity (to call it nothing more) as part of a tragedy written by Gray.   These persons well know, that till
style and sentiment be a little more regarded, mere action and
passion will never secure reputation to the author, whatever
they may do to the actor.   It is the business of the one ' to
strut and fret his hour upon the stage; ' and if he frets and
struts enough, he is sure to find his reward in the plaudit of an
upper gallery; but the other ought to have some regard to the
cooler judgment of the closet: for I will be bold to say that
if Shakespeare himself had not written a multitude of passages
which please there as much as they do on the stage, his reputation would not stand so universally high as it does at present.
Many of these passages, to the shame of our theatrical taste,
are omitted constantly in the representation: but I say not
this from conviction that the mode of writing, which Gray pursued, is the best for dramatic purposes.   I think myself, what

---

* See Tacitus's Annals, book xiii. xiv.   *Mason.*

I have asserted elsewhere,* that a medium between the French
and English taste would be preferable to either; and yet this
medium, if hit with the greatest nicety, would fail of success
on our theatre, and that for a very obvious reason. Actors (I
speak of the troop collectively) must all learn to speak as well
as act, in order to do justice to such a drama.

"But let me hasten to give the reader what little insight I
can into Gray's plan, as I find and select it from two detached
papers. The Title and Dramatis Personæ are as follow."
(See Mason. Life of Gray, vol. iii. p. 8.)

AGRIPPINA, A TRAGEDY.

[It appears that Lord Hervey left in MS. a tragedy of Agrippina, in rhymed verse: see Walpole's Noble Authors, p. 453.
There is a tragedy of Agrippina by Lohenstein: see Resumé
de l' Hist. Allemande par A. L. Veimars, p. 271. See Cibber's Lives of the Poets, vol. ii. p. 8.]

DRAMATIS PERSONÆ

AGRIPPINA, the Empress-mother.
NERO, the Emperor.
POPPÆA, believed to be in love with OTHO.
OTHO, a young man of quality, in love with POPPÆA.
SENECA, the Emperor's Preceptor.
ANICETUS, Captain of the Guards.
DEMETRIUS, the Cynic, friend to SENECA.
ACERONIA, Confidante to AGRIPPINA.

SCENE — *The Emperor's villa at Baiæ.*

"THE argument drawn out by him, in these two papers, under
the idea of a plot and under-plot, I shall here unite; as it will
tend to show that the action itself was possessed of sufficient
unity.

"The drama opens with the indignation of Agrippina, at re-
ceiving her son's orders from Anicetus to remove from Baiæ,
and to have her guard taken from her. At this time, Otho,

---

* See Letters prefixed to Elfrida, particularly Letter II.

having conveyed Poppæa from the house of her husband Rufus Crispinus, brings her to Baiæ, where he means to conceal her among the crowd; or, if his fraud is discovered, to have recourse to the Emperor's authority; but, knowing the lawless temper of Nero, he determines not to have recourse to that expedient but on the utmost necessity.   In the mean time he commits her to the care of Anicetus, whom he takes to be his friend, and in whose age he thinks he may safely confide.   Nero is not yet come to Baiæ : but Seneca, whom he sends before him, informs Agrippina of the accusation concerning Rubellius Plancus, and desires her to clear herself, which she does briefly : but demands to see her son, who, on his arrival, acquits her of all suspicion, and restores her to her honours.   In the mean while, Anicetus, to whose care Poppæa had been intrusted by Otho, contrives the following plot to ruin Agrippina : he betrays his trust to Otho, and brings Nero, as it were by chance, to the sight of the beautiful Poppæa; the Emperor is immediately struck with her charms, and she, by a feigned resistance, increases his passion: though, in reality, she is from the first dazzled with the prospect of empire, and forgets Otho : she therefore joins with Anicetus in his design of ruining Agrippina, soon perceiving that it will be for her interest.   Otho, hearing that the Emperor had seen Poppæa, is much enraged; but not knowing that this interview was obtained through the treachery of Anicetus, is readily persuaded by him to see Agrippina in secret, and acquaint her with his fears that her son Nero would marry Poppæa.   Agrippina, to support her own power, and to wean the Emperor from the love of Poppæa, gives Otho encouragement, and promises to support him.   Anicetus secretly introduces Nero to hear their discourse, who resolves immediately on his mother's death, and, by Anicetus's means, to destroy her by drowning.   A solemn feast, in honour of their reconciliation, is to be made; after which, she being to go by sea to Bauli, the ship is so contrived as to sink or crush her: she escapes by accident, and returns to Baiæ.   In this interval, Otho has an interview with Poppæa; and being duped a second time by Anicetus and her, determines to fly with her into Greece, by means of a vessel which is to be furnished by Anicetus; but he, pretending to remove Poppæa on board in the night, conveys her to Nero's apartment: she then encourages and determines Nero to banish Otho, and finish the horrid deed he had attempted on his mother.   Anicetus undertakes to execute his resolves; and, under pretence of a plot upon the Emperor's life, is sent with a guard to murder Agrippina, who is still at Baiæ in imminent fear, and irresolute how to conduct herself.   The account of her death, and the Emperor's horror and fruitless remorse, finishes the drama."   *Mason.*

ACT I. SCENE 1.

AGRIPPINA. ACERONIA.

AGRIP. 'Tis well, begone! your errand is per-
  form'd,   [*Speaks as to* Anicetus *entering.*
The message needs no comment. Tell your master,
His mother shall obey him. Say you saw her
Yielding due reverence to his high command:
Alone, unguarded and without a lictor,   5
As fits the daughter of Germanicus.
Say, she retir'd to Antium; there to tend
Her household cares, a woman's best employment.
What if you add, how she turn'd pale and trembled:
You think, you spied a tear stand in her eye,   10
And would have dropp'd, but that her pride re-
  strain'd it?
(Go! you can paint it well) 'twill profit you,
And please the stripling. Yet 'twould dash his joy
To hear the spirit of Britannicus
Yet walks on earth: at least there are who know
Without a spell to raise, and bid it fire   16
A thousand haughty hearts, unus'd to shake
When a boy frowns, nor to be lured with smiles
To taste of hollow kindness, or partake
His hospitable board: they are aware   20
Of th' unpledg'd bowl, they love not aconite.

V. 19. So in the Britannicus of Racine, act. iv. sc. 2, Agrip-
pina says:
  " Vous êtes un ingrat, vous le fûtes toujours.
   Des vos plus jeunes ans, mes soins et mes tendresses
   N'ont arraché de vous, que de *feintes caresses.*"

Acer. He's gone: and much I hope these
    walls alone
And the mute air are privy to your passion.
Forgive your servant's fears, who sees the danger
Which fierce resentment cannot fail to raise   25
In haughty youth, and irritated power.

    Agrip. And dost thou talk to me, to me of dan-
Of haughty youth and irritated power,   [ger,
To her that gave it being, her that arm'd
This painted Jove, and taught his novice hand   30
To aim the forked bolt; while he stood trembling,
Scar'd at the sound, and dazzled with its bright-
    ness?

    'Tis like, thou hast forgot, when yet a stranger
To adoration, to the grateful steam
Of flattery's incense, and obsequious vows   35
From voluntary realms, a puny boy,
Deck'd with no other lustre than the blood
Of Agrippina's race, he liv'd unknown
To fame or fortune; haply eyed at distance
Some edileship, ambitious of the power   40
To judge of weights and measures; scarcely dar'd
On expectation's strongest wing to soar
High as the consulate, that empty shade

V. 29.
    " Il mêle avec l'orgueil qu'il a pris dans leur sang,
    La fierté des Nerons, *qu'il puisa dans mon flanc.*"
                                Britannicus, act i. sc. 1
    V. 38. So Elegy (Epitaph): " A youth, *to fortune and to
fame unknown.*"
    V. 45.
    " Ce jour, ce triste jour, frappe encor ma mémoire;
    Où Néron fut lui-même *ébloui de sa gloire.*"
                                Britannicus, act i. sc. 1

Of long-forgotten liberty: when I   44
Oped his young eye to bear the blaze of greatness;
Shew'd him ·where empire tower'd, and bade him
    strike
The noble quarry. Gods! then was the time
To shrink from danger; fear might then have worn
The mask of prudence; but a heart like mine,
A heart that glows with the pure Julian fire,   50
If bright ambition from her craggy seat
Display the radiant prize, will mount undaunted,
Gain the rough heights, and grasp the dangerous
    honour.   [steps,
  ACER. Thro' various life I have pursued your
Have seen your soul, and wonder'd at its daring:
Hence rise my fears. Nor am I yet to learn   55
How vast the debt of gratitude which Nero
To such a mother owes; the world, you gave him,
Suffices not to pay the obligation.

  I well remember too (for I was present)   60
When in a secret and dead hour of night,
Due sacrifice perform'd with barb'rous rites
Of mutter'd charms, and solemn invocation,
You bade the Magi call the dreadful powers,
That read futurity, to know the fate   65

"Hæc (exclamat) mihi pro tanto
Munere reddis præmia, gnate?
Hac sum, fateor, digna carinâ
Quæ te genui, quæ tibi lucem
Atque imperium, nomenque dedi
Cæsaris, amens."
  Agrippina's Speech in Seneca's Octavia, ver. 333
V. 64. On Nero's *Magical* studies, consult Plinii. Nat. Hist.
lib. xxx. cap. 5.

Impending o'er your son : their answer was,
If the son reign, the mother perishes.
Perish (you cried) the mother ! reign the son !
He reigns, the rest is heav'n's ; who oft has bade,
Ev'n when its will seem'd wrote in lines of blood, 70
Th' unthought event disclose a whiter meaning.
Think too how oft in weak and sickly minds
The sweets of kindness lavishly indulg'd
Rankle to gall ; and benefits too great
To be repaid, sit heavy on the soul,   75
As unrequited wrongs.   The willing homage
Of prostrate Rome, the senate's joint applause,
The riches of the earth, the train of pleasures
That wait on youth, and arbitrary sway :
These were your gift, and with them you bestow'd
The very power he has to be ungrateful.   81

    AGRIP. * Thus ever grave and undisturb'd re-
      flection
Pours its cool dictates in the madding ear
Of rage, and thinks to quench the fire it feels not.
Say'st thou I must be cautious, must be silent, 85
And tremble at the phantom I have raised ?
Carry to him thy timid counsels.   He
Perchance may heed 'em : tell him too, that one
Who had such liberal power to give, may still

---

    * In Gray's MS. Agrippina's was one continued speech
from this line to the end of the scene.   Mr. Mason informs us,
that he has altered it to the state in which it now stands.

    V. 91. " Et c'est trop respecter l' ouvrage de mes mains."
Britannicus, act iii. sc. 3.

    V 98. " And silken dalliance in the wardrobe lies."
               Hen. V. act ii. Chor. *Rogers.*

With equal power resume that gift, and raise   90
A tempest that shall shake her own creation
To its original atoms — tell me! say
This mighty emperor, this 'dreaded hero,
Has he beheld the glittering front of war?
Knows his soft ear the trumpet's thrilling voice, 95
And outcry of the battle? Have his limbs
Sweat under iron harness? Is he not
The silken son of dalliance, nurs'd in ease
And pleasure's flow'ry lap? — Rubellius lives,
And Sylla has his friends, though school'd by fear
To bow the supple knee, and court the times   101
With shows of fair obeisance; and a call,
Like mine, might serve belike to wake pretensions
Drowsier than theirs, who boast the genuine blood
Of our imperial house.   [passion,

  ACER. Did I not wish to check this dangerous
I might remind my mistress that her nod   107
Can rouse eight hardy legions, wont to stem
With stubborn nerves the tide, and face the rigour
Of bleak Germania's snows. Four, not less brave,
That in Armenia quell the Parthian force   111
Under the warlike Corbulo, by you
Mark'd for their leader: these, by ties confirm'd,
Of old respect and gratitude, are yours.
Surely the Masians too, and those of Egypt,   115

V. 99. v. Senecæ Octav. 437. Nero enters, "Perage im-
perata, mitte qui *Plauti* mihi, Sullæque cæsi referat abscissum
caput." i. e. Plauti Rubellii.
  V. 110. But Tacitus says: "Sed *Corbuloni* plus molis ad-
versus *ignaviam militum,* quam contra perfidium hostium, erat."
v. Annales, xiii. 35.

Have not forgot your sire: the eye of Rome,
And the Prætorian camp, have long rever'd,
With custom'd awe, the daughter, sister, wife,
And mother of their Cæsars.

    AGRIP.   Ha! by Juno,
It bears a noble semblance. On this base   120
My great revenge shall rise; or say we sound
The trump of liberty; there will not want.
Even in the servile senate, ears to own
Her spirit-stirring voice; Soranus there,
And Cassius; Vetus too, and Thrasea,   125
Minds of the antique cast, rough, stubborn souls
That struggle with the yoke. How shall the spark
Unquenchable, that glows within their breasts,
Blaze into freedom, when the idle herd
(Slaves from the womb, created but to stare,   130
And bellow in the Circus) yet will start,
And shake 'em at the name of liberty,
Stung by a senseless word, a vain tradition,
As there were magic in it? Wrinkled beldams
Teach it their grandchildren, as somewhat rare
That anciently appear'd, but when, extends   135
Beyond their chronicle — oh! 'tis a cause

V. 118.
  " Et moi, qui sur le trône ai suivi mes ancêtres,
    Moi, fille, femme, sœur, et mere de vos maîtres."
                          Britannicus, act i. sc. 2.
  V. 124. " The *spirit-stirring* drum, the ear-piercing fife."
                             Othello, act iii. sc. 3.
       —— " the *spirit-stirring* form
Of Cæsar, raptur'd with the charms of rule." Dyer. Rome.
  V. 147. " The swarm that in thy noontide beam were born.'
Bard.

To arm the hand of childhood, and rebrace
The slacken'd sinews of time-wearied age.

Yes, we may meet, ungrateful boy, we may!
Again the buried Genius of old Rome   141
Shall from the dust uprear his reverend head,
Rous'd by the shout of millions: there before
His high tribunal thou and I appear.
Let majesty sit on thy awful brow,   145
And lighten from thy eye: around thee call
The gilded swarm that wantons in the sunshine
Of thy full favour; Seneca be there
In gorgeous phrase of labour'd eloquence
To dress thy plea, and Burrhus strengthen it   150
With his plain soldier's oath, and honest seeming.
Against thee, liberty and Agrippina:
The world, the prize; and fair befall the victors.

But soft! why do I waste the fruitless hours
In threats unexecuted? Haste thee, fly   155
These hated walls that seem to mock my shame,
And cast me forth in duty to their lord.

ACER. 'Tis time to go, the sun is high advanc'd,
And, ere mid-day, Nero will come to Baiæ.

V. 148. "Hi rectores imperatoriæ juventæ, et pari in so-
cietate potentiæ, concordes, diversâ arte, ex æquo pollebant.
Burrus militaribus curis, et severitate morum: *Seneca* præ-
ceptis eloquentiæ, et comitate honestâ." Taciti Annales, xiii.
c. 2.

V. 149. See Senecæ Octav. v. 377.

V. 150. So in the speech of Burrhus in the Britannicus of
Racine, act i. sc. 2:
    " Je répondrai, madame; avec la liberté
     D'un soldat, que sait mal farder la vérité."
And again, act i. sc. 2:
    " Burrhus pour le mensonge, eut toujours trop d'horreur."

K

AGRIP. My thought aches at him; not the
basilisk
More deadly to the sight, than is to me   160
The cool injurious eye of frozen kindness.
I will not meet its poison. Let him feel
Before he sees me.
    ACER.   Why then stays my sovereign,
Where he so soon may —
    AGRIP.   Yes, I will be gone,   165
But not to Antium — all shall be confess'd,
Whate'er the frivolous tongue of giddy fame
Has spread among the crowd; things, that but
   whisper'd
Have arch'd the hearer's brow, and riveted
His eyes in fearful extasy: no matter   170
What; so't be strange and dreadful. — Sorceries,
Assassinations, poisonings — the deeper
My guilt, the blacker his ingratitude.

    And you, ye manes of ambition's victims,
Enshrined Claudius, with the pitied ghosts   175
Of the Syllani, doom'd to early death,
(Ye unavailing horrors, fruitless crimes!)

V. 169. " Whom have I hurt? has poet yet or peer
        Lost the *arch'd eyebrow*, or Parnassian sneer?"
            Pope. Prol. to the Satires, ver. 95.
" To *arch the brows* which on them gaz'd."
                V. Marvell. Poems, i. 45.
V. 172. " Pour rendre sa puissance, et la vôtre odieuses,
        J' avoûrai les rumeurs les plus injurieuses,
        Je confesserai tout, exils, assassinâts,
        Poison même."   Britannicus, act iii. sc. 3.
See also Taciti Annales, lib. xiii. c. 15.
V. 176. " Prò facinus ingens ! fœminæ est munus datus

If from the realms of night my voice ye hear,
In lieu of penitence, and vain remorse,
Accept my vengeance.   Though by me ye bled,
He was the cause.   My love, my fears for him,
Dried the soft springs of pity in my heart,
And froze them up with deadly cruelty.
Yet if your injur'd shades demand my fate,
If murder cries for murder, blood for blood,   185
Let me not fall alone; but crush his pride,
And sink the traitor in his mother's ruin.

[*Exeunt.*

SCENE II. — OTHO, POPPÆA.

OTHO. Thus far we're safe.   Thanks to the
      rosy queen
Of amorous thefts: and had her wanton son
Lent us his wings, we could not have beguil'd 190
With more elusive speed the dazzled sight
Of wakeful jealousy.   Be gay securely;
Dispel, my fair, with smiles, the tim'rous cloud
That hangs on thy clear brow.   So Helen look'd,
So her white neck reclin'd, so was she borne 195

Silanus, et cruore fœdavit suo
Patrios Penates, criminis ficti reus."
                              Senecæ Octavia, ver. 148.
And see Taciti Annales, xii. c. 3, 4.
    V. 195. "Obstipum caput et *tereti cervice reflexum.*"
                              Cic. de Nat. Deor. ii. 42.
    " Et caput *inflexâ* lentum *cervice* recumbit
      Marmoreâ."   Virgilii Ciris. 449.
        " *Niveâ cervice reclinis*
      Mollitur ipsa."   Manil. Astron. 5. v. 555.
This particular beauty is also given to Helen by Constantine

By the young Trojan to his gilded bark   196
With fond reluctance, yielding modesty,
And oft reverted eye, as if she knew not
Whether she fear'd, or wish'd to be pursued.

*   *   *   *   *   *   *

HYMN TO IGNORANCE.

A FRAGMENT.

[See Mason's Memoirs, vol. iii. p. 75. Supposed to be written
about the year 1742, when Gray returned to Cambridge.]

HAIL, horrors, hail! ye ever gloomy bowers,
Ye gothic fanes, and antiquated towers,
Where rushy Camus' slowly winding flood
Perpetual draws his humid train of mud:

Manasses, in his " Annales," (see Meursii Opera, vol. vii.
p. 390):

Δειρὴ μακρὰ κάταλευκος, ὅθεν ἐμυθουργήθη
Κυκνογενῆ τὴν εὐόπτον Ἑλένην χρημάτιζειν.

And so also in the Antehomerica of Tzetzes, ed. Jacobs. p. 115
(though the passage is corrupted).

" That soft cheek springing to the *marble neck,*
Which *bends aside* in vain."
Akenside. Pl. of Imag. b. i. p. 112. ed. Park.

V. 197. See Milton. Par. L. iv. 310:

" *Yielded* with coy submission, *modest* pride,
And sweet, *reluctant* amorous delay."   *Luke.*

V. 1. "Hail, horrors, hail ! " Milton. Par. L. i. 205.

V. 3. "Jam nec *arundiferum* mihi cura revisere *Camum,*"
Miltoni Eleg. i. 11. and 89. "*juncosas* Cami remeare *paludes.*"
Luke.

Glad I revisit thy neglected reign,   5
Oh take me to thy peaceful shade again.   [high
But chiefly thee, whose influence breathed from
Augments the native darkness of the sky;
Ah, ignorance! soft salutary power!
Prostrate with filial reverence I adore.   10
Thrice hath Hyperion roll'd his annual race,
Since weeping I forsook thy fond embrace.
Oh say, successful dost thou still oppose
Thy leaden ægis 'gainst our ancient foes?
Still stretch, tenacious of thy right divine,   15
The massy sceptre o'er thy slumb'ring line?
And dews Lethean through the land dispense
To steep in slumbers each benighted sense?
If any spark of wit's delusive ray
Break out, and flash a momentary day,   20
With damp, cold touch forbid it to aspire,
And huddle up in fogs the dang'rous fire.

   Oh say — she hears me not, but, careless grown,
Lethargic nods upon her ebon throne.

V. 4.   —— " Where rivers now
   Stream, and *perpetual draw their humid train.*"
             Milton. Par. Lost, vii. 310.

V. 14. " To hatch a new Saturnian age of lead."
             Pope. Dunciad, i. 28.

And so in the speech of Ignorance in " Henry and Minerva,"
by I. B. 1729 (one among the poetical pieces bound up by Pope
in his library, and now in my possession):

   "Myself behind this *ample shield of lead,*
    Will to the field my daring squadrons head."

V. 17. " Let Fancy still my sense in Lethe steep."
       Shakesp. T. Night. act iv. sc. 1.   *Luke.*

V. 22. " Here *Ignorance* in steel was arm'd, and there
    Cloath'd in a cowl, dissembled fast and pray'r;

Goddess! awake, arise! alas, my fears!   25
Can powers immortal feel the force of years?
Not thus of old, with ensigns wide unfurl'd,
She rode triumphant o'er the vanquish'd world;
Fierce nations own'd her unresisted might,
And all was ignorance, and all was night.   30
    Oh! sacred age! Oh! times for ever lost!
(The schoolman's glory, and the churchman's
      boast.)
For ever gone — yet still to fancy new,
Her rapid wings the transient scene pursue,
And bring the buried ages back to view.   35
    High on her car, behold the grandam ride
Like old Sesostris with barbaric pride;
* * * a team of harness'd monarchs bend
     *   *   *   *   *   *

    Against my sway her pious hand stretch'd out,
    And *fenc'd* with *double fogs* her idiot rout."
                       Henry and Minerva.
And so in the Dunciad, b. i. ver. 80:
    " All these, and more, the cloud-compelling queen
    Beholds thro' *fogs* that magnify the scene."
    V. 25.   Awake, arise, or be for ever fallen!"
                   Milt. P. L. i. 330. *Luke.*
    V. 37. " *Sesostris*-like, such charioteers as these
        May drive *six harness'd monarchs* if they please."
                Young. Love of Fame, Sat. v.
    " High on his car, Sesostris struck my view,
    Whom sceptred slaves in golden harness drew."
                 Pope. T. of Fame. *Luke.*
And so S. Philips. Blenheim, v. 16:
    " As curst Sesostris, proud Egyptian king,
    That *monarchs harness'd* to his chariot yok'd."

EDUCATION AND GOVERNMENT.

A FRAGMENT.*

[See Mason's Memoirs, vol. iii. p. 99; and Musæ Etonenses,
vol. ii. p. 152.]

ESSAY I.

―――― Πόταγ' ὦ 'γαθέ· τὰν γὰρ ἀοιδὰν
Οὔτι πα εἰς Ἀίδαν γε τὸν ἐκλελάθοντα φυλαξεῖς.
Theocritus, Id. I. 63.

As sickly plants betray a niggard earth,
Whose barren bosom starves her generous birth,
Nor genial warmth, nor genial juice retains,
Their roots to feed, and fill their verdant veins:
And as in climes, where winter holds his reign, 5
The soil, though fertile, will not teem in vain,
Forbids her gems to swell, her shades to rise,
Nor trusts her blossoms to the churlish skies:

Var. V. 2. *Barren*] Flinty. MS.

---

* In a note to his Roman history, Gibbon says: "Instead
of compiling tables of chronology and natural history, why
did not Mr. Gray apply the powers of his genius to finish the
philosophic poem of which he has left such an exquisite specimen?" Vol. iii. p. 248. 4to. — Would it not have been more
philosophical in Gibbon to have lamented the situation in
which Gray was placed; which was not only not favourable to
the cultivation of poetry, but which naturally directed his
thoughts to those learned inquiries, that formed the amusement or business of all around him?

So draw mankind in vain the vital airs,
Unform'd, unfriended, by those kindly cares,   10
That health and vigour to the soul impart, [heart:
Spread the young thought, and warm the opening
So fond instruction on the growing powers
Of nature idly lavishes her stores,
If equal justice with unclouded face   15
Smile not indulgent on the rising race,
And scatter with a free, though frugal hand,
Light golden showers of plenty o'er the land:
But tyranny has fix'd her empire there,
To check their tender hopes with chilling fear,   20
And blast the blooming promise of the year.
    This spacious animated scene survey,
From where the rolling orb, that gives the day,
His sable sons with nearer course surrounds
To either pole, and life's remotest bounds,   25
How rude so e'er th' exterior form we find,
Howe'er opinion tinge the varied mind,
Alike to all, the kind, impartial heav'n
The sparks of truth and happiness has giv'n:

Var. V. 19. *But tyranny has*] Gloomy sway have. MS.
      V. 21. *Blooming*] Vernal. MS.

V. 9. "Vitales auras carpis," Virg. Æn. i. 387. *Luke.*

V. 14. "And *lavish nature* laughs and throws her *stores* around," Dryden. Virgil, vii. 76. *Luke.*

V. 21. "Destroy the promise of the youthful year."
               Pope. Vert. and Pomona, 108. *Luke.*

V 36. "On mutual wants, build mutual happiness."
               Pope. Ep. iii. 112.

V. 47. "Bellica nubes," Claudiani Laus Seren. 196. *Luke.*

V. 48. So Claudian calls it, Bell. Getico, 641. "Cimbrica

With sense to feel, with memory to retain,　　30
They follow pleasure, and they fly from pain;
Their judgment mends the plan their fancy draws,
The event presages, and explores the cause;
The soft returns of gratitude they know,
By fraud elude, by force repel the foe;　　　35
While mutual wishes, mutual woes endear
The social smile, the sympathetic tear.

　　Say then, through ages by what fate confin'd
To different climes seem different souls assign'd?
Here measur'd laws and philosophic ease　　40
Fix, and improve the polish'd arts of peace;
There industry and gain their vigils keep,
Command the winds, and tame th' unwilling deep:
Here force and hardy deeds of blood prevail;
There languid pleasure sighs in every gale.　　45
Oft o'er the trembling nations from afar
Has Scythia breath'd the living cloud of war;
And, where the deluge burst, with sweepy sway
Their arms, their kings, their gods were roll'd
　　away.
As oft have issued, host impelling host,　　50
The blue-eyed myriads from the Baltic coast.

---

tempestas." Pope. Hom. Od. 5, 303, "And next a wedge to
drive with *sweepy sway*." See note on Bard, v. 75.
　V. 50. So Thomson. Liberty, iv. 803:
　　"Hence many a people, fierce with freedom, rush'd
　　From the rude iron regions of the *North*
　　To Libyan deserts, *swarm protruding swarm*."
And Winter, 840:
　　"Drove martial *horde on horde, with dreadful sweep*
　　Resistless rushing o'er the enfeebled South."
　V. 51. So Pope. Dunciad, iii. 89:
　　"The *North by myriads* pours her mighty sons."

The prostrate south to the destroyer yields
Her boasted titles, and her golden fields:
With grim delight the brood of winter view
A brighter day, and heav'ns of azure hue;   55
Scent the new fragrance of the breathing rose,
And quaff the pendent vintage as it grows.
Proud of the yoke, and pliant to the rod,
Why yet does Asia dread a monarch's nod,
While European freedom still withstands   60
Th' encroaching tide that drowns her lessening
          lands;
And sees far off, with an indignant groan,
Her native plains, and empires once her own?
Can opener skies and suns of fiercer flame
O'erpower the fire that animates our frame;   65
As lamps, that shed at eve a cheerful ray,
Fade and expire beneath the eye of day?
Need we the influence of the northern star
To string our nerves and steel our hearts to war?
And, where the face of nature laughs around,   70
Must sick'ning virtue fly the tainted ground?

Var. V. 55. *Heav'ns*] Skies. MS.
       V. 56. *Scent*] Catch. MS.

" The fair complexion of the *blue-eyed warriors of Germany*
formed a singular contrast with the swarthy or olive hue, which
is derived from the neighbourhood of the torrid zone." Gibbon.
Rom. Hist. iii. 337. Ausonius gives them this distinguished
feature: " *Oculos cærula*, flava comas," De Bissula. 17. p. 341.
ed. Tollii. " *Cærula* quis stupuit Germani *lumina*," Juv. Sat.
xiii. 164.
    V. 54. " Mirantur nemora et rorantes Sole racemos." Sta-
tius. v. Plin. Nat. H. l. xiii. c. ii. 1.
    V. 56. Milton. Arcades. 32, " And ye, ye *breathing roses* of
the wood." *Luke.*

Unmanly thought! what seasons can control,
What fancied zone can circumscribe the soul,
Who, conscious of the source from whence she
    springs,
By reason's light, on resolution's wings,   75
Spite of her frail companion, dauntless goes
O'er Libya's deserts and through Zembla's snows?
She bids each slumb'ring energy awake,
Another touch, another temper take,
Suspends th' inferior laws that rule our clay: 80
The stubborn elements confess her sway;
Their little wants, their low desires, refine,
And raise the mortal to a height divine.

   Not but the human fabric from the birth
Imbibes a flavour of its parent earth: 85
As various tracts enforce a various toil,
The manners speak the idiom of their soil.
An iron-race the mountain-cliffs maintain,
Foes to the gentler genius of the plain:
For where unwearied sinews must be found   90
With side-long plough to quell the flinty ground,
To turn the torrent's swift-descending flood,

V. 57. Claudian, in his poem De Bello Getico, ver. 504, makes the Gothic warriors mention the vines of Italy: "Quid palmitis uber Etrusci," &c. " Et dulces rapuit de collibus uvas," Statii Silv. ii.; and "Carpite de plenis *pendentes* vitibus uvas," Ovid. Am. i. x. 55. "*Pendet* vindemia," Virg. Georg. ii. 89.

V. 66. " And as these mighty tapers disappear,
       When day's bright lord ascends our hemisphere."
                    Dryd. Rel. Laici. *Rogers.*

V. 91. " And side-long lays the glebe."
                    Thomson. Spring. *Luke*

To brave the savage rushing from the wood,
What wonder if to patient valour train'd,
They guard with spirit, what by strength they
    gain'd ?   95
And while their rocky ramparts round they see,
The rough abode of want and liberty,
(As lawless force from confidence will grow)
Insult the plenty of the vales below ?   99
What wonder, in the sultry climes, that spread
Where Nile redundant o'er his summer-bed
From his broad bosom life and verdure flings,
And broods o'er Egypt with his wat'ry wings,
If with advent'rous oar and ready sail
The dusky people drive before the gale;   105

"Or drives his venturous *ploughshare* to the steep,
Or seeks the den, where snow-tracks mark the way,
And drags the struggling *savage* into day."
                          Goldsmith. Traveller.

V. 101. "Gaudet aquis, quas ipsa vehit *Niloque redundant.*"
Claudiani Nilus, ver. 7. "The *broad redundant Nile.*" Young.
Busiris, act v. sc. 1.

    V. 103.   —— "On the watery calm
His brooding wings the Spirit of God outspread."
                          Milt. P. L. vii. 235.

"O'er which he kindly *spreads his spacious wing,*
And *hatches* plenty for th' ensuing spring."
                Denham. Cooper's Hill. W.

V. 105. "Cepheam hic *Meröen, fuscaque regna* canat," Propert. iv. vi. 78. " *Fuscis* Ægyptus alumnis," ii. xxiv. 15.

"Jam proprior tellusque natans Ægyptia Nilo;
Lenius irriguis *infuscat* corpora campis."
                          Manil. iv. 727.

And so Dryden's version of Virg. Georg. iv. 409, pointed out
by Wakefield:

"And where in pomp the *sun-burnt people* ride
On painted barges o'er the *teeming tide.*"

V. Martial. Ep. iv. 42. "Mareotide fuscâ." "Spread the

Or on frail floats to neighb'ring cities ride,
That rise and glitter o'er the ambient tide

*   *   *   *   *

[The following couplet, which was intended to have been introduced in the poem on the Alliance of Education and
Government, is much too beautiful to be lost.   Mason, vol.
iii. p. 114.]

When love could teach a monarch to be wise,*
And gospel-light first dawned from Bullen's eyes.

Var. V. 106. *Neighb'ring*] Distant. MS.

---

thin oar, and catch the *driving gale.*" Pope. Ess. on Man, iii.
178. See Gifford's Juvenal. Sat. xv. 175. p. 460.

V. 106. Lucan will explain the meaning of the *frail float:*

—— " Sic cum tenet omnia *Nilus,*
Conseritur *bibula Memphitis cymba papyro.*"
Pharsal. iv. 135.

But Gilpin gives another explanation in his Western Tour, see
p. 34. Add Brown's Travels in Africa, p. 66. 4to.. Arbuth-
not on Coins, p. 215. 4to. Denon. Trav. ii. p. 224.

* The last couplet of this poem: " *When love could teach,*"
&c. has been imitated by H. Walpole, in an inscription on a
Gothic column to Queen Katharine ; but with a loss of the
metaphorical beauty in the original:

" From Katharine's wrongs a nation's bliss was spread,
And Luther's light from Henry's lawless bed."

" If (says Dryden) Conscience had any part in moving the
king to sue for a divorce, she had taken a long nap of almost
twenty years together before she was awakened; and, perhaps,
had slept on till doomsday, if Anne Boleyn, or some other fair
lady, had not given her a jog: so the satisfying of an inordi-
nate passion cannot be denied to have had a great share at
least in the production of that schism which led the very way
to our pretended Reformation." Dryden. ed. Malone, vol. iii.
p. 522.

COMMENTARY.

THE author's subject being (as we have seen) *the necessary alliance between a good form of government and a good mode of education, in order to produce the happiness of mankind*, the Poem opens with two similes; an uncommon kind of exordium: but which I suppose the poet intentionally chose, to intimate the analogical method he meant to pursue in his subsequent reasonings. 1st, He asserts that men without education are like sickly plants in a cold or barren soil (line 1 to 5, and 8 to 12); and, 2dly, he compares them, when unblest with a just and well-regulated government, to plants that will not blossom or bear fruit in an unkindly and inclement air (l. 5 to 9, and l. 13 to 22). Having thus laid down the two propositions he means to prove, he begins by examining into the characteristics which (taking a general view of mankind) all men have in common one with another (l. 22 to 39); they covet pleasure and avoid pain (l. 31); they feel gratitude for benefits (l. 34); they desire to avenge wrongs, which they effect either by force or cunning (l. 35); they are linked to each other by their common feelings, and participate in sorrow and in joy (l. 36, 37). If then all the human species agree in so many moral particulars, whence arises the diversity of national characters ? This question the poet puts at line 38, and dilates upon to l. 64. Why, says he, have some nations shewn a propensity to commerce and industry; others to war and rapine; others to ease and pleasure? (l. 42 to 46). Why have the northern people overspread, in all ages, and prevailed over the southern? (l. 46 to 58). Why has Asia been, time out of mind, the seat of despotism, and Europe that of freedom? (l. 59 to 64). Are we from these instances to imagine men necessarily enslaved to the inconveniences of the climate where they were born? (l. 64 to 72). Or are we not rather to suppose there is a natural strength in the human mind, that is able to vanquish and break through them? (l. 72 to 84). It is confest, however, that men receive an early tincture from the situation they are placed in, and the climate which produces them (l. 84 to 88). Thus the inhabitants of the mountains, inured to labour and patience, are naturally trained to war (l. 88 to 96); while those of the plain are more open to any attack, and softened by ease and plenty (l. 96 to 99). Again, the Ægyptians, from the nature of their situation, might be the inventors of home navigation, from a necessity of keeping up an intercourse between their towns during the inundation of the Nile (l. 99 to ***). Those persons would naturally have the first turn to commerce, who inhabited a barren coast like the Tyrians, and were persecuted by some neighbouring tyrant; or were drove to take refuge on some shoals, like the Venetian and Hollander: their discovery of some rich island, in the infancy of the world, described. The Tartar hardened to war by his rigorous climate and pastoral life, and by his disputes for water and herbage in a country without land-marks, as also by skirmishes between his rival clans, was consequently fitted to conquer his rich southern neighbours, whom ease and luxury had enervated: yet this is no proof that liberty and valour may not exist in southern climes, since the Syrians and Carthaginians gave noble instances of both; and the Arabians carried their conquests as far as the Tartars. Rome also (for many centuries) repulsed those very nations, which, when she grew weak, at length demolished † her extensive empire.****

---

† The reader will perceive that the Commentary goes further than the text. The reason for which is, that the Editor found it so on the paper from which he formed that comment; and as the thoughts seemed to be those which Gray would have next graced with the harmony of his numbers, he held it best to give them in continuation. There are other maxims on different papers, all apparently relating to the same subject, which are too excellent to be lost; these, therefore, (as the place in which he meant to employ them cannot be ascertained) I shall subjoin to this note, under the title of detached Sentiments:

" Man is a creature not capable of cultivating his mind but in society, and in that only where he is not a slave to the necessities of life.

" Want is the mother of the inferior arts, but Ease that of the finer ; as eloquence, policy, morality, poetry, sculpture, painting, architecture, which are the improvements of the former.

" The climate inclines some nations to contemplation and pleasure; others to hardship, action, and war; but not so as to incapacitate the former for courage and discipline, or the latter for civility, politeness, and works of genius.

" It is the proper work of education and government united to redress the faults that arise from the soil and air.

" The principal drift of education should be to make men *think* in the northern climates, and *act* in the southern.

" The different steps and degrees of education may be compared to the artificer's operations upon marble; it is one thing to dig it out of the quarry, and another to square it, to give it gloss and lustre, call forth every beautiful spot and vein, shape it into a column, or animate it into a statue.

" To a native of free and happy governments his country is always dear:

    ' He loves his old hereditary trees.   (COWLEY.)

while the subject of a tyrant has no country; he is therefore selfish and base-minded; he has no family, no posterity, no desire of fame; or, if he has, of one that turns not on its proper object.

" Any nation that wants public spirit, neglects education, ridicules the desire of fame, and even of virtue and reason, must be ill governed.

"Commerce changes entirely the fate and genius of nations, by communicating arts and opinions, circulating money, and introducing the materials of luxury; she first opens and polishes the mind, then corrupts and enervates both that and the body.

" Those invasions of effeminate southern nations by the warlike northern people, seem (in spite of all the terror, mischief, and ignorance which they brought with them) to be necessary evils; in order to revive the spirit of mankind, softened and broken by the arts of commerce, to restore them to their native liberty and equality, and to give them again the power of supporting danger and hardship ; so a comet, with all the horrors that attend it as it passes through our system, brings a supply of warmth and light to the sun, and of moisture to the air.

" The doctrine of Epicurus is ever ruinous to society; it had its rise when Greece was declining, and perhaps hastened its dissolution, as also that of Rome; it is now propagated in France and in England, and seems likely to produce the same effect in both.

" One principal characteristic of vice in the present age is the contempt of fame.

" Many are the uses of good fame to a generous mind: it extends our existence and example into future ages ; continues and propagates virtue, which otherwise would be as short-lived as our frame; and prevents the prevalence of vice in a generation more corrupt even than our own. It is impossible to conquer that natural desire we have of being remembered ; even criminal ambition and avarice, the most selfish of all passions, would wish to leave a name behind them."

Thus, with all the attention that a connoisseur in painting employs in collecting every slight outline as well as finished drawing which led to the completion of some capital picture, I have endeavoured to preserve every fragment of this great poetical design. It surely deserved this care, as it was one of

the noblest which Mr. Gray ever attempted; and also, as far
as he carried it into execution, the most exquisitely finished.
That he carried it no further is, and must ever be, a most
sensible loss to the republic of letters. *Mason*.

STANZAS TO MR. BENTLEY.

A FRAGMENT.

[See Mason's Memoirs, vol. iii. p. 148.]

These were in compliment to Bentley, who drew a set of
designs for Gray's poems, particularly a head-piece to the
Long Story.   The original drawings are in the library at
Strawberry Hill. See H. Walpole's Works, vol. ii. p. 447.

In silent gaze the tuneful choir among,
   Half pleas'd, half blushing, let the Muse admire,
While Bentley leads her sister-art along,
   And bids the pencil answer to the lyre.

See, in their course, each transitory thought   5
   Fix'd by his touch a lasting essence take;
Each dream, in fancy's airy colouring wrought,
   To local symmetry and life awake!

V. 3. So Pope. Epist. to Jervas, 13:
   " Smit with the love of *sister-arts* we came;
    And met congenial, mingling flame with flame."
V. Dryden to Kneller, " Our arts are sisters," " Long time
the *sister-arts* in iron sleep."
V. 7. " Thence endless streams of fair ideas flow,
    Strike on the sketch, or in the picture glow."
            Pope. Epist. to Jervas, ver. 42.
V. 8. " When *life awakes* and dawns at every line." Pope.
Ep. to Jervas, v. 4. See also Kidd's note to Hor. A. P. v. 66,
from Plato.

L

The tardy rhymes that us'd to linger on,
 To censure cold, and negligent of fame, 10
In swifter measures animated run,
 And catch a lustre from his genuine flame.

Ah! could they catch his strength, his easy grace,
 His quick creation, his unerring line;
The energy of Pope they might efface, 15
 And Dryden's harmony submit to mine.

But not to one in this benighted age
 Is that diviner inspiration giv'n,
That burns in Shakespeare's or in Milton's page,
 The pomp and prodigality of heav'n. 20

As when conspiring in the diamond's blaze,
 The meaner gems that singly charm the sight,
Together dart their intermingled rays,
 And dazzle with a luxury of light.

Enough for me, if to some feeling breast 25
 My lines a secret sympathy 'impart;'
And as their pleasing influence 'flows confest,'
 A sigh of soft reflection 'heaves the heart.' †

   * * * * * *

V. 20. " Heaven, that but once was *prodigal* before,
  To Shakspear gave as much, she could not give him
   more."   Dryden to Congreve. *Luke.*

 † The words within the inverted commas were supplied by
Mason, a corner of the old manuscript copy being torn: with all
due respect to his memory, I do not consider that he has been
successful in the selection of the few words which he has added

SKETCH OF HIS OWN CHARACTER.

WRITTEN IN 1761, AND FOUND IN ONE OF HIS POCKET-
BOOKS.

TOO poor for a bribe, and too proud to importune,
He had not the method of making a fortune:
Could love, and could hate, so was thought some-
    what odd;
No very great wit, he believed in a God:
A post or a pension he did not desire,   5
But left church and state to Charles Townshend
    and Squire.

---

to supply the imperfect lines: my own opinion is, that Gray
had in his mind Dryden's Epistle to Kneller, from which he
partly took his expressions: under the shelter of that sup-
position, I shall venture to give another reading:

    " Enough for me, if to some feeling breast
      My lines a secret sympathy ' convey; '
      And as their pleasing influence ' is exprest,'
      A sigh of soft reflection ' dies away.'

V. 1. This is similar to a passage in one of Swift's letters
to Gay, speaking of poets : "I have been considering why
poets have such ill success in making their court. They are
too libertine to haunt ante-chambers, too *poor to bribe* porters,
and too *proud to cringe* to second-hand favourites in a great
family." See Pope. Works, xi. 36. ed. Warton.

V. 4. "I pay my debts, *believe*, and say my prayers."
                    Pope. Prol. to Satires, ver. 268.

V. 6. *Squire*] At that time Fellow of St. John's College,
Cambridge, and afterwards Bishop of St. David's. Dr. S.
Squire died 1766, see Nicholl. Poems, vol. vii. p. 231. Bishop
Warburton one day met Dean Tucker, who said that he hoped
his Lordship liked his situation at Gloucester; on which the
sarcastic Bishop replied, that never bishopric was so *bedeaned*,
for that his predecessor Dr. Squire had made *religion his trade,*

AMATORY LINES.

The following lines by Gray first appeared in Warton's* edition of Pope, vol. i. p. 285.

WITH beauty, with pleasure surrounded, to languish —
To weep without knowing the cause of my anguish:
To start from short slumbers, and wish for the morning —
To close my dull eyes when I see it returning;

Sighs sudden and frequent, looks ever dejected —
Words that steal from my tongue, by no meaning connected!
Ah! say, fellow-swains, how these symptoms befell me?
They smile, but reply not—Sure Delia will tell me!

---

and that he Dr. Tucker had made *trade his religion.* See Cradock. Mem. iv. 335.

Perhaps these lines of Gray gave a hint to Goldsmith for his character of Burke in the 'Retaliation:'

'Tho' equal to all things, for all things unfit,
  Too nice for a statesman, too proud for a wit;
  For a patriot too cool, for a drudge disobedient,
  And too fond of the right to pursue the expedient.'

* As Dr. Warton has here favoured us with some manuscript lines by Gray, it will be a species of poetical justice to give the reader some lines from a manuscript of Dr. Warton, which he intended to insert in his Ode to Fancy, and which are placed within the inverted commas:

In converse while methinks I rove
With Spenser through a fairy grove,
'Or seem by powerful Dante led
To the dark chambers of the dead,

SONG.*

THYRSIS, when we parted, swore
  Ere the spring he would return —
Ah! what means yon violet flower,
  .And the bud that decks the thorn?
'Twas the lark that upward sprung!   5
'Twas the nightingale that sung!

Var. V. 1. *Thyrsis, when we parted*] In Mr. Park's edition,
for " when *we parted*," it is printed " when *he left me*." And,
for " *Ere* the spring," " *In* the spring."
  Var. V. 3. *Yon violet flower*] In Mr. Park's edition, " *the
    opening flower*."
    V. 5. *'Twas the lark*] In Mr. Park's edition, this and
    the following line are transposed.

    Or to the $\frac{silent}{gloomy}$ towers where pine
    The sons of famish'd Ugoline;
    Or by the Tuscan wizard's power
    Am wafted to Alcina's bower'
    Till suddenly, &c.
And after the couplet —
    On which thou lov'st to sit at eve,
    Musing o'er thy darling's grave —
Add, from the MS. —
    ' To whom came trooping at thy call
    Thy spirits from their airy hall,
    From sea and earth, from heaven and hell,
    Stern Hecate, and sweet Ariel.'

  * Written at the request of Miss Speed, to an old air of
Geminiani: — the thought from the French. This and the
preceding Poem were presented by Miss Speed, then Countess
de Viry, to the Rev. Mr. Leman of Suffolk, while on a visit
at her castle in Savoy, where she died in 1783. Admiral Sir
T. Duckworth, whose father was vicar of Stoke from 1756 to
1794, remembers Gray and Miss Speed at that place. Gray
left Stoke about the year 1758, on the death of his aunt Mrs.
Rogers: when his acquaintance with Miss Speed probably
closed.

Idle notes! untimely green!
  Why this unavailing haste?
Western gales and skies serene
  Speak not always winter past.   10
Cease, my doubts, my fears to move,
Spare the honour of my love.

[This Song is in this edition printed from the copy as it
appears in H. Walpole's Letters to the Countess of Ailesbury.
See his Works, vol. v. p. 561.]

Var. V. 8. *Why* this] In Mr. Park's edition, "why *such*."
  V. 9. *Western*, &c.] In Mr. Park's edition, these lines
    are printed thus :
      " *Gentle* gales and *sky* serene
        Prove not always winter past."

TOPHET.

AN EPIGRAM.

Thus Tophet look'd; so grinn'd the brawling fiend,
Whilst frighted prelates bow'd, and call'd him
friend.

Our mother-church, with half-averted sight,
Blush'd as she bless'd her grisly proselyte;
Hosannas rung thro' hell's tremendous borders,
And Satan's self had thoughts of taking orders.*

---

* The Rev. Henry Etough, of Cambridge University, the person satirized, was as remarkable for the eccentricities of his character, as for his personal appearance. Mr. Tyson, of Bene't College, made an etching of his head, and presented it to Gray, who embellished it with the above lines. Information respecting Mr. Etough, (who was rector of Therfield, Herts, and of Colmworth, Bedfordshire, and patronized by Sir Robert Walpole,) may be found in the Gentleman's Magaz. vol. lvi. p. 25. 281 ; and in Nichols's Literary Anecdotes of the xviiith Century, vol. viii. p. 261, and Brydges' Restituta, vol. iv. p. 246, and Polwhele's Recollect. i. 212. "Etough was originally a Jew, but renounced his religion for the sake of a valuable living. To understand the second line, it is necessary to inform you, that Tophet kept the conscience of the minister." See Neville. Imit. of Horace, p. 59. "The slanderous pests, the ETOUGHS of the age." See an account of Dr. Etough in Coxe's Life of Sir R. Walpole, vol. i. p. xxvi. "Etough was a man of great research and eager curiosity, replete with prejudice, but idolizing Sir R. Walpole, &c."

IMPROMPTU,

SUGGESTED BY A VIEW, IN 1766, OF THE SEAT AND
RUINS OF A DECEASED NOBLEMAN, AT
KINGSGATE, KENT.*

[Written at Denton in the spring of 1766. See Nichols' Select Poems, vol. vii. p. 350, and W. S Landori Poemata,
p. 196.]

OLD, and abandon'd by each venal friend,
 Here H——d form'd the pious resolution
To smuggle a few years, and strive to mend
 A broken character and constitution.

On this congenial spot he fix'd his choice; 5
 Earl Goodwin trembled for his neighbouring
  sand;
Here sea-gulls scream, and cormorants rejoice,
 And mariners, though shipwreck'd, dread to
  land.

Here reign the blustering North and blighting
 East,
 No tree is heard to whisper, bird to sing; 10

Var. V. 2. *Form'd*] Took. MS.
 V. 3. *A*] Some. MS.
 V. 9. *Dread*] Fear. Nichols.

---

 * Dallaway, in his Anecdotes of the Arts, p. 385, says, that
this house was built by Lord Holland as a correct imitation
of Cicero's Formian villa, at Baiæ, under the superintendence
of Sir Thomas Wynne, Bart. afterwards Lord Newborough.
See Gent. Mag. vol. lxxvii. p. 1116.

Yet Nature could not furnish out the feast,
   Art he invokes new horrors still to bring.

Here mouldering fanes and battlements arise,
   Turrets and arches nodding to their fall,
Unpeopled monast'ries delude our eyes,   15
   And mimic desolation covers all.

" Ah!" said the sighing peer, "had B—te been
     true,
   Nor M—'s, R—'s, B—'s friendship vain,
Far better scenes than these had blest our view,
   And realiz'd the beauties which we feign: 20

" Purg'd by the sword, and purified by fire,
   Then had we seen proud London's hated walls;
Owls would have hooted in St. Peter's choir,
   And foxes stunk and litter'd in St. Paul's."

Var. V. 11. *Could*] Cannot. MS.
     V. 12. *Horrors*] Terrors. Nich.
     V. 13. *Here*] Now. MS.
     V. 14. *Turrets and arches*] Arches and turrets. MS.
     V. 15. *Monast'ries, our*] Palaces, his. MS.
     V. 17. *B—te*] Bute. MS.
     V. 18. *M—'s, R—'s, B—'s*] Shelburne's, Rigby's, Cal-
        craft's. MS.
        Nor C—'s nor B—d's promises been vain. Nich.
     V. 19. *Better*] Other. MS. Grac'd our view. N.
     V. 20. *Beauties which*] Ruins that. MS.   Horrors
        which. N.
     V. 21. *Purified*] Beautified. MS.
     V. 23. *Would*] Might. MS. Should. N.

    V. 18. These initials stand for "Mungo's, Rigby's, Brad-
shaw's. See Heroic Epistle, v. 95; and Verses by Lord Holland in returning from Italy, 1767, in Asylum for Fug. Pieces,
ii. p. 10:

THE CANDIDATE:

OR, THE CAMBRIDGE COURTSHIP.*

[See character of Lord Sandwich in "Chrysal." See Scott's
Lives of the Novelists, i. p. 169 ; Davies. Biog. and Lit.
Anecdotes; Churchill's Verses on Lord Sandwich, in Candi-
date and Duellist; "From his youth upwards," &c. Cradock's Memoirs, vol. i. p. 117. 148. vol. iv. p. 163. 223; Miss
Hawkins's Anecdotes, p. 239 ; Bell's Fugitive Poetry, v.
xvi. p. 93. 172 ; Wilkes. Letters, i. p. 211. ii. p. 220 ;
Walpole. Letters to Lord Hertford, p. 51—65. 102. by which
it appears that Warburton had dedicated his Sermons to
Lord Sandwich, but expunged his name for Pitt's. I have
seen " A letter of advice from Alma Mater to her beloved
son, Jemmy Twitcher, 1764."]

WHEN sly Jemmy Twitcher had smugg'd up his
    face,
With a lick of court whitewash, and pious grimace,
A wooing he went, where three sisters of old
In harmless society guttle and scold.   4

  "Lord! sister," says Physic to Law, "I declare,
Such a sheep-biting look, such a pick-pocket air!
Not I for the Indies: — you know I'm no prude, —
But his nose is a shame, — and his eyes are so
    lewd!

" But, *Rigby*, what did I for thee endure,
  Thy serpent's tooth admitted of no lure:
  Shelburne and Calcraft ! O ! the holy band
  See, see, with Gower caballing where they stand," &c.

 * These verses were written a short time previous to the
election of a high-steward of the University of Cambridge, for
which office the noble lord alluded to (Lord Sandwich) made
an active canvass.

 V. 8. *Nose*] In all editions printed by mistake "Name."

Then he shambles and straddles so oddly — I
   fear —
No — at our time of life 'twould be silly, my dear."
  "I don't know," says Law, "but methinks for
    his look,   11
'Tis just like the picture in Rochester's book;
Then his character, Phyzzy, — his morals — his
   life —
When she died, I can't tell, but he once had a wife.
They say he's no Christian, loves drinking and
   w——g,   15
And all the town rings of his swearing and roaring!
His lying and filching, and Newgate-bird tricks; —
Not I — for a coronet, chariot and six."
  Divinity heard, between waking and dozing,
Her sisters denying, and Jemmy proposing: 20
From table she rose, and with bumper in hand,
She strok'd up her belly, and strok'd down her
   band —   [ing!
 "What a pother is here about wenching and roar-
Why, David lov'd catches, and Solomon w——g:
Did not Israel filch from th' Egyptians of old 25
Their jewels of silver and jewels of gold?
The prophet of Bethel, we read, told a lie:
He drinks — so did Noah; — he swears — so do I:

V. 9.   —— " That babe of grace
      Who ne'er before at sermon show'd his face,
      See *Jemmy Twitcher shambles*." ——
                      Heroic Epistle, 125, note.
See Hurd. Obs. on this word, in Cradock. Memoirs, vol. i. 117;
and Anecdote, p. 164.
  V. 16. But see Cradock. Memoirs, vol. iv. 166.

To reject him for such peccadillos, were odd;
Besides, he repents — for he talks about G** —
[*To* Jemmy]
' Never hang down your head, you poor penitent
elf,
Come buss me — I'll be Mrs. Twitcher myself.' "

*   *   *   *   *   *

[The concluding couplet is too gross to give. Ed.]

" From recollection I am sure Lord Sandwich was aware of
Gray; for about the time he offered himself as high-steward,
contrary to his usual maxim of not seeing an enemy on public
occasions, he once said to me, ' I have my private reasons for
knowing his absolute inveteracy.' " Cradock. iv. 223.

EXTRACTS.

PROPERTIUS, LIB. III. ELEG. V. v. 19.

" Me juvat in primâ coluisse Helicona juventâ," &c.

IMITATED.

Long as of youth the joyous hours remain,
Me may Castalia's sweet recess detain,
Fast by the umbrageous vale lull'd to repose,
Where Aganippe warbles as it flows;   4
Or roused by sprightly sounds from out the trance,
I'd in the ring knit hands, and join the Muses'
dance.
Give me to send the laughing bowl around,
My soul in Bacchus' pleasing fetters bound;
Let on this head unfading flowers reside,
There bloom the vernal rose's earliest pride;   10

And when, our flames commission'd to destroy,
Age step 'twixt Love and me, and intercept the
    joy;
When my changed head these locks no more shall
And all its jetty honours turn to snow; [know,
Then let me rightly spell of Nature's ways;   15
To Providence, to HIM my thoughts I'd raise,
Who taught this vast machine its steadfast laws,
That first, eternal, universal cause;
Search to what regions yonder star retires,
That monthly waning hides her paly fires,   20
And whence, anew revived, with silver light
Relumes her crescent orb to cheer the dreary
    night:
How rising winds the face of ocean sweep,
Where lie the eternal fountains of the deep,
And whence the cloudy magazines maintain   25
Their wintry war, or pour the autumnal rain;
How flames perhaps, with dire confusion hurl'd,
Shall sink this beauteous fabric of the world;
What colours paint the vivid arch of Jove;
What wondrous force the solid earth can move, 30
When Pindus' self approaching ruin dreads,
Shakes all his pines, and bows his hundred heads;
Why does yon orb, so exquisitely bright,
Obscure his radiance in a short-liv'd night;
Whence the Seven Sisters' congregated fires, 35
And what Bootes' lazy waggon tires;
How the rude surge its sandy bounds control;
Who measured out the year, and bade the sea-
    sons roll;

If realms beneath those fabled torments know,
Pangs without respite, fires that ever glow, 40
Earth's monster brood stretch'd on their iron bed,
The hissing terrors round Alecto's head,
Scarce to nine acres Tityus' bulk confined,
The triple dog that scares the shadowy kind,
All angry heaven inflicts, or hell can feel, 45
The pendent rock, Ixion's whirling wheel,
Famine at feasts, or thirst amid the stream;
Or are our fears the enthusiast's empty dream,
And all the scenes, that hurt the grave's repose,
But pictured horror and poetic woes. 50
 These soft inglorious joys my hours engage;
Be love my youth's pursuit, and science crown
  my age.

       * 1738. Æt. 22.

———

PROPERTIUS, LIB. II. ELEG. I. v. 17.

"Quod mihi si tantum, Mæcenas, fata dedissent," &c.

YET would the tyrant Love permit me raise
My feeble voice, to sound the victor's praise,
To paint the hero's toil, the ranks of war,
The laurell'd triumph, and the sculptured car;
No giant race, no tumult of the skies, 5
No mountain-structures in my verse should rise.
Nor tale of Thebes, nor Ilium there should be,
Nor how the Persian trod the indignant sea;
Not Marius' Cimbrian wreaths would I relate,
Nor lofty Carthage struggling with her fate. 10

Here should Augustus great in arms appear,
And thou, Mæcenas, be my second care;
Here Mutina from flames and famine free,
And there the ensanguined wave of Sicily,
And scepter'd Alexandria's captive shore,   15
And sad Philippi, red with Roman gore:
Then, while the vaulted skies loud ïos rend,
In golden chains should loaded monarchs bend,
And hoary Nile with pensive aspect seem
To mourn the glories of his sevenfold stream,   20
While prows, that late in fierce encounter met,
Move through the sacred way and vainly threat,
Thee too the Muse should consecrate to fame,
And with her garlands weave thy ever-faithful
          name.
    But nor Callimachus' enervate strain   25
May tell of Jove, and Phlegra's blasted plain;
Nor I with unaccustomed vigour trace
Back to its source divine the Julian race.
Sailors to tell of winds and seas delight,
The shepherd of his flocks, the soldier of the fight,
A milder warfare I in verse display;   31
Each in his proper art should waste the day:
Nor thou my gentle calling disapprove,
To die is glorious in the bed of Love.
    Happy the youth, and not unknown to fame,
Whose heart has never felt a second flame.   36
Oh, might that envied happiness be mine!
To Cynthia all my wishes I confine;
Or if, alas! it be my fate to try
Another love, the quicker let me die: 40

But she, the mistress of my faithful breast,
Has oft the charms of constancy confest,
Condemns her fickle sex's fond mistake,
And hates the tale of Troy for Helen's sake.
Me from myself the soft enchantress stole;   45
Ah! let her ever my desires control,
Or if I fall the victim of her scorn,
From her loved door may my pale corse be borne.
The power of herbs can other harms remove,
And find a cure for every ill, but love.   50
The Lemnian's hurt Machaon could repair,
Heal the slow chief, and send again to war;
To Chiron Phœnix owed his long-lost sight,
And Phœbus' son recall'd Androgeon to the light.
Here arts are vain, e'en magic here must fail,   55
The powerful mixture and the midnight spell;
The hand that can my captive heart release,
And to this bosom give its wonted peace,
May the long thirst of Tantalus allay,
Or drive the infernal vulture from his prey.   60
For ills unseen what remedy is found?
Or who can probe the undiscover'd wound?
The bed avails not, nor the leech's care,
Nor changing skies can hurt, nor sultry air.
'Tis hard th' elusive symptoms to explore: 65
To-day the lover walks, to-morrow is no more;
A train of mourning friends attend his pall,
And wonder at the sudden funeral.
    When then the fates that breath they gave shall
        claim,
And the short marble but preserve a name,   70

M

A little verse my all that shall remain;
Thy passing courser's slacken'd speed restrain;
(Thou envied honour of thy poet's days,
Of all our youth the ambition and the praise!)
Then to my quiet urn awhile draw near,   75
And say, while o'er that place you drop the tear,
Love and the fair were of his youth the pride;
He lived, while she was kind; and when she
    frown'd, he died.

                     April, 1742. Æt. 26.

———

TASSO GERUS. LIB. CANT. XIV. ST. 32.

"Preser commiato, e sì 'l desio gli sprona," &c.

DISMISS'D at length, they break through all delay
To tempt the dangers of the doubtful way;
And first to Ascalon their steps they bend,
Whose walls along the neighbouring sea extend,
Nor yet in prospect rose the distant shore;   15
Scarce the hoarse waves from far were heard to
    roar,
When thwart the road a river roll'd its flood
Tempestuous, and all further course withstood;
The torrent stream his ancient bounds disdains,
Swoll'n with new force, and late-descending rains.
Irresolute they stand; when lo, appears
The wondrous Sage: vigorous he seem'd in years,
Awful his mien, low as his feet there flows
A vestment unadorn'd, though white as new-fall'n
    snows;

Against the stream the waves secure he trod, 15
His head a chaplet bore, his hand a rod.
  As on the Rhine, when Boreas' fury reigns,
And winter binds the floods in icy chains,
Swift shoots the village-maid in rustic play
Smooth, without step, adown the shining way, 20
Fearless in long excursion loves to glide,
And sports and wantons o'er the frozen tide.
  So mov'd the Seer, but on no harden'd plain;
The river boil'd beneath, and rush'd toward the
    main.
Where fix'd in wonder stood the warlike pair, 25
His course he turn'd, and thus relieved their care·
  " Vast, oh my friends, and difficult the toil
To seek your hero in a distant soil!
No common helps, no common guide ye need,
Art it requires, and more than winged speed. 30
What length of sea remains, what various lands,
Oceans unknown, inhospitable sands!
For adverse fate the captive chief has hurl'd
Beyond the confines of our narrow world:
Great things and full of wonder in your ears 35
I shall unfold; but first dismiss your fears;
Nor doubt with me to tread the downward road
That to the grotto leads, my dark abode."
  Scarce had he said, before the warriors' eyes
When mountain-high the waves disparted rise; 40
The flood on either hand its billows rears,
And in the midst a spacious arch appears.
Their hands he seized, and down the steep he led
Beneath the obedient river's inmost bed;

The watery glimmerings of a fainter day   45
Discover'd half, and half conceal'd their way;
As when athwart the dusky woods by night
The uncertain crescent gleams a sickly light.
Through subterraneous passages they went,
Earth's inmost cells, and caves of deep descent; 50
Of many a flood they view'd the secret source,
The birth of rivers rising to their course,
Whate'er with copious train its channel fills,
Floats into lakes, and bubbles into rills;
The Po was there to see, Danubius' bed,   55
Euphrates' fount, and Nile's mysterious head.
Further they pass, where ripening minerals flow,
And embryon metals undigested glow,
Sulphureous veins and living silver shine,
Which soon the parent sun's warm powers refine,
In one rich mass unite the precious store,
The parts combine and harden into ore:
Here gems break through the night with glitter-
        ing beam,
And paint the margin of the costly stream,
All stones of lustre shoot their vivid ray,   65
And mix attemper'd in a various day;
Here the soft emerald smiles of verdant hue,
And rubies flame, with sapphire's heavenly blue,
The diamond there attracts the wondrous sight,
Proud of its thousand dyes and luxury of light.

                                  1738. Æt. 22.

POEMATA.

HYMENEAL

ON THE MARRIAGE OF HIS ROYAL HIGHNESS THE PRINCE OF WALES.*

Ignaræ nostrûm mentes, et inertia corda,
Dum curas regum, et sortem miseramur iniquam,
Quæ solio affixit, vetuitque calescere flammâ
Dulci, quæ dono divûm, gratissima serpit   4
Viscera per, mollesque animis lene implicat æstus ;
Nec teneros sensus, Veneris nec præmia nôrunt,
Eloquiumve oculi, aut facunda silentia linguæ :

  Scilicet ignorant lacrymas, sævosque dolores,
Dura rudimenta, et violentæ exordia flammæ ;

---

  * Printed in the Cambridge Collection, 1736, fol. In this Collection is also a Latin Copy of Hendecasyllables, by Horace Walpole; a short Copy by Thomas Ashton, the friend of Walpole, &c. ; and there are some Greek verses by Richard Dawes, the author of ' Miscellanea Critica.'

  V. 1. " Heu, vatum ignaræ mentes ! " Virg. Æn. iv. 65. " Teucrûm mirantur inertia corda," Æn. ix. 55.

  V. 2. " Sortemque animo miseratus iniquam," Æn. vi. 332.

  V. 4. " Dono divûm gratissima serpit," Æn. ii. 269.

  V. 6. " Nec dulces natos, Veneris nec præmia noris ? " Æn. iv. 33.

  V. 7. " Vide Hor. Od. iv. i. 35. And Pope. Homer, b. xiv. ver. 252:
    " Silence that spoke, and *eloquence* of eyes."
And Fairfax. Tasso, iv. 85:
    " *Dumb eloquence*, persuading more than speech."

Scilicet ignorant, quæ flumine tinxit amaro   10
Tela Venus, cæcique armamentaria Divi,
Irasque, insidiasque, et tacitum sub pectore vulnus;
Namque sub ingressu, primoque in limine Amoris
Luctus et ultrices posuere cubilia Curæ;
Intus habent dulces Risus, et Gratia sedem,   15
Et roseis resupina toris, roseo ore Voluptas :
Regibus huc faciles aditus; communia spernunt
Ostia, jamque expers duris custodibus istis
Panditur accessus, penetraliaque intima Templi.

Tuque Oh! Angliacis, Princeps, spes optima
   regnis,   20
Ne tantum, ne finge metum : quid imagine captus
Hæres, et mentem pictura pascis inani ?
Umbram miraris : nec longum tempus, et ipsa
Ibit in amplexus, thalamosque ornabit ovantes.
Ille tamen tabulis inhians longum haurit amo-
   rem,   25
Affatu fruitur tacito, auscultatque tacentem
Immemor artificis calami, risumque, ruboremque

V. 10. " Bis *flumine* corpora *tingat*," Ovid. Met. xii. 413.
V. 11. " Quidquid habent telorum armamentaria cœli,"
Juv. Sat. xiii. 83.
V. 12. This line, which is unmetrical, is so printed in the
Cambridge Collection; and in Park's edition, without remark.
The fault is probably in the author, and not in the printer;
as the line is composed of two hemistichs of Virgil; Æn. xii.
336, " Iræque, Insidiæque, Dei comitatus, aguntur;" and
Æn. iv. 67, " Tacitum vivit sub pectore vulnus." Or perhaps
a line is omitted, which should intervene.
V. 14. This line is from Virgil, Æn. vi. 274:
   " Luctus et ultrices posuére cubilia Curæ."
V. 18. " Quos *dura* premit *custodia* matrum," Hor. Ep. i.
i. 22.

Aspicit in fucis, pictæque in virginis ore: 28
Tanta Venus potuit; tantus tenet error amantes.

Nascere, magna Dies, qua sese AUGUSTA Bri-
tanno
Committat Pelago, patriamque relinquat amœnam;
Cujus in adventum jam nunc tria regna secundos
Attolli in plausus, dulcique accensa furore
Incipiunt agitare modos, et carmina dicunt:
Ipse animo sed enim juvenis comitatur euntem 35
Explorat ventos, atque auribus aëra captat,
Atque auras, atque astra vocat crudelia; pectus
Intentum exultat, surgitque arrecta cupido;
Incusat spes ægra fretum, solitoque videtur
Latior effundi pontus, fluctusque morantes. 40
[tanno
Nascere, Lux major, qua sese AUGUSTA Bri-
Committat juveni totam, propriamque dicabit;

V. 22. "Atque animum picturâ pascit inani," Æn. i. 464.
V. 23. "Nec longum tempus et ingens," &c. Virg. Georg.
ii. 80.
V. 30. "*Magnus* ab integro sæclorum *nascitur* ordo," Virg.
Ecl. iv. 5.
V. 31. "Commisit pelago ratem," Hor. Od. i. iii. 11
V. 33. "Subitoque accensa furore," Æn. iv. 697.
V. 35. "Virum qui sic comitatur euntem?" Æn. vi. 863.
V. 36. This line is from Virgil, Æn. iii. 514:
    "Explorat ventos, atque auribus aëra captat."
V. 37. From Virg. Georg. iv. 495: "Crudelia retro Fata
vocant." Æn. v. 138: "Laudumque arrecta cupido."
V. 41. "Nascere, præque diem veniens age, Lucifer, al-
mum," Virg. Ecl. viii. 118.
V. 42. "Connubio jungam stabili, *propriamque dicabo*,"
Virg. Æn. i. 73.

At citius (precor) Oh! cedas melioribus astris ;
Nox finem pompæ, finemque imponere curis
Possit, et in thalamos furtim deducere nuptam ;   45
Sufficiat réquiemque viris, et amantibus umbras :
Adsit Hymen, et subridens cum matre Cupido
Accedant, sternantque toros, ignemque ministrent ;
Ilicet haud pictæ incandescit imagine formæ
Ulterius juvenis, verumque agnoscit amorem.   50

Sculptile sicut ebur, faciemque arsisse venustam
Pygmaliona canunt : ante hanc suspiria ducit,
Alloquiturque amens, flammamque et vulnera nar-
    rat ;
Implorata Venus jussit cum vivere signum,   54
Fœmineam inspirans animam ; quæ gaudia sur-
    gunt,
Audiit ut primæ nascentia murmura linguæ,
Luctari in vitam, et paulatim volvere ocellos

V. 44. So in Gray's Epistle from Sophonisba:
    " Pompæ finis erat. Totâ vix nocte quievi."
V. 46. " On the position of the ' que,' see Burman. Virgil,
Æn. vi. 395.
V. 47. " Prò Venus, et tenerâ volucer cum matre Cupido,"
Ov. Met. ix. 481.
V. 50. " Veros exponit amores," Ovid. Met x. 439. " Ve-
ros parce profitemur amores," Ovid. Art. Am. ii. 639.
V. 51 is from Ovid. Met. x. 247:
    " Interea niveum mira feliciter arte
    Sculpit ebur; formamque dedit, qua fœmina nasci
    Nulla potest: operisque sui concepit amorem:
    Virginis est veræ facies, quam vivere credas;
    Et, si non obstet reverentia, velle moveri:
    Ars adeo latet arte suâ. Miratur, et haurit
    Pectore Pygmalion simulati corporis ignes."
V 56. " Sed parvæ murmura linguæ," Ov. Met. xii. 49.

Sedulus, aspexitque novâ splendescere flammâ ;
Corripit amplexu vivam, jamque oscula jungit
Acria confestim, recipitque rapitque ; prioris   60
Immemor ardoris, Nymphæque oblitus eburneæ.

THO. GRAY, Pet. Coll.

LUNA HABITABILIS.*

DUM Nox rorantes, non incomitata per auras
Urget equos, tacitoque inducit sidera lapsu ;
Ultima, sed nulli soror inficianda sororum,
Huc mihi, Musa ; tibi patet alti janua cœli,
Astra vides, nec te numeri, nec nomina fallunt.   5
Huc mihi, Diva veni ; dulce est per aperta serena
Vere frui liquido, campoque errare silenti ;

V. 59. " Excipis amplexu, feliciaque oscula jungis," Ov.
Ep. xviii. 101.   And Met. x. 256: "Oscula dat, reddique
putat; loquiturque tenetque."

V. 61. " Sit conjux opto, (non ausus, eburnea virgo,
        Dicere Pygmalion,) similis mea, dixit eburneæ."
                                       Ov. Met. x. 275.

* This copy of verses was written by desire of the College,
in 1737.   It has never been printed, but in the " Musæ Etonenses," vol. ii. p. 107; and has not there the name of the
author.   It is referred to in Mason's Memoirs; a copy of
verses on the subject, " Planetæ sunt habitabiles," is in the
same work.   See also in V. Bourne's Poems, p. 261, 4to.

V. 2. " Tacito lapsu," Claudian, xxii. 430.   And xxxi. 40:
" Tacito defluxit fistula lapsu."

V. 4. " Noctes atque dies patet atri janua Ditis."
                                       Virg. Æn. vi 127

V. 7.   —— " Ver inde serenum
        Protinus, et liquidi clementior aura favoni."
                                       Claudian, i. 272.

Vere frui dulce est; modo tu dignata petentem
Sis comes, et mecum gelidâ spatiere sub umbrâ.
Scilicèt hos orbes, cœli hæc decora alta putandum
    est,   10
Noctis opes, nobis tantum lucere; virûmque
Ostentari oculis, nostræ laquearia terræ,
Ingentes scenas, vastique aulæa theatri?
Oh! quis me pennis æthræ super ardua sistet
Mirantem, propiusque dabit convexa tueri;   15
Teque adeo, undè fluens reficit lux mollior arva
Pallidiorque dies, tristes solata tenebras?
    Sic ego, subridens Dea sic ingressa vicissim:
Non pennis opus hìc, supera ut simul illa petamus:
Disce, Puer, potiùs cœlo deducere Lunam;   20
Neu crede ad magicas te invitum accingier artes,
Thessalicosve modos; ipsam descendere Phœben
Conspicies novus Endymion; seque offeret ultrò
Visa tibi ante oculos, et notâ major imago.

And Virg. Georg. i. 43:
    " *Vere* novo, gelidus canis cum montibus humor
      Liquitur."
    V. 13. " Vel *scena* ut versis discedat frontibus; utque
        Purpurea intexti tollant *aulæa* Britanni."
                  Virg. Georg. iii. 24.
    V. 14. This and the following line are from Virg. Georg. ii.
489; and Æn. iv. 451.
    V. 20. " Disce, puer," Æn. xii. 435.   " Vel cœlo possunt
deducere lunam," Eclog. viii. 69.
    V. 21. " Magicas invitam adcingier artes," Æn. iv. 493.
    V. 22. " Quæ sidera excantata voce Thessala
          Lunamque cœlo deripit." Hor. Epod. v. 45.
    V. 24. This line is from Virgil, Æn. ii. 773:
      " Visa *mihi* ante oculos, et notâ major imago."
    V. 25. " Ingrediturque solo, et caput inter nubila condit."
                  Virg. Æn. iv. 177

Quin tete admoveas (tumuli super aggere spec-
 tas),   25
Compositum tubulo; simul imum invade canalem
Sic intentâ acie, cœli simul alta patescent
Atria; jamque, ausus Lunaria visere regna,
Ingrediêre solo, et caput inter nubila condes.   29
 Ecce autem! vitri se in vertice sistere Phœben
Cernis, et Oceanum, et crebris Freta consita terris.
Panditur *ille* atram faciem caligine condens
Sublustri; refugitque oculos, fallitque tuentem;
Integram Solis lucem quippè haurit aperto   34
Fluctu avidus radiorum, et longos imbibit ignes:
Verum *his*, quæ, maculis variata nitentibus, auro
Cœrula discernunt, celso sese insula dorso
Plurima protrudit, prætentaque littora saxis;
Liberior datur his quoniàm natura, minusque

V. 31. " Et crebris legimus freta consita terris."
          Virg. Æn. iii. 127.

V. 35. There is no authority in Latin poetry for the use of
the word "imbibit" in this sense. It is a word unusual in
poetry, though twice found in Lucretius (iii. 1010, and vi. 71):
but it is there used in another construction : as " Imbibit
petere," *i. e.* " Induxit in animum petere." There is a note
on this word in Mureti Var. Lectiones, lib. i. cap. 6. (In
Gesner's Thesaurus, and Havercamp's Lucretius, the reference
to Muretus is wrong, l. cap. 5.) The word which Gray should
have used is "bibit." See Æn. i. 749: xi. 804: Georg. ii.
506, &c. "Lympha bibit solem." Sid. Apoll. xi. 12. See
the notes of the commentators, on Gratii Cyneg. 60. Burm.
Poet. Lat. Minor. vol. i. p. 60.

V. 38. This word is unusual in Latin poetry. It may be
defended on the authority of Lucretius, iv. 247: " Extemplo
protrudit, agitque aëra:" — where, however, some manuscripts
read " procudit."

V. 39.   —— " *Natura* videtur
     Libera " ——.   Lucret. ii. 1090.

Lumen depascunt liquidum; sed tela diei   40
Detorquent, retròque docent se vertere flammas.

Hinc longos videas tractus, terrasque jacentes
Ordine candenti, et claros se attollere montes ;
Montes queîs Rhodope assurgat, quibus Ossa nivali
Vertice: tum scopulis infrà pendentibus antra 45
Nigrescunt clivorum umbrâ, nemorumque tene-
    bris.
Non rores illi, aut desunt sua nubila mundo ;
Non frigus gelidum, atque herbis gratissimus
    imber ;
His quoque nota ardet picto Thaumantias arcu,
Os roseum Auroræ, propriique crepuscula cœli. 50
Et dubitas tantum certis cultoribus orbem
Destitui? exercent agros, sua mœnia condunt
Hi quoque, vel Martem invadunt, curantque trium-
Victores: sunt hic etiam sua præmia laudi ; ⌈phos
His metus, atque amor, et mentem mortalia tan-
    gunt.   55

V. 40. "Lucida tela diei," Lucret. i. 148. "Luciferique
pavent letalia tela diei," Ausonii Mosell. 260.

V. 45. "Fronte sub adversâ scopulis pendentibus antrum,"
Virg. Æn. i. 166.

V. 48. "Quum ros in tenerâ pecori gratissimus herbâ."
Virg. Eclog. viii. 15.

V. 49. "Roseo Thaumantias ore locuta est," Virg. Æn.
ix. 5. "In terram *pictos* delapsa per *arcus*," Ov. Met. xiv. 838.

V. 53. "Invadunt Martem clypeis," Æn. xii. 712.

V. 54. —— "Sunt hic etiam sua præmia laudi,
    Sunt lacrymæ rerum, et mentem mortalia tangunt."
        Æn. i. 461.

V. 56. Scaliger, like Gray, uses the final vowel in 'uti'
short; and a short vowel at the end of the first form of the
Elegiac verse. V. Bibl. Parriana, p. 322.

Quin, uti nos oculis jam nunc juvat ire per arva,
Lucentesque plagas Lunæ, pontumque profundum;
Idem illos etiàm ardor agit, cum se aureus effert
Sub sudum globus, et terrarum ingentior orbis;
Scilicèt omne æquor tum lustrant, scilicèt omnem 60
Tellurem, gentesque polo sub utroque jacentes;
Et quidam æstivi indefessus ad ætheris ignes
Pervigilat, noctem exercens, cœlumque fatigat;
Jam Galli apparent, jam se Germania latè
Tollit, et albescens pater Appeninus ad auras; 65
Jam tandem in Borean, en! parvulus Anglia nævus
(Quanquam aliis longè fulgentior) extulit oras;
Formosum extemplò lumen, maculamque nitentem
Invisunt crebri Proceres, serùmque tuéndo
Hærent, certatimque suo cognomine signant: 70
Forsitan et Lunæ longinquus in orbe Tyrannus
Se dominum vocat, et nostrâ se jactat in aulâ.
Terras possim alias propiori sole calentes
Narrare, atque alias, jubaris queîs parcior usus,
Lunarum chorus, et tenuis penuria Phœbi; 75
Nî meditans eadem hæc audaci evolvere cantu,
Jam pulset citharam soror, et præludia tentet.
　Non tamen has proprias laudes, nec facta silebo

V. 63. "Et quidam seros hiberni ad luminis ignes
　　　Pervigilat." Virg. Georg. i. 292.
V. 65. "Vertice se attollens pater Apenninus ad auras."
　　　Æn. xii. 703.
V. 72. "Illâ se jactat in aulâ," Æn. i. 140.
V. 75. So Virgil. Georg. i. 424: "Lunasque sequentes."
　V. 75. This expression "Penuria Phœbi" is not, I believe,
warranted by the authority of any of the Latin poets. There
would have been less objection, if the plain term, instead of
the figurative, had been used.

Jampridèm in fatis, patriæque oracula famæ.
Tempus erit, sursùm totos contendere cœtus   80
Quo cernes longo excursu, primosque colonos
Migrare in lunam, et notos mutare Penates:
Dum stupet obtutu tacito vetus incola, longèque
Insolitas explorat aves, classemque volantem.
    Ut quondàm ignotum marmor, camposque na-
        tantes   85
Tranavit Zephyros visens, nova regna, Columbus;
Litora mirantur circùm, mirantur et undæ
Inclusas acies ferro, turmasque biformes,
Monstraque fœta armis, et non imitabile fulmen.
Fœdera mox icta, et gemini commercia mundi, 90
Agminaque assueto glomerata sub æthere cerno.
Anglia, quæ pelagi jamdudum torquet habenas,
Exercetque frequens ventos, atque imperat undæ;
Aëris attollet fasces, veteresque triumphos
Hùc etiam feret, et victis dominabitur auris.   95

V. 79. "Esse quoque *in fatis* reminiscitur," Ov. Met. i. 256.
    V. 83. "Obtutu tacito stetit," Æn. xii. 666.
    V. 84. "Innumeræ comitantur aves, stipantque volantem,"
Claud. Phœnix, 76.
    V. 85. "Campique natantes," Georg. iii. 198.
    V. 89. "Fœta armis," Æn. ii. 238. "Non imitabile ful-
men," Æn. vi. 590.
    V. 90. "Geminoque facis commércia mundo," Claud. xxxiii.
90.
    V. 92. Æquoreas habenas," Claud. viii. 422.
    V. 95. "Servitio premet, ac victis dominabitur Argis," Æn.
i. 285.

SAPPHIC ODE: TO MR. WEST.*

[See Mason's Memoirs, vol. ii. p. 42; on a version of Gray's
Latin Odes by Green, in English, see H. Walpole's Letters
to Cole, p. 116.]

BARBARAS ædes aditure mecum
Quas Eris semper fovet inquieta,
Lis ubi latè sonat, et togatum
           Æstuat agmen;

Dulcius quanto, patulis sub ulmi   5
Hospitæ ramis temerè jacentem

---

* Mason considered this as the first original production of
Gray's Muse; the two former poems being imposed as ex-
ercises by the College.

V. 1. Comp. Hor. Od. ii. vi. 1: "Septimi, Gades aditure
mecum," &c. *Luke.*

V. 3. " *Lis* nunquam, *toga* rara," Martial. Ep. x. 47.

V. 4. So Claudian, xi. 24:
    " Quot *æstuantes* ancipiti gradu
    Furtiva carpent oscula *Naïdes.*"

V. 5. " Platanus ... patulis est diffusa ramis," Cic. de
Oratore, Lib. I. cap. vii. " Hospita umbra," Ovid. Trist.
III. iii. 64. Hor. Od. ii. iii. 9.

V. 6. There is no authority for the *last* syllable of " temere "
being made *long.* See Burmanni. Anth. Lat. vol. ii. 458, and
Class. Journal, No. xviii. p. 340. Yet Casimir Sarbievus has
erred in the quantity of this word, as well as Gray:
    " Te sibilantis lenior halitus
    Perflabit Euri; me juvet interim
    Collum reclinasse; et virenti
    Sic tem*ere* jacuisse ripa."   Ad. Testudinem.
And Cowley (Solitudo) " Hic jaciens vestris *temere* sub um
bris." Lowth Ode ad orn. Puellam. " Ducit aquas *temere*
sequentes." Carmin. Quadrig. ii. 81. " Defessus *temere* se."
See Woty's Poet. Calendar, Part xii. p. 34. In Horace, Vir-

Sic libris horas, tenuique inertes
            Fallere Musâ ?

Sæpe enim curis vagor expeditâ
Mente ; dum, blandam meditans Camænam,
Vix malo rori, meminive seræ   11
            Cedere nocti ;

Et, pedes quò me rapiunt, in omni
Colle Parnassum videor videre
Fertilem sylvæ, gelidamque in omni   15
            Fonte Aganippen.

Risit et Ver me, facilesque Nymphæ
Nare captantem, nec ineleganti,
Manè quicquid de violis eundo
            Surripit aura :   20

---

gil, and Ovid the final syllable of this word is always *elided*.
— A friend observed, that the last syllable of *temere* is made
long in the 'Gradus' on the authority of Tertullian : "Immemor ille Dei temerē committere tale." It is hardly necessary to observe that the authority of Tertullian on a question
of a doubtful quantity would not be esteemed sufficient. The
last syllable of *temere* being *always elided* by Virgil, Horace,
and Ovid, sufficiently shows their opinion to have been, that it
was *short;* and therefore that it could not be used in Hexa-
meter verse, without lengthening its final syllable by elision.
See Menagiana, vol. iii. p. 418. (Hor. Od. ii. xi. 13, " Pinu
jacentes sic temere." *Luke.*)

V. 7. " Tenui deducta poemata filo," Hor. Ep. II. i. 225.
" Graciles Musas," Propert. Eleg. II. x. 3. Virg. Eclog. i. 2.
Hor. S. ii. 6, 61, " Nunc veterum *libris*, nunc somno et *inertibus
horis*." *Luke.*

V. 9.   —— " ultra
            Terminum, curis vagor expeditis."
Hor. Od. I. xxii. 10. Virg. Eclog. viii. 88, " Nec seræ memi-
nit decedere nocti." *Luke.*

Me reclinatum teneram per herbam;
Quà leves cursus aqua cunque ducit,
Et moras dulci strepitu lapillo
          Nectit in omni.

Hæ novo nostrum ferè pectus anno   25
Simplices curæ tenuere, cœlum
Quamdiù sudum explicuit Favonî
          Purior hora:

Otia et campos nec adhuc relinquo,
Nec magis Phœbo Clytie fidelis;   35
(Ingruant venti licet, et senescat
          Mollior æstas.)

Namque, seu, lætos hominum labores

V. 13, 14. "I, pedes quo te rapiunt," Hor. Od. iii. xi. 49. "Videre magnos jam videor duces," Od. ii. i. 21.

V. 17. "Sed faciles nymphæ risere," Virg. Eclog. iii. 9.

V. 18. Virg. Georg. i. 376, "Patulis captavit naribus auras."

V. 19. On the Cæsura post alterum pedem, see Fabricius on the Metres of Seneca.

V. 21. Virg. Eclog. viii. 15, "Cum ros in tenera pecori gratissimus herba." Luke.

V. 22. "Levis cursu," Virg. Æn. xii. 489. "Cursus ducebat," Æn. v. 667.

V. 23. Hor. Od. iv. 37, "Dulcem quæ strepitum, Pieri, temperas." Luke.

V. 26.   —— " Cœli in regione serenâ
    Per sudum rutilare vident."   Virg. Æn. viii. 528.

V. 30. See Ov. Metam. iv. 234. 264.

V 31. "Senescit ager," Ovid. Art. Am. iii. 82, ex Pont. I. iv. 14. "Molles anni," Ovid. Ep. iii. 3. Tristia, iv. 43. "Mollior æstas," Virg. Georg. i. 312.

N

Prataque et montes recreante curru,
Purpurâ tractus oriens Eoos   35
        Vestit, et auro;

Sedulus servo veneratus orbem
Prodigum splendoris; amœniori
Sive dilectam meditatur igne
        Pingere Calpen;   40

Usque dum, fulgore magìs magìs jam
Languido circum, variata nubes
Labitur furtim, viridisque in umbras
        Scena recessit.

O ego felix, vice si (nec unquam   45
Surgerem rursus) simili cadentem
Parca me lenis sineret quieto
        Fallere Letho!

V. 34. V. Lucret. v. 402, " Solque * * *recreavit* cuncta gubernans." *Luke.*

V. 41. See Tate in the Class. Journ. No. ix. p. 120. " Horace makes the division after the 5th, 6th, or 7th foot, never after the 3rd, as the Moderns do."

V. 45. The last syllable of *ego* is short, and so used by the best writers; nor will the example of Ausonius, or an instance or two of its being found *long* in Plautus and Catullus, authorize a modern poet in this license. See the note by Heinsius on Ovid. Ep. xiii. 135, vol. i. p. 180, and Burmann on Propertii Eleg. I. viii. 41. " Recte Heinsius, qui nunquam a Nasone, p. 93, 94, 733, hujus voculæ ultimam *produci* notat; et falsos esse illos qui ab ullo Augustei ævi poetâ id factum contendunt, dicit ad Albinov. Epiced. Drusi. x. 193." See also Vossius de Arte Grammaticâ, lib. ii. cap. 27. Drakenborch, in his note on Sil. Italicus xvii. 358, p. 865, (where the last syllable of *ego* is long), relies on the authorities produced by Vossius; and thinks that it may be lengthened, even without the power of the cæsura.

Multa flagranti radiisque cincto
Integris ah! quam nihil inviderem,   50
Cum Dei ardentes medius quadrigas
                    Sentit Olympus.

———

ALCAIC FRAGMENT.

[See Mason's Memoirs, vol. ii. p. 43.]

O LACRYMARUM fons,* tenero sacros
Ducentium ortus ex animo; quater
    Felix! in imo qui scatentem
    Pectore te, pia Nympha, sensit.

———

V. 47. See Stewart's Moral Philosophy, vol. iii. p. 201.
V. 48. " Natus moriensque fefellit," Hor. Ep. I. xvii. 10.
V. 49. Mason has improperly accented this word, as if it were an adverb (multà). All the other editions have followed him. It is the " nomen pro adverbio," as Hor. Od. iv. ii. 25.
V. 52. Virg. Æn. x. 206, " Phœbe medium pulsabat Olympum." *Luke.*
* So Sophocles, Antigone, ver. 803:
——— ἴσχειν
δ' οὐκ ἔτι πηγὰς δύναμαι δάκρυων.
V. Chariton. ed. Dorville, p. 5, and Chrysostom in laud. Pauli ed. Hemsterh. p. xxvi. καὶ πηγὰς δάκρυων ἡ φιει.

LATIN LINES

ADDRESSED TO MR. WEST, FROM GENOA.

[See Mason's Memoirs, vol. ii. p. 94.]

HORRIDOS tractus, Boreæque linquens
Regna Taurini fera, molliorem *
Advehor brumam, Genuæque amantes
                    Litora soles.

———

ELEGIAC VERSES,

OCCASIONED BY THE SIGHT OF THE PLAINS WHERE THE
BATTLE OF TREBIA WAS FOUGHT.

[See Mason's Memoirs, vol. ii. p. 104.]

QUA Trebie glaucas salices intersecat undâ,
    Arvaque Romanis nobilitata malis.
Visus adhuc amnis veteri de clade rubere,
    Et suspirantes ducere mœstus aquas ;
Maurorumque ala, et nigræ increbescere turmæ,   5
    Et pulsa Ausonidum ripa sonare fugâ.

————

* So in the Sapphic Ode, " Mollior æstas." Ovid in his
Epist. ex Ponto, i. ii. 62: " Litora mollia."
V. 1. I do not know on what authority Gray has used the
word " Trebie " with the final *e*. The word which is used in
the Classic authors is *Trebia*, Τρεβίας. See Sil. Ital. iv. 661,
xi. 140, &c. sæpe. Lucan, ii. 46. Livy, xxi. c. 48. Pliny,
N. H. 3. 20, &c. Claudian, xxiv. 145, Manilius, iv. 661.—
It is most probable that Gray thought that the final syllable
of Trebia could not be lengthened; therefore used the word

CARMEN AD C. FAVONIUM ZEPHYRINUM.*

[See Mason's Memoirs, vol. ii. p. 120.]

MATER rosarum, cui teneræ vigent
Auræ Favonî, cui Venus it comes
Lasciva, Nympharum choreis
Et volucrum celebrata cantu!

Trebie, as Libya, Libye. But in Ovid the words Leda, Rhea, Hybla, Phædra, Andromeda, Amalthea, &c. lengthen the final syllable. " Mittit Hypermnestrā de tot modo fratribus uni," Ov. Ep. xiv. 1. In Propertius, ii. xi. 5. the *a* in Electra is long; also in Ovid. Fast. iv. 177. See on this point D'Orville. Misc. Obs. ii. 202, and Burmann. notes to Anthol. Latin. i. 215. ii. 78. Jortin. Tracts. vol. ii. 421. Burmann. Propert. iv. 7. 63. p. 844. In the Herc. Fur. of Seneca, 203: " Megarā parvum comitata gregem." Gray therefore would have had sufficient authority for the use of Trebia in this place. So Sil. Italicus, iv. 661, describing the appearance of Trebia:

"Tum madidos crines, et *glauca* † *fronde* revinctum
   Attollit cum voce caput."
Virg. Georg. iv. 182: "Et glaucas salices." *Luke.*

V. 5. Sil. Ital. describes the army of Hannibal, iii. 407:
"Talia Sidonius per *campos* agmina ductor
   Pulvere *nigrantes* raptat."

* Written by Gray immediately after his journey to Frascati and the cascades of Tivoli, which he had described in a preceding letter to his friend West.

V. 1. " Et reserata *viget* genitalis *aura Favonî.*"
                                                    Lucret. i. 2.

---

† When the epithet *glauca* is applied to the foliage of a tree, and the tree itself not particularized, as in the passage of Sil. Italicus; we must refer it to the "salix," the "populus," or the "oliva;" according to situation, and other circumstances; as "Cæruleus" is generally applied to the Pine, Fir, and Cypress.

Dic, non inertem fallere quâ diem　　5
　　Amat sub umbrâ, seu sinit aureum
　　　Dormire plectrum, seu retentat
　　　　Pierio Zephyrinus antro
Furore ˌdulci plenus, et immemor
Reptantis inter frigora Tusculi　　10
　　Umbrosa, vel colles Amici
　　　Palladiæ superantis Albæ.
Dilecta Fauno, et capripedum choris
Pineta, testor vos, Anio minax
　　Quæcunque per clivos volutus　　15
　　　Præcipiti tremefecit amne,
Illius altum Tibur, et Æsulæ
Audîsse sylvas nomen amabiles,
　　Illius et gratas Latinis
　　　Naisin ingeminâsse rupes;　　20

V. 6. "Et te sonantem plenius *aureo*,
　　　Alcæe, *plectro*." 　　　　Hor. Od. ii. xiii. 26.
V. 8. "Pierio recreatis antro," Hor. Od. iii. iv. 40.
V. 14. "Et præceps Anio, ac Tiburni lucus," Hor. Od. i.
vii. 13. "Preceps Anien," Stat. Silv. i. v. 25.
V. 20. In Mason's, and all the subsequent editions, the
word "Naïasin" is ˑhere placed; which would make the line
unmetrical. Gray indeed might have written "Naïasin gemi-
nâsse rupes." But the word "Naides" in the following line,
which has also the same error in the editions as the former
word, would make an objection to that reading. I have therefore restored the metre, by reading "Naisin" and "Naides."
See Gronovius on Senecæ Hippol. 778. Jortin. Tracts, vol. i.
p. 321.
V. 20. See Propert. i. xx. 12: "Non minor Ausonius est
amor ah ! Dryasin." And i. xx. 32: "Ah ! dolor ibat Hylas,
ibat Hamadryasin." And Ov. Art. Am. iii. 672. See Burmann. note to Ovid, Ep. xiii. 137, and Trist. v. 5. 43. V.
Lotichii. Poem. i. p. 226. ed Burm. and Burm. Anthol. Lat.
vol. ii. p. 508. Burm. ad Virg. Eclog. x. 10. Salmasii Ling.
Helen. p. 142.

Nam me Latinæ Naides uvidâ
Vidêre ripâ, quâ niveas levi
   Tam sæpe lavit rore plumas
     Dulcè canens Venusinus ales;
Mirum! canenti conticuit nemus,   25
Sacrique fontes, et retinent adhuc
   (Sic Musa jussit) saxa molles
     Docta modos, veteresque lauri.
Mirare nec tu me citharæ rudem
Claudis laborantem numeris: loca   30
   Amœna, jucundumque ver in-
     compositum docuere carmen;

V. 23. In this, the following, and the last stanza, the third line of the Alcaic stanza ends with two dissyllables; which can be defended but by very few examples of Horace. See the *fictitious* ode, lib. i. 40. ad Librum suum, (published by Villoison in Long. Past.) v. 11. "Huic ara stabit, fama cantu." Another error in this verse is the absence of the *accent* on the *fifth* or sixth syllable.

V. 26. " Κρήνης ἱερὸν ῥόον," Apoll. Rhod. i. 1208. iv. 134. Theocr. Idyll. ii. 1. 69. " Ad *aquæ* lene caput *sacræ*," Hor. Od. i. i. 22. " Nec *sacros* pollue *fontes*," Ovid. Metam. ii. 464. " Fonte sacro," Virg. Æn. vii. 84. and Jortin's remarks on Spenser, vol. i. p. 63.

V. 30. This is the only instance in this ode in which Gray has not conformed to the rule of the "divisio versûs post quintam syllabam." In the other Alcaic Ode on the Chartreuse, there is also one instance similar to this:

    " Per invias rupes, fera per juga."

The practice of Horace certainly seems to authorize this rule. Three exceptions are to be found: Od. lib. i. xxxvii. 5, i. xxxvii. 14, and Od. iv. xiv. 16. I do not know that there are any more; of course, the case of an *elided syllable* being excepted.

V. 31. In Horace there are but nine instances of an amphibrachys, as " Amœna," beginning the third line of the Alcaic stanza. As the places where it occurs in that poet have not, I believe, been ever pointed out, I will set them down here,

Hærent sub omni nam folio nigri
Phœbea lucî (credite) somnia,
    Argutiusque et lympha et auræ   35
    Nescio quid solito loquuntur.

FRAGMENT OF A LATIN POEM * ON THE GAURUS.

[See Mason's Memoirs, vol. ii. p. 145.]

NEC procul infelix se tollit in æthera Gaurus,
Prospiciens vitreum lugenti vertice pontum:
Tristior ille diu, et veteri desuetus olivâ
Gaurus, pampineæque eheu jam nescius umbræ;

---

to save any trouble to those desirous of seeing them : i. xvii.
7, i. xxix. 7, i. xxxv. 15, i. xxxvii. 15, ii. iii. 3, ii. xvii. 3, ii.
xx. 11, iii. iii. 71, iii. xxix. 11.

V. 31, 32. There is no instance in Horace of a *broken word*
ending the third line of the Alcaic stanza, or, indeed, of its
being used at all; and therefore it must be considered as not
defended by authority; though it may be found ending the
third line of the Sapphic stanza, in Horace, i. xxv. 11. i. ii.
19, ii. xvi. 7, iii. xxvii. 60, but, I believe, that no example
even of this can be found in the Sapphics of Seneca. It ends
the first line, in Hor. Od. iv. ii. 1, and the second line in ii. ii.
18, and iv. ii. 22, in which latter passage it is to be observed,
that the "divisio vocis" takes place in two successive lines.

V. 33.   —— "Quam sedem Somnia vulgò
Vana tenere ferunt, foliisque sub omnibus hærent."
                         Virg. Æn. vi. 283.

* Sent by Gray to his friend West, with a reference to Sandys's Travels, book iv. pag. 275, 277, and 278. A translation
of this poem may be seen in the Gent. Mag. for July, 1775.

V. 2. "Vitreo ponto," Hor. Od. iv. ii. 3. "Vitrea unda,"
Virg. Æn. vii. 759. Georg. iv. 350.

V 4. "Bacchei vineta madentia Gauri," Statii Silv. iii. v
99. "Icario nemorosus palmite Gaurus," Silv. iii. i. 147.

Horrendi tam sæva premit vicinia montis,   5
Attonitumque urget latus, exuritque ferentem.
  Nam fama est olim, mediâ dum rura silebant
Nocte, Deo victa, et molli perfusa quiete,
Infremuisse æquor ponti, auditamque per omnes
Latè tellurem surdùm immugire cavernas: 10
Quo sonitu nemora alta tremunt: tremit excita tuto
Parthenopæa sinu, flammantisque ora Vesevi.
At subitò se aperire solum, vastosque recessus
Pandere sub pedibus, nigrâque voragine fauces;
Tum piceas cinerum glomerare sub æthere nubes
Vorticibus rapidis, ardentique imbre procellam. 16
Præcipites fugere feræ, perque avia longè
Sylvarum fugit pastor, juga per deserta,
Ah, miser! increpitans sæpè altâ voce per umbram
Nequicquam natos, creditque audire sequentes. 20
Atque ille excelso rupis de vertice solus
Respectans notasque domos, et dulcia regna,
Nil usquàm videt infelix præter mare tristi
Lumine percussum, et pallentes sulphure campos

V. 5. "Vicinia Persidis urget," Georg. iv. 290. "Pampi-
neas invidit collibus umbras," Virg. Ec. vii. 58.

V. 9. "Immania ponti æquora," Lucret. vi. 624.

V. 10. "Curvisque immugiit Ætna cavernis." Æn. iii. 674.

V. 11. "Tum *sonitu* Prochyta alta *tremit*."
                Virg. Æn. ix. 715. *Luke.*

V 15. "Piceâ crassam caligine nubem," Virg. Georg. ii.
309. "Vorago, pestiferas aperit fauces," Æn. vii. 569.

V. 17. "Terra tremit: fugere feræ," Virg. Georg. i. 330.

V 24.   —— "tum longo limite sulcus
Dat *lucem*, et latè circùm loca *sulphure* fumant."
                Virg. Æn. ii. 698.

Fumumque, flammasque, rotataque turbine saxa.

Quin ubi detonuit fragor, et lux reddita cœlo;
Mæstos confluere agricolas, passuque videres
Tandem iterum timido deserta requirere tecta :
Sperantes, si forte oculis, si forte darentur
Uxorum cineres, miserorumve ossa parentum   30
Tenuia, sed tanti saltem solatia luctûs)
Unà colligere et justâ componere in urnâ.

Uxorum nusquam cineres, nusquam ossa parentum

And, " *Sulphurei* cum per juga consita *Gauri*," Ausonii Mosell.
p. 387, ed. Tollii. "Anhelantem cœlesti sulfure campum,"
v. Stat. Theb. xi. 17.

V. 25. In the modern Latin poetry, this license of lengthening the "que" before the mute and liquid, even with the
power of the cæsura, ought to be avoided, as it is supported
by so few examples. See Virg. Æn. vii. 186. Georg. i. 164.
And see also Æn. iii. 91. Ov. Met. v. 484, and Class. Journal, No. xxi. p. 174, xxii. 364.

V. 26. This is not a common expression in Latin poetry.
Val. Flaccus has, " Dum detonet ira : " iv. 294. See also
Quintilian (Gesn. xii. ix. 4): "Cum illa dicendi vitiosa jac-
tatio inter plausores sero detonuit." Petron. Sat. c. xvii.
p. 37. Sid. Apollin. c. xiv. 24.

V. 31. See Virg. Georg. i. 397: "Tenuia nec lanæ," &c.—
ii. 121 : "Depectant tenuia Seres." Lucret. iv. 747. And
Terent. Maur. ver. 474.

V. 31.   —— " Solatia luctûs
     Exigua ingentis misero sed debita patri."

                              Æn. xi. 62.

V. 32. I should conceive the proper phrase to be " Colligere
in unum," and not *unà*. Virg. Ecl. vii. 2 : " Compulerant-
que greges Corydon et Thyrsis in unum." Cicero de In-
ventione, i. 56 : " *Colligere* et conferre *in unum*." Again,
" Militibus in unum conductis." And Philip. ix.: "Si omnes
juris consulti in unum conferantur." Ovidii Met. iii. 715.
See the note on Ovid. Metam. xiii. 910.

V. 33.   —— " Alas !
     Nor wife, nor children more shall he behold,
     Nor friends, nor sacred home."

                       Thomson. Winter, 315.

(Spem miseram!) assuetosve Lares, aut rura vide-
Quippe ubi planities campi diffusa jacebat; [bunt.
Mons novus: ille supercilium, frontemque favillâ
Incanum ostentans, ambustis cautibus, æquor
Subjectum, stragemque suam, mæsta arva, minaci
Despicit imperio, soloque in littore regnat.

Hinc infame loci nomen, multosque per annos
Immemor antiquæ laudis, nescire labores   41
Vomeris, et nullo tellus revirescere cultu.
Non avium colles, non carmine matutino
Pastorum resonare; adeo undique dirus habebat
Informes latè horror agros saltusque vacantes. 45
Sæpius et longè detorquens navita proram
Monstrabat digito littus, sævæque revolvens
Funera narrabat noctis, veteremque ruinam.

Montis adhuc facies manet hirta atque aspera
        saxis: 49
Sed furor extinctus jamdudum, et flamma quievit,
Quæ nascenti aderat; seu fortè bituminis atri
Defluxere olìm rivi, atque effœta lacuna
Pabula sufficere ardori, viresque recusat;
Sive in visceribus meditans incendia jam nunc
(Horrendùm) arcanis glomerat genti esse futuræ
Exitio, sparsos tacitusque recolligit ignes.   56

V. 41. "Res antiquæ laudis," Virg. Georg. ii. 174.
V. 43. "Matutini cantus," Æn. viii. 456. Par. Lost, v. 7.
V. 45. "Longe *saltus*, lateque *vacantes*."
                        Virg. Georg. iii. 476. *Luke.*
V. 47. "Indice monstraret digito," Hor. Sat. ii. viii. 26.
And Pers. i. 28
V. 56. "Sparsosque recolligit ignes," Lucan. i. 157. "Dum
tacitas vires, et flammam colligit ignis," Sil. Ital. iv. 307;

Raro per clivos haud secius ordine vidi
Canescentem oleam : longum post tempus amicti
Vite virent tumuli ; patriamque revisere gaudens
Bacchus in assuetis tenerum caput exerit arvis 60
Vix tandem, infidoque audet se credere cœlo.

A FAREWELL TO FLORENCE.

[See Mason's Memoirs, vol. ii. p. 157.]

* * Oh Fæsulæ amœna
Frigoribus juga, nec nimiùm spirantibus auris !
Alma quibus Tusci Pallas decus Apennini
Esse dedit, glaucâque suâ canescere sylvâ !
Non ego vos posthàc Arni de valle videbo   5
Porticibus circum, et candenti cincta coronâ
Villarum longè nitido consurgere dorso,   [sus
Antiquamve Ædem, et veteres præferre Cupres-
Mirabor, tectisque super pendentia tecta.

----

and Virg. Georg. i. 427. The position of "que" is wrong.
See note to Burm. Ovid. Metam. xiv. 30 ; but also consult
Class. Journal. No. xxii. p. 22.

V. 58. "Fœtum canentis olivæ," Ov. Met. vi. 81.

V. 60. "Jam modò cœruleo nitidum caput exsere ponto,"
Ov. Met. xiii. 838. And Fast. i. 458.

V. 61. " Pennis ausus se credere cœlo," Virg. Æn. vi. 15.

V. 1 In Sil. Ital. Pun. viii. 478, the second syllable of this
word is short: " Fæsula, et antiquus Romanis mœnibus horror." Polybius also (lib. ii. cap. 9,) writes Φαίσολα. In
other authors, as Appian. Civ. Bell. ii. c. 2. Dion. xxxvii. it

IMITATION OF AN ITALIAN SONNET

OF SIGNIOR ABBATE BUONDELMONTE.

[See Mason's Memoirs, vol. ii. p. 158.]

Spesso Amor sotto la forma
D'amistà ride, e s'asconde:
Poi si mischia, e si confonde
Con lo sdegno, e col rancor.
In Pietade ei si trasforma;
Par trastullo, e par dispetto;
Mà nel suo diverso aspetto
Sempr' egli, è l' istesso Amor.

Lusit amicitiæ interdum velatus amictu,   1
   Et benè compositâ veste fefellit Amor.

---

is written Φισουλαῖ, which appears to be the more ancient orthography. See Cluver. Ital. Antiq. vol. i. p. 509.

V. 5. " Non ego vos posthac, viridi projectus in antro,
    Dumosâ pendere procul de rupe videbo."
                   Virg. Ecl. i. 76.

V. 7. " Conspicitur *nitidis* fundata pecunia villis," Hor. Ep.
i. xv. 46. " Superni villa candens Tusculi," Epod. i. 29.
" Candida qua geminas ostendunt culmina turres," Propert.
Eleg. iii. xvi. 3. " Nitidos lares," Martial. Ep. i. 71. 2.

V. 8. " Præferimus manibus vittas," Æn. vii. 237.

V. 9. " Talia despectant longo per cœrula tractu
    Pendentes saxis instanti culmine, *villæ*."
                Ausonii Mosell. ver. 283.
And, " Culmina *villarum pendentibus* edita ripis." v. 20.

V. 1. " Intrat amicitiæ nomine, tectus Amor."
                Ovid. Ar. Am. i. 720.
   " Ut mihi prætextæ pudor exvelatus amictu."
               Propert. iii. xxiii. 3.

V. 2. " At me compositâ pace fefellit amor," Propert. El.
ii. ii. 6. " Cum bene compositis," Manil. iv. 58.

Mox iræ assumpsit cultus, faciemque minantem,
Inque odium versus, versus et in lacrymas:
Ludentem fuge, nec lacrymanti, aut crede furenti;
Idem est dissimili semper in ore Deus.   6

ALCAIC ODE,*

WRITTEN IN THE ALBUM OF THE GRANDE CHARTREUSE,
IN DAUPHINY, AUGUST 1741.

[See Mason's Memoirs, vol. ii. p. 160, and W. S. Landori
Poemata, p. 195. An imitation of this ode appeared by Mr.
Seward in Europ. Mag. 1791, and it is translated in E. Cart-
wright's Poems, 1803, p. 91.]

On Tu, severi Religio loci,
Quocunque gaudes nomine (non leve
Nativa nam certè fluenta
Numen habet, veteresque sylvas;

V. 5. So Moschus, Idyll. i. 25:

Κἢν ποτ' ἴδῃς κλαίοντα, φυλάσσεο μή σε πλανήσῃ.
Κἢν γελάα, τὺ νιν ἕλκε, καὶ ἢν ἐθέλῃ σὲ φιλᾶσαι
Φεῦγε.

This little poem has been translated into English verse by
Mr. Walpole; see his works, vol. iv. p. 454; and also by the
author of "The Pleasures of Memory:' see Rogers's Poems,
p. 165.

* In Heron's [Pinkerton] "Letters of Literature," p. 299,
is a translation of this ode; and, after that, a most extraordinary assertion, which I wish the author of that book had not
given me an opportunity of producing: as, to say no worse, it
is erroneous in every instance. "This exquisite ode," says he,
"*is by no means in the Alcaic measure, which Mr. Gray seems to*

Præsentiorem et conspicimus Deum   5
Per invias rupes, fera per juga,
   Clivosque præruptos, sonantes
     Inter aquas, nemorumque noctem;
Quàm si repostus sub trabe citreâ
Fulgeret auro, et Phidiacâ manu)   10
   Salve vocanti ritè, fesso et
     Da placidam juveni quietem.

---

have intended it for. The Alcaic measure, as used by Horace, consists of six feet, or twelve syllables, in the two first lines; three feet and a half, or seven syllables, in the third; and four feet, or eight syllables, in the fourth. ' Truly, Master Holofernes, the epithets are sweetly varied, like a scholar at the least.' " (Love's Labour's Lost.) And yet I am afraid that this ingenious commentator has not experienced how **true is** the admonition given by the Moorish grammarian.

    " Quid sit litera, quid duæ,
    Junctæ quid sibi syllabæ.
    Dumos inter, et aspera
    Scruposis sequimur vadis.
    Fronte exile negotium
    Et dignum pueris putes.
    Aggressis labor arduus
    Nec tractibile pondus est."
          Terent. Maur. Præf. 6. ed. Brissæo

V. 2. " Neque enim leve nomen Amatæ," Æn. vii. 581. V. Cas. Sarb. Carm. p. 216. ed. Barbou.

V. 6. This verse would be reckoned faulty, from the absence of the cæsura in its right place. See the note to the " Carmen ad Favonium," ver. 30.

V. 8. " Veteris sub *nocte cupressi*," Val. Flac. i. 774. " Nox propria luce est," Senecæ Thyestes, ver. 678.
" Each tree whose thick and spreading growth hath made
    Rather *a night* between the boughs than shade."
         Davenant. v. Dryden. Misc. vi. 318.

V. 9. " Ponit marmoream sub *trabe citrea.*"
            Hor. Od. iv. i. 20

V. 10. " Phidiacâ manu," Martial. vi. 73. x. 89.

V. 11. " Mihi cumque salve
      Rite vocanti." Hor. Od. i. xxxii. 15.

Quod si invidendis sedibus, et frui
Fortuna sacrâ lege silentii
    Vetat volentem, me resorbens   15
    In medios violenta fluctus :
Saltem remoto des, Pater, angulo
Horas senectæ ducere liberas;
    Tutumque vulgari tumultu
    Surripias, hominumque curis.   20

PART OF AN HEROIC EPISTLE

FROM SOPHONISBA TO MASINISSA.

[See Mason's Memoirs, vol. iii. p. 46, " I thank him (Mason)
  for one, thinking, as I do, many of the lines fully equal to
  Ovid's." MS. note of Bennett, Bishop of Cloyne.]

EGREGIUM accipio promissi Munus amoris,
  Inque manu mortem, jam fruitura, fero :
Atque utinam citius mandasses, luce vel unâ ;
  Transieram Stygios non inhonesta lacus.
Victoris nec passa toros, nova nupta, mariti,   5
  Nec fueram fastus, Roma superba, tuos.

V. 14. " Utrumque sacro digna silentio." Hor. Od. ii. xiii.
29. " Resorbens," Hor. Od. ii. vii. 15.

V. 4. " Quamvis ista mihi mors est *inhonesta* futura,
    Mors *inhonesta* quidem." Propert. El. ii. vii. 89.

V. 5. " Virgineo nullum corpore passa virum," Ovid. Fast.
v. 146. Virg. Georg. iii. 60.

Scilicet hæc partem tibi, Masinissa, triumphi
  Detractam, hæc pompæ jura minora suæ
Imputet, atque uxor quòd non·tua pressa catenis,
  Objecta et sævæ plausibus orbis eo :   10
Quin tu pro tantis cepisti præmia factis,
  Magnum Romanæ pignus amicitiæ !
Scipiadæ excuses, oro, si, tardius utar
  Munere.   Non nimiùm vivere, crede, velim. 14
Parva mora est, breve sed tempus mea fama re-
    quirit :
Detinet hæc animam cura suprema meam.
Quæ patriæ prodesse meæ Regina ferebar,
  Inter Elisæas gloria prima nurus,
Ne videar flammæ nimis indulsisse secundæ,
  Vel nimis hostiles extimuisse manus.   20
Fortunam atque annos liceat revocare priores,

V. 7. In Mason's edition it is spelt 'Massinissa;' which,
however, will only partially correct the quantity ; as the
second syllable will still be short.   See Ovid. Fast. vi. 769:
"Postera lux melior, superat Masinissa Syphacem."   And
Sil. Ital. xvi. 117:

  "Cultuque Aeneadum nomen *Masinissa* superbum."

  That 'Masinissa' is the right orthography, see Drakenborch's note on Sil. Italicus; Gronovius on Livy, lib. xxv. c.
xxxiv. 11; Vorstius on Val. Max. i. i. 31.   Tortellius, in his
Grammatical Commentaries, under the word 'Masanissa,' says,
'Non enim primum aliquo pacto duplicari potuit: ut ignari
quidam syllabarum voluerunt."   See also Noltenii Lexicon,
vol. i. p. 112.   Cellarii Orthog. Lat. i. p. 285.

  V. 12. " I liber absentis pignus amicitiæ."
                                       Martial. ix. cii.
  V. 15. "Parva mora est," Ovid. Met. i. 671.   Ep. ii. 144.
  V. 18. See Sil. Italicus. ii. 239; vi. 346; xiv. 257.
  V. 20. " Pallet, et *hostiles* credit adesse *manus*," Ov. Fast.
ii. 468.
  V. 21. " Non annis revocare tuis," Ov. Met. vii. 177.

Gaudiaque heu! quantis nostra repensa malis.
Primitiasne tuas meministi atque arma Syphacis
    Fusa, et per Tyrias ducta trophæa vias?
(Laudis at antiquæ forsan meminisse pigebit,   25
    Quodque decus quondam causa ruboris erit.)
Tempus ego certe memini, felicia Pœnis
    Quo te non puduit solvere vota deis;
Mœniaque intrantem vidi: longo agmine duxit
    Turba salutantum, purpureique patres.   30
Fœminea ante omnes longe admiratur euntem
    Hæret et aspectu tota caterva tuo.
Jam flexi, regale decus, per colla capilli,
    Jam decet ardenti fuscus in ore color!
Commendat frontis generosa modestia formam,   35
    Seque cupit laudi surripuisse suæ.

V. 26. " Aut ubi cessaras, *causa ruboris eram.*"
                      Ov. Trist. iii. vii. 26.

V. 27. Here the last syllable of *ego* is again made long.
See the note to the Sapphic Ode to West, ver. 45, p. 186. I
have only to add to that note, that *ego* is said to be found with
this quantity in the ' Diræ Catonis,' ver. 156; but which line
is thus given by Wernsdorf, vol. iii. p. 19:

    " Ausus egon' primus custos violare pudores?"

and by all the other editors prior to him. See Pithæi Catul.
p. 219. Scaligeri Collect. p. 61. Boxhornii Poet. Sat. p. 117.
Burmanni Anthol. ii. 674; but erroneously: see Bentley's
Canon, Heaut. Terentii, act v. sc. 1. and Clas. Journ. No. lxii.
p. 352.

V. 30. " Turba salutantum," Claudian. iii. 213, p. 30. ed
Gesn. Virgil. Georg. ii. 462.

V. 31. " Omnia fœmineis quare dilecta catervis," Martial.
xi. 48. " Venit in exsequias tota caterva meas," Prop. iv
xi. 68. And " aspectu hæsit," Virg. Æn. iii. 597.

V. 34. " Et enim *fusco* grata *colore* Venus," Ov. Amor.
ii. 440. And Propert. El. ii. xix. 78.

V. 35. Ov. Medicam. ver. 1. " Quæ faciem commendat
cura." And ad Liv. 259.

Prima genas tenui signat vix flore juventas,
  Et dextræ soli credimus esse virum.
Dum faciles gradiens oculos per singula jactas,
  (Seu rexit casus lumina, sive Venus)   40
In me (vel certè visum est) conversa morari
  Sensi; virgineus perculit ora pudor.
Nescio quid vultum molle spirare tuendo,
  Credideramque tuos lentius ire pedes.
Quærebam, juxta æqualis si dignior esset,   45
  Quæ poterat visus detinuisse tuos :
Nulla fuit circum æqualis quæ dignior esset,
  Asseruitque decus conscia forma suum.
Pompæ finis erat. Totâ vix nocte quievi,
  Sin premat invitæ lumina victa sopor,   50
Somnus habet pompas, eademque recursat imago ;
  Atque iterum hesterno munere victor ades.†

   * * * * *

V. 37. " Ora puer *prima signans* intonsa *juventa*," Virg.
Æn. ix. 181. Also Ovid. Met. xiii. 754. Virg. Æn. vii. 162.
viii. 160.
 V. 39. " *Facilesque oculos* fert omnia circum," Virg. Æn.
viii. 310.
 V. 40. " Ad fratrem *casu* lumina flexa tulit," Ov. Trist.
iii. ix. 22.
 V. 43. Gray has in this instance preserved a metrical canon,
which has been broken through by many of the modern Latin
poets ; — repeatedly by Milton, Addison, Buchanan, and T.
Warton. See the Classical Journal, 1. 71. 283, xxi. 174. xxii.
364. and Barthius and Burman on Nemesian Eclog. ii. 32. see
Poet. Lat. Minor. vol. i. p. 570. and Dawes. Misc. Crit. ed.
Kidd. p. 3.
 V. 46. " Sæpe oculos etiam detinuisse tuos," Ov. Trist. ii.
520.
 V. 49. " Infelix *totâ* quicumque *quiescere nocte*," Ovid.
Amor. ii. 9. 39.
 V. 50. " *Lumina* cum placido *victa sopore* jacent," Ov. Ep
xvi. 100.
 † Ellis, in his Historical Sketch of English Poetry, (p. 224,)

DIDACTIC POEM UNFINISHED:

ENTITLED

DE PRINCIPIIS COGITANDI.

LIBER PRIMUS.   AD FAVONIUM.

[See Mason's Memoirs, vol. iii. p. 55.]

UNDE Animus scire incipiat; quibus inchoet orsa
Principiis seriem rerum, tenuemque catenam
Mnemosyne : Ratio unde rudi sub pectore tardum
Augeat imperium ; et primum mortalibus ægris
Ira, Dolor, Metus, et Curæ nascantur inanes,   5
Hinc canere aggredior. Nec dedignare canentem,
O decus! Angliacæ certe O lux altera gentis!
Si quà primus iter monstras, vestigia conor
Signare incertâ, tremulâque insistere plantâ.
Quin potius duc ipse (potes namque omnia) sanc-
    tum   10
Ad limen (si ritè adeo, si pectore puro,)

---

thinks that the description of the entry of Troilus into Troy,
in Chaucer's Romance of Troilus and Creseida, suggested to
Gray some very beautiful lines in this Epistle: "Jam flexi,
regale decus," &c. (See Chaucer, b. xi. st. 83. fol. 151. ed.
1602.)
    " This Troilus sat on his baye steed,
      All armed, save his head, full richely," &c.
   V. 4. Virg. Georg. i. 237, " Mortalibus ægris," and Lucret.
vi. 1. *Luke.*
   V. 5. Virg. Georg. iv. 345, " *Curam* Clymene narrabat
inanem." *Luke.*
   V. 7. " Magnæ spes altera Romæ," Virg. Æn. xii. 168.
This apostrophe is addressed to ' Locke.'
   V. 9. " Tremulis possunt insistere plantis," Juv. Sat. vi. 96

Obscuræ reserans Naturæ ingentia claustra.
Tu cæcas rerum causas, fontemque severum
Pande, Pater; tibi enim, tibi, veri magne Sacerdos,
Corda patent hominum, atque altæ penetralia
    Mentis.   15
Tuque aures adhibe vacuas, facilesque, Favonî,
(Quod tibi crescit opus) simplex nec despice car-
    men,
Nec vatem: non illa leves primordia motus,
Quanquam parva, dabunt. Lætum vel amabile
    quicquid   [auras,
Usquam oritur, trahit hinc ortum; nec surgit ad
Quin ea conspirent simul, eventusque secundent.
Hinc variæ vitaï artes, ac mollior usus,   22
Dulce et amicitiæ vinclum: Sapientia dia
Hinc roseum accendit lumen, vultuque sereno
Humanas aperit mentes, nova gaudia monstrans,
Deformesque fugat curas, vanosque timores: 26
Scilicet et rerum crescit pulcherrima Virtus.
Illa etiam, quæ te (mirùm) noctesque diesque

V. 12. *Naturæ* primus portarum *claustra* cupiret," Lucret.
i. 72. " Cæcas causas," Ibid. iii. 317. Virg. Æn. vii. 15
" portarum ingentia claustra." *Luke.*

V. 13. " *Amnemque severum*," Virg. Æn. vi. 374. And
Georg. iii. 7: *Amnemque severum* Cocyti metuet."

V. 15. " Mentis penetralia nudat," Claud. Rap. Pros. i. 213.

V. 16. " *Faciles* habuit *aures*," Quintil. Inst. Orat. vi. v.
p. 576. " Vacuas aures adhibe," Lucret. i. 45.

V. 21. " Eventusque secundet," Virg. Georg. iv. 397.

V. 24. " Rubens accendit lumina Vesper," Virg. Georg.
i. 251.

V. 26. Hor. Epod. xiii. 18, " Deformis ægrimoniæ." *Luke.*

V. 27. " Scilicet et rerum facta est pulcherrima Roma,"
Georg. ii. 534.

Assiduè fovet inspirans, linguamque sequentem
Temperat in numeros, atque horas mulcet inertes;
Aurea non aliâ se jactat origine Musa.   31

    Principio, ut magnum fœdus Natura creatrix
Firmavit, tardis jussitque inolescere membris
Sublimes animas; tenebroso in carcere partem
Noluit ætheream longo torpere veterno: 35
Nec per se proprium passa exercere vigorem est,
Ne sociæ molis conjunctos sperneret artus,
Ponderis oblita, et cœlestis conscia flammæ.
Idcircò innumero ductu tremere undique fibras
Nervorum instituit: tum toto corpore miscens 40
Implicuit latè ramos, et sensile textum,
Implevitque humore suo (seu lympha vocanda,
Sive aura est) tenuis certè, atque levissima quæ-
    dam
Vis versatur agens, parvosque infusa canales
Perfluit; assiduè externis quæ concita plagis, 45
Mobilis, incussique fidelis nuntia motûs,
Hinc indè accensâ contage relabitur usque
Ad superas hominis sedes, arcemque cerebri.

V. 31. "At non *Venus aurea* contra," Virg. Æn. x. 16.
" Qui nunc *te* fruitur credulus *aurea*," Hor. Od. i. v. 9.

V. 32. Rerum *natura creatrix*," Lucret. i. 623.

V. 33. See note at p. 176, on the position of " que," and
Burman on Antholog. Lat. vol. i. p. 607.

V. 35. " Nec *torpere* gravi passus sua regna *veterno*," Virg.
Georg. i. 124.

V. 45. " *Sequenti concita plaga*," Lucret. iv. 189. " Externis plagis," Ibid. ii. 1140.

V. 48. —— " Stetit unis in *arcem*
    Erectus *capitis*."   Manil. Astron. iv. 905.
    —— " Penitusque supremum,
In cerebrum."   Claud. xviii. 52.

Namque illìc posuit solium, et sua templa sacravit
Mens animi : hanc circum coëunt, densoque fe-
    runtur   50
Agmine notitiæ, simulacraque tenuia rerum :
Ecce autem naturæ ingens aperitur imago
Immensæ, variique patent commercia mundi.

Ac uti longinquis descendunt montibus amnes
Velivolus Tamisis, flaventisque Indus arenæ,   55
Euphratesque, Tagusque, et opimo flumine Ganges,
Undas quisque suas volvens, cursuque sonoro
In mare prorumpunt : hos magno acclinis in antro
Excipit Oceanus, natorumque ordine longo
Dona recognoscit venientûm, ultròque serenat 60

---

v. Macrob. S. Scipionis, i. p. 46. v. Gronovii Not. Apuleii
Apolog. " *Verticem* hominis velat *arcem* et regiam." Coripp.
de Laud. Justini. ii. 190. Claudiani Cons. Honor, iv. " *Summa* capitis pendavit in *arce.*"   Sid. Apoll. v. 239, " Arce
cerebri." Prudent. Ham. 312, " Mediaque ex arce cerebri,"
and many other examples. Roscommon has the " Caverns of
the Brain," on Poetry, v. 27, and see Sprat. Plague of Athens,
st. 11.

            —— " Tum vapor ipsam,
   Corporis arcem flammis urit."   Senecæ Œdip. 185.
See also Shakespeare: —— " And his pure *brain*,
   Which some suppose the *soul's frail dwelling-house.*"
                         K. John, act v. sc. 7.
And see ver. 135 of this poem.

   V. 51. So Lucret. iii. 244:
    " Qua nec mobilius quidquam neque *tenuius* exstat."
And Virg. Georg. i. 398:
    " *Tenuia* nec lanæ per cœlum vellera ferri."

   V. 51. " *Rerum simulachra* ferantur," Lucret. iv. 165.
" Geminoque facis commercia mundo," Claud. xxxiii. 91.

   V. 59. " Te tuus Oceanus *natali* gurgite lassum Excipit,"
Claud. vii. 176.

   V. 60. " Dona recognoscit populorum," Virg. Æn. viii. 721

Cæruleam faciem, et diffuso marmore ridet.
Haud aliter species properant se inferre novellæ
Certatim menti, atque aditus quino agmine com-
    plent.
    Primas tactus agit partes, primusque minutæ
Laxat iter cæcum turbæ, recipitque ruentem.   5
Non idem huic modus est, qui fratribus: amplius
    ille
Imperium affectat senior, penitusque medullis,
Visceribusque habitat totis, pellîsque recentem
Funditur in telam, et latè per stamina vivit.
Necdum etiam matris puer eluctatus ab alvo   70
Multiplices solvit tunicas, et vincula rupit;
Sopitus molli somno, tepidoque liquore
Circumfusus adhuc: tactus tamen aura lacessit
Jamdudum levior sensus, animamque reclusit.
Idque magis simul, ac solitum blandumque calo-
    rem   75
Frigore mutavit cœli, quod verberat acri
Impete inassuetos artus: tum sævior adstat
Humanæque comes vitæ Dolor excipit; ille
Cunctantem frustrà et tremulo multa ore queren-
    tem
Corripit invadens, ferreisque amplectitur ulnis. 80

V. 61. "Diffuso lumine ridet," Lucret. iii. 22.

V. 69. So Pope. Essay on Man, i. 217:

    "The spider's touch, so exquisitely fine,
      Feels at each thread, and lives along the line."

V. 70. "Tum porro *puer.* — *Nixibus ex alvo matris* natura profudit," Lucret. v. 223. "Cum veteres ponunt tunicas," Ibid. iv. 56.

V. 80. "Cupidisque *amplectitur ulnis*," Ovid. Met. xi. 63.

Tum species primùm patefacta est candida Lucis
(Usque vices adeò Natura bonique, malique,
Exæquat, justâque manu sua damna rependit)
Tum primùm, ignotosque bibunt nova lumina soles.

Carmine quo, Dea, te dicam, gratissima cœli   85
Progenies, ortumque tuum; gemmantia rore
Ut per prata levi lustras, et floribus halans
Purpureum Veris gremium, scenamque virentem
Pingis, et umbriferos colles, et cærula regna?
Gratia te, Venerisque Lepos, et mille Colorum,   90
Formarumque chorus sequitur, motusque decentes.
At caput invisum Stygiis Nox atra tenebris
Abdidit, horrendæque simul Formidinis ora,
Pervigilesque æstus Curarum, atque anxius Angor.

V. 81. "Nam simul ac *species patefacta est* verna diei!"
Lucret. i. x.

V. 84. " *Editus ex utero cæcus nova lumina* sensit,
        Et stupet *ignotum* se meruisse *diem.*"
                                        Claud. xcix. 10.

V. 85. —— " Dignissima cœli,
        Progenies."   Achill. Statii. ii. 372.

V. 86. Lucret. ii. 319, " Invitant herbæ *gemmantes rore*
recenti." *Luke.*

V. 87. Virg. Georg. iv. 109, " Croceis *halantes floribus*
horti." *Luke.*

V. 88. " Hic ver purpureum," Virg. Eclog. ix. 41.

V. 89. " Umbriferum nemus," Lucret. vi. 703. " Cœruleo
regno," Virg. Ciris. 483.

V. 91. " Quove color? decens
        Quo motus?"   Hor. Od. iv. xiii. 17.

V. 92. " Invisum hoc detrude caput sub Tartara," Æn. ix.
476. " Stygiis tenebris," Georg. iii. 551.

V. 93. " Subit *horrida* mentem *formido,*" Sil. Ital. x. 544;
Lucret. vi. 253. " Curarum fluctuat æstu," Virg. Æn. viii.
19. xii. 335.

V. 94. Lucret. iii. 1006, " Exest anxius angor." *Luke.*

Undique lætitiâ florent mortalia corda,   95
Purus et arridet largis fulgoribus Æther.

    Omnia nec tu ideò invalidæ se pandere Menti
(Quippe nimis teneros posset vis tanta diei
Perturbare, et inexpertos confundere visus)
Nec capere infantes animos, neu cernere credas 100
Tam variam molem, et miræ spectacula lucis:
Nescio quâ tamen hæc oculos dulcedine parvos
Splendida percussit novitas, traxitque sequentes;
Nonne videmus enim, latis inserta fenestris
Sicubi se Phœbi dispergant aurea tela,   105
Sive lucernarum rutilus colluxerit ardor,
Extemplo hùc obverti aciem, quæ fixa repertos
Haurit inexpletum radios, fruiturque tuendo?

    Altior huic verò sensu, majorque videtur
Addita, Judicioque arctè connexa potestas,   110
Quod simul atque ætas volventibus auxerit annis,
Hæc simul, assiduo depascens omnia visu,
Perspiciet, vis quanta loci, quid polleat ordo,
Juncturæ quis honos, ut res accendere rebus
Lumina conjurant inter se, et mutua fulgent.   115

V. 96. "Improviso vibratus ab Æthere fulgor," Virg. Æn. viii. 524.

V. 102. "Nescio qua præter solitum dulcedine læti," Virg. Georg. i. 413.

V. 104. "Plena per insertas fundebat luna fenestras," Virg. Æn. iii. 152.

V. 105. "Lucida tela diei," Lucret. i. 128.

V. 108. "*Expleri mentem* nequit, ardescitque *tuendo*," Virg. Æn. i. 713.

V. 113. "Tantum series, *juncturaque pollet*," Horat. Art. Poet. 242. "Ita *res accendent* lumina *rebus*," Lucret. i. 1110.

Nec minor in geminis viget auribus insita virtus,
Nec tantum in curvis quæ pervigil excubet antris
Hinc atque hinc (ubi Vox tremefecerit ostia pulsu
Aëriis invecta rotis) longèque recurset:
Scilicet Eloquio hæc sonitus, hæc fulminis alas,
Et mulcere dedit dictis et tollere corda,   121
Verbaque metiri numeris, versuque ligare
Repperit, et quicquid discant Libethrides undæ,
Calliope quotiès, quotiès Pater ipse canendi
Evolvat liquidum carmen, calamove loquenti 125
Inspiret dulces animas, digitisque figuret.

At medias fauces, et linguæ humentia templa
Gustus habet, quà se insinuet jucunda saporum
Luxuries, dona Autumni, Bacchique voluptas.

Naribus interea consedit odora hominum vis, 130
Docta leves captare auras, Panchaïa quales
Vere novo exhalat, Floræve quod oscula fragrant,

V. 115. On this use of the *indicative*, 'conjurant,' 'fulgent,'
for the *subjunctive mood*, see Parr's Letter to Dr. Gabell, in the
Class. Journ. lxxix. Sept. 1829, p. 45, and Parr's Correspond.
vol. i. p. 476.

V. 119. "Puniceis *invecta rotis*," Virg. Æn. xii. 77.

V. 122. "Nec *numeris* nectere *verba* juvat," Ovid. Pont. ii.
30.

V. 123. "Nymphæ, noster amor, Libethrides," Virg. Eclog. vii. 21. Pomp. Mela, ii. 3.

V. 126. "Mobilibus *digitis* expergefacta *figurant*."
                           Lucret. ii. 412.

V. 128. "Jucundus sapores," Tibull. i. vii. 35.

V. 130. "Odora canum vis," Lucret. vi. 778. Virg. Æn.
iv. 132.

V. 132. Compare Par. Lost, b. v. 16 : "Then with voice,
mild as when Zephyrus on Flora breathes." Virg. Georg. i.
43. "Vere novo gelidus canis cum montibus humor." *Luke.*

Roscida, cum Zephyri furtìm sub vesperis horâ
Respondet votis, mollemque aspirat amorem.

Tot portas altæ capitis circumdedit arci   135
Alma Parens, sensûsque vias per membra reclusit;
Haud solas: namque intùs agit vivata facultas,
Quâ sese explorat, contemplatusque repentè
Ipse suas animus vires, momentaque cernit.
Quid velit, aut possit, cupiat, fugiatve, vicissìm
Percipĭt imperio gaudens; neque corpora fallunt
Morigera ad celeres actus, ac numina mentis.

Qualis Hamadryadum quondam si fortè sororum
Una, novos peragrans saltus, et devia rura;
(Atque illam in viridi suadet procumbere ripâ
Fontis pura quies, et opaci frigoris umbra)
Dum prona in latices speculi de margine pendet,
Mirata est subitam venienti occurrere Nympham:
Mox eosdem, quos ipsa, artus, eadem ora gerentem
Unà inferre gradus, unà succedere sylvæ   150
Aspicit alludens; seseque agnoscit in undis.
Sic sensu interno rerum simulacra suarum
Mens ciet, et proprios observat conscia vultus.

V. 134. "Votis respondet avari," Georg. i. 47. "Divinum
adspirat amorem," Virg. Æn. viii. 373.

V. 137. "Vivata potestas," Lucret. iii. 410. 557. 680.

V. 139. —— "*Animus* vario labefactus vulnere nutat
Huc levis, atque illùc; *momentaque* sumit utroque."
Ovid. Met. x. 375

V. 144. "Mater virideis saltus orbata peragrans."
Lucret. ii. 355. *Luke*

V. 147. "Lympharum in speculo," Phædrus, i. iv. 3.

V. 149. The same synæresis is found in Propert. iv. vii. 7:
"*Eosdem* habuit secum, quibus est elata capillos."

And, "*Eosdem* oculos; lateri vestis adusta fuit."

Nec verò simplex ratio, aut jus omnibus unum
Constat imaginibus. Sunt quæ bina ostia nôrunt ;
Hæ privos servant aditus ; sine legibus illæ
Passìm, quà data porta, ruunt, animoque propin-
    quant.   157
Respice, cui à cunis tristes extinxit ocellos,
Sæva et in eternas mersit natura tenebras :
Illi ignota dies lucet, vernusque colorum   160
Offusus nitor est, et vivæ gratia formæ.
Corporis at filum, et motus, spatiumque, locique
Intervalla datur certo dignoscere tactu :   [plex,
Quandoquidem his iter ambiguum est, et janua du-
Exclusæque oculis species irrumpere tendunt   165
Per digitos.   Atqui solis concessa potestas
Luminibus blandæ est radios immittere lucis.
  Undique proporrò sociis, quacunque patescit
Notitiæ campus, mistæ lasciva feruntur
Turba voluptatis comites, formæque dolorum   170
Terribiles visu, et portâ glomerantur in omni.
Nec vario minus introïtu magnum ingruit Illud,
Quo facere et fungi, quo res existere circùm
Quamque sibi proprio cum corpore scimus, et ire

V. 154. " Nec *ratio* solis *simplex*," Lucret. v. 613.   " Constat imago," iv. 108.   " Privas aures," iv. 570.

V. 157. Virg. Æn. i. 83.   " Qua data porta ruunt."
                                                    Luke.

V. 161. " Ea gratia formæ," Ovid. Met. vii. 44.

V. 167. " Radios inter quasi rumpere lucis," Lucret. v. 288.
' Radiis ardentem lucis," Virg. Æn. vii. 142.

V. 171. " Terribiles visu formæ," Æn. vi. 277.

V. 173. " At *facere, et fungi* sine corpore nulla potestas."
                                       Lucret. i. 444

Ordine, perpetuoque per ævum flumine labi.   175
    Nunc age quo valeat pacto, quâ sensilis arte
Affectare viam, atque animi tentare latebras
Materies (dictis aures adverte faventes)
Exsequar.   Imprimìs spatii quam multa per
        æquor
Millia multigenis pandant se corpora seclis,   180
Expende.   Haud unum invenies, quod mente li-
        cebit
Amplecti, nedum propriùs deprendere sensu,
Molis egens certæ, aut solido sine robore, cujus
Denique mobilitas linquit, texturave partes,
Ulla nec orarum circumcæsura coërcet.   185
Hæc conjuncta adeò totâ compage fatetur
Mundus, et extremo clamant in limine rerum,
(Si rebus datur extremum) primordia.   Firmat
Hæc eadem tactus (tactum quis dicere falsum
Audeat?) hæc oculi nec lucidus arguit orbis.   190
    Inde potestatum enasci densissima proles:
Nam quodcunque ferit visum, tangive laborat,

V. 175. "*Perpetuo* possint *ævi labentia* tractu."
                                        Lucret. v. 1215.
    V. 177. " Viamque adfectat Olympo," Georg. iv. 562.
"Tentare latebras," Æn. ii. 38.
    V. 185. " Extima membrorum *circumcæsura coercet*."
                                        Lucret. iv. 651.
    V. 189.   —— " Solem quis dicere falsum
        Audeat."   Virg. Georg. i. 463.
    V. 190. " At si tantula pars *oculi* media illa peresa est,
        Incolumis quamvis alioqui *splendidus orbis*."
                                        Lucret. iii. 415.
    V. 191. "Densior hinc soboles," Virg. Georg. iii. 308.
    V. 192. " Quæ *feriunt oculorum acies*, visumque lacessant,"
Lucret. iv. 329.

Quicquid nare bibis, vel concava concipit auris,
Quicquid lingua sapit, credas hoc omne, necesse
    est
Ponderibus, textu, discursu, mole, figurâ   195
Particulas præstare leves, et semina rerum.
Nunc oculos igitur pascunt, et luce ministrâ
Fulgere cuncta vides, spargique coloribus orbem,
Dum de sole trahunt alias, aliasque supernè
Detorquent, retròque docent se vertere flammas.

V. 193. " Nare bibis." Is this expression warranted by the
authority of any of the Latin poets? Horace has " Bibit aure,"
Od. ii. xiii. 32 ; and Statius, in Ach. ii. 120, " Aure bibentem."
" Naso videt," Plautius. See Martini. Var. Lect. p. 10. Shake-
speare transfers the same word to *sight:* " And with mine *eyes*
I'll *drink* the words you send," Cymbel. act i. sc. 2. And
Thomson. Spring, 106: " Or *taste* the *smell* of dairy." " Elap-
susque *cavâ* fingitur *aure* lapis," Ov. Art. Am. i. 432.

V. 196. " Multorum semina rerum," Lucret. ii. 676. *Luke.*

V. 197. " Oculos qui pascere possunt," Lucret. ii. 419.
Luke.

" Consulit ardentes radios, et *luce magistra.*"
Claud. Cons. Honor. vi. 7.

V. 198. " Grammatici veteres notaverunt à Virgilio et anti-
quioribus poetis, *stridere* in tertiâ conjugatione cum aliis verbis,
ut *fervere, fulgere* esse usitatum ; à Lucano autem, et Statio,
et ejus ætatis poetis in secundâ." *Vide* Priscian. Col. 837.
866. 893. Dousam. ad Lucil. lib. ix. p. 119. N. Marcell.
voce "fulgere," ed. Mercer. Coripp. Laud. Justini, iii. 257.
Virg. Georg. iv. 262. Æn. iv. 689. vii. 334. xii. 691. Lucan.
ii. 250. vi. 179. ed. Oudendorp. Gesner, in a note to Claudian
de Cons. Stilich. iii. 142, "Siculas obsident urbes," says, " *Ob-
sidere* tertiâ conjugatione, nec optimos refugisse docent The-
sauri nostri." It was on the authority of the use of these
verbs in the third conjugation, that Vossius, in his treatise " De
Arte Grammatica," (lib. ii. p. 90), attempted to defend *respon-
děre* in the well-known passage of Manilius, lib. v. 753, and
that Scaliger and Bronkhusius read " Jam canis ætas mea
canaret annis." v. Propert. El. ii. 14. 7.

V. 200. " Faciunt ignem *se vertere* in auras."
Lucret. i. 783.

Nunc trepido inter se fervent corpuscula pulsu,
Ut tremor æthera per magnum, latèque natantes
Aurarum fluctus avidi vibrantia claustra
Auditûs queat allabi, sonitumque propaget.
Cominùs interdum non ullo interprete per se   ₂₀₅
Nervorum invadunt teneras quatientia fibras,
Sensiferumque urgent ultrò per viscera motum.

*   *   *   *   *   *   *

LIBER QUARTUS.

HACTENUS haud segnis Naturæ arcana retexi
Musarum interpres, primusque Britanna per arva
Romano liquidum deduxi flumine rivum.
Cum Tu opere in medio, spes tanti et causa laboris,
Linquis, et æternam fati te condis in umbram!
Vidi egomet duro graviter concussa dolore
Pectora, in alterius non unquam lenta dolorem;

V. 207. "*Sensiferos motus* quæ dedit prima per artus," Lucret. ii. 246, and iii. 937. "Longe ab *sensiferis* primordia *motibus* errant."

V. 2. See Lucret. i. 95; iv. 5. And Columella de Cult. Hort. 435:

"Qui primus veteres ausus recludere fontes,
Ascræum cecinit Romana per oppida carmen."

Virg. Georg. ii. 175. And iii. 12:

"Aonio rediens deducam vertice Musas."

And see note to Ennius, ed. Hesselii. p. 10.

V. 8. "Languescent lumina morte," Catull. lxiv. 188. "Vultus amatos," Ov. Fast. vi. 579.

Et languere oculos vidi, et pallescere amantem
Vultum, quo nunquam Pietas nisi rara, Fidesque,
Altus amor Veri, et purum spirabat Honestum. 10
Visa tamen tardi demùm inclementia morbi
Cessare est, reducemque iterum roseo ore Salutem
Speravi, atque unà tecum, dilecte Favoni!
Credulus heu longos, ut quondàm, fallere Soles:
Heu spes nequicquam dulces, atque irrita vota!
Heu mæstos Soles, sine te quos ducere flendo 16
Per desideria, et questus jam cogor inanes!

At Tu, sancta anima, et nostri non indiga luctûs,
Stellanti templo, sincerique ætheris igne,
Unde orta es, fruere; atque ô si secura, nec ultra
Mortalis, notos olìm miserata labores 21
Respectes, tenuesque vacet cognoscere curas;
Humanam si fortè altâ de sede procellam
Contemplêre, metus, stimulosque cupidinis acres,
Gaudiaque et gemitus, parvoque in corde tumultum
Irarum ingentem, et sævos sub pectore fluctus;

V. 9. " Incorrupta *fides*, nudaque *veritas*."
                                    Hor. Od. i. xxiv. 7.
V. 11. " Rapit inclementia mortis," Virg. Georg. iii. 68.
                                                       Luke.
V. 14. " Tecum etenim longos memini consumere soles."
                       Pers. Sat. v. 41. Virg. Eclog. ix. 51.
V. 17. ." *Questus* ad nubila rumpit *inanes*," Claud. xxxv.
249. " Questu volvebat inani," Ciris. v. 401.
V. 18. " *Sancta* ad vos *anima*," Virg. Æn. xii. 648.
  " Opisque haud indiga nostræ," Georg. ii. 428.
V. 21. " Oh ! sola infandos Trojæ miserata labores ! " Æn.
i. 597. " Tenuisque piget cognoscere curas," Georg. i. 177
V. 21. ———" Si quid pietas antiqua *labores*
  Respicit humanos."   Æn. v. 688.
V. 24. " Et stimulos acres sub pectore vertit," Æn. ix. 718.

P

Respice et has lacrymas, memori quas ictus amore
Fundo; quod possum, juxtà lugere sepulchrum
Dum juvat, et mutæ vana hæc jactare favillæ. 29
*   *   *   *   *   *   *

GREEK EPIGRAM.

[See Mason's Memoirs, vol. iii. p. 45.]

Αζόμενος πολύθηρον ἐκηβόλου ἄλσος ἀνάσσας,
Τᾶς δεινᾶς τεμένη λεῖπε κυναγὲ θεᾶς,
Μοῦνοι ἄρ' ἔνθα κύνων ζαθέων κλαγγεῦσιν ὑλάγμοι,
'Ανταχεῖς Νυμφᾶν ἀγροτερᾶν κελάδῳ.

V. 29. " Taliaque illacrymans *mutæ jace* verba *favillæ.*"
Propert. Eleg. ii. i. 77.

219

EXTRACTS.

PETRARCA PART I. SONETTO 170.

"Lasso ch' i' ardo, ed altri non mel crede;" &c.

IMITATED.*

Uror, io; veros at nemo credidit ignes:
Quin credunt omnes; dura sed illa negat,
Illa negat, soli volumus cui posse probare;
Quin videt, et visos improba dissimulat.   4
Ah, durissima mî, sed et, ah, pulcherrima rerum!
Nonne animam in miserâ, Cynthia, fronte vides?
Omnibus illa pia est; et, si non fata vetâssent,
Tam longas mentem flecteret ad lacrymas.
Sed tamen has lacrymas, hunc tu, quem spreveris, ignem,
Carminaque auctori non bene culta suo,   10
Turba futurorum non ignorabit amantûm:
Nos duo, cumque erimus parvus uterque cinis,
Jamque faces, eheu! oculorum, et frigida lingua,
Hæ sine luce jacent, immemor illa loqui;
Infelix musa æternos spirabit amores,   15
Ardebitque urnâ multa favilla meâ.

---

* Great judgment is evinced in the imitation of this sonnet in elegiac Propertian verse; and the substitution of the name of Cynthia, for the Laura of Petrarch, gives it an air of originality in the Latin language, and marks that propriety which distinguishes *every* composition of Mr. Gray. *Mason.*

MR. GRAY paid very particular attention to the Anthologia
Græca, and he enriched an interleaved edition of it (by Henry
Stephens in 1566) with copious notes, with parallel passages
from various authors, and with some conjectural emendations
of the text. He translated, or imitated, a few of the epigrams;
and as the editor thinks that the reader may not be displeased
with the terse, elegant, and animated manner in which Mr.
Gray transfused their spirit into the Latin language, he is
presented with a specimen.

FROM THE ANTHOLOGIA GRÆCA.

EDIT. HEN. STEPH. 1566.

IN BACCHÆ FURENTIS STATUAM.[1]

CREDITE, non viva est Mænas; non spirat imago :
Artificis rabiem miscuit ære manus.

IN ALEXANDRUM, ÆRE EFFICTUM.[2]

QUANTUM audet, Lysippe, manus tua! surgit in
    ære
Spiritus, atque oculis bellicus ignis adest :
Spectate hos vultus, miserisque ignoscite Persis :
Quid mirum, imbelles si leo sparsit oves ?

IN MEDEÆ IMAGINEM, NOBILE TIMOMACHI OPUS.[3]

EN ubi Medeæ varius dolor æstuat ore,
    Jamque animum nati, jamque maritus, habent!

---

[1] Anthol. p. 296.   [2] Ib. p. 314.   [3] Ib. p. 317.

Succenset, miseret, medio exardescit amore,
  Dum furor inque oculo gutta minante tremit.
Cernis adhuc dubiam; quid enim? licet impia
    matris
  Colchidos, at non sit dextera Timomachi.

IN NIOBES STATUAM.[4]

FECERAT e vivâ lapidem me Jupiter; at me
  Praxiteles vivam reddidit e lapide.

A NYMPH OFFERING A STATUE OF HERSELF TO VENUS.

TE tibi, sancta, fero nudam; formosius ipsa
  Cum tibi, quod ferrem, te, Dea, nil habui.

IN AMOREM DORMIENTEM.[5]

DOCTE puer vigiles mortalibus addere curas,
  Anne potest in te somnus habere locum?
Laxi juxta arcus, et fax suspensa quiescit,
  Dormit et in pharetrâ clausa sagitta suâ;
Longè mater abest; longè Cythereïa turba:
  Verùm ausint alii te prope ferre pedem,
Non ego: nam metui valdè, mihi, perfide, quiddam
  Forsan et in somnis ne meditere mali.

---

[4] Anthol. p. 315.
[5] Ib. p. 332. Catullianam illam spirat mollitiem. *Gray.*

FROM A FRAGMENT* OF PLATO.[6]

Itur in Idalios tractus, felicia regna,
  Fundit ubi densam myrtea sylva comam,
Intus Amor teneram visus spirare quietem,
  Dum roseo roseos imprimit ore toros ;
Sublimem procul a ramis pendere pharetram,
  Et de languidulâ spicula lapsa manu,
Vidimus, et risu molli diducta labella
  Murmure quæ assiduo pervolitabat apis.

IN FONTEM AQUÆ CALIDÆ.[7]

Sub platanis puer Idalius prope fluminis undam
  Dormiit, in ripâ deposuitque facem.
Tempus adest, sociæ, Nympharum audentior una,
  Tempus adest, ultra quid dubitamus ? ait.
Ilicet incurrit, pestem ut divûmque hominumque
  Lampada collectis exanimaret aquis :
Demens ! nam nequiit sævam restinguere flam-
      mam
  Nympha, sed ipsa ignes traxit, et inde calet.

Irrepsisse suas murem videt Argus in ædes,
  Atque ait, heus, a me nunquid, amice, velis ?
Ille autem ridens, metuas nihil, inquit ; apud te,
  O bone, non epulas, hospitium petimus.

---

* " Elegantissimum hercle fragmentum, quod sic Latinè
nostro modo adumbravimus." *Gray.*
  [6] The second of the name. Anthol. p. 332.
  [7] Anthol. p. 354.   [8] Ib. p. 186.

[9] HANC tibi Rufinus mittit, Rodoclea, coronam,
   Has tibi decerpens texerat ipse rosas;
Est viola, est anemòne, est suave-rubens hyacyn-
      thus,
   Mistaque Narcisso lutea caltha suo:
Sume; sed aspiciens, ah, fidere desine formæ;
   Qui pinxit, brevis est, sertaque teque, color.

AD AMOREM.[10]

PAULISPER vigiles, oro, compesce dolores,
   Respue nec musæ supplicis aure preces;
Oro brevem lacrymis veniam, requiemque furori:
   Ah, ego non possum vulnera tanta pati!
Intima flamma, vides, miseros depascitur artus,
   Surgit et extremis spiritus in labiis:
Quòd si tam tenuem cordi est exsolvere vitam,
   Stabit in opprobrium sculpta querela tuum.
Juro perque faces istas, arcumque sonantem,
   Spiculaque hoc unum figere docta jecur;
Heu fuge crudelem puerum, sævasque sagittas!
   Huic fuit exitii causa, viator, Amor.

------

[9] Anthol. p. 474.   [10] Ib. p. 452.

THE END.

CPSIA information can be obtained
at www.ICGtesting.com
Printed in the USA
LVOW01s0024060216

473972LV00008B/216/P